About the Author

John Fiennes was born in Melbourne, Australia, in 1934, and is of mostly Irish descent with a dash of French and English mixed in. He completed university studies in Australia and France, interspersed with National Service in the Australian Army. His working life included time as a farm-hand, teacher, civil servant and guesthouse-keeper variously in Australia, England, France and Ireland. His studies of French in high school under a gifted languages teacher sparked a lifelong affair with all things French and his spare time and money have been largely spent on travel, particularly in the French-speaking world. He now lives in retirement in Brisbane, Australia, a mere two-hour flight, as he points out, from the *ambience française* of Nouméa, New Caledonia. John Fiennes is also the author of *The Good Boy*, published in 2013 by Hybrid Publishers, Melbourne, Australia.

French Letters

John Fiennes
Illustrations by Stewart Free

French Letters

Olympia Publishers
London

www.olympiapublishers.com
OLYMPIA PAPERBACK EDITION

Copyright © John Fiennes 2023

The right of John Fiennes to be identified as author of
this work has been asserted in accordance with sections 77 and 78
of the Copyright, Designs and Patents Act 1988.

All Rights Reserved

No reproduction, copy or transmission of this publication
may be made without written permission.
No paragraph of this publication may be reproduced,
copied or transmitted save with the written permission of the
publisher, or in accordance with the provisions
of the Copyright Act 1956 (as amended).

Any person who commits any unauthorised act in relation to
this publication may be liable to criminal
prosecution and civil claims for damage.

A CIP catalogue record for this title is
available from the British Library.

ISBN: 978-1-80074-516-2

First Published in 2023

Olympia Publishers
Tallis House
2 Tallis Street
London
EC4Y 0AB

Printed in Great Britain

Contents

Foreword 9
Chapter 1 Australia to Europe on The *Oceania* 13
Chapter 2 Italy to Aquitaine 42
   (i) Passing through Paris 42
   (ii) A student in Bordeaux 48
Chapter 3 Condom-En-Armagnac 58
Chapter 4 Zig-Zagging Through France 66
   (i) Cherbourg to Conques 66
   (ii) Conques to Marseille 103
Chapter 5 Quiche Lorraine And Savoiardi 122
   (i) Nancy 122
   (ii) The fighting nuns of Lorraine. 126
   (iii) Savoiardi 132
Chapter 6 Bourbon and Burgundy 136
   (i) Arnay-le-Duc 136
   (ii) The Morvan 141
   (iii) Moulins 146
Chapter 7 Through the Massif Central 150
   (i) Clermont-Ferrand 150
      (a) The Allier valley and the Cévennes 153
      (b) The Cantal and the Aubrac. 159
   (ii) Figeac 161
   (iii) Lyon 170
   (iv) Saint-Flour 176

Chapter 8 Heading North to Go South 178
  (i) Amiens 178
  (ii) Lille 185
  (iii) Brussels 187
Chapter 9 In the Midi 191
  (i) Grignan 191
  (ii) Béziers 201
  (iii) Narbonne 213
  (iv) Nice 217
  (v) Corsica 227
Chapter 10 A Tale of Four Rivers: Loire, Maine, Aure And Seine 232
  (i) Beaugency 232
  (ii) Angers 246
  (iii) Bayeux 250
  (iv) Rouen 255
Chapter 11 Outremer 262
  (i) Indochina 262
  (ii) Réunion Island 290
  (iii) New Caledonia 300
  (iv) Tahiti via the New Hebrides 314
  (v) Madagascar 332
  (vi) Madagascar to Marseille 348
  (vii) Quebec to Europe on the *Marco Polo* 360
Chapter 12 The Last Time I Saw Paris 371

Foreword

These tales of travelling around France and the French-speaking world are based on diaries, postcards and letters sent to family and friends in Australia in the course of over sixty years of such travel. The stories are more about personal experiences than about tourist sites and they largely relate to the less well-known parts of Francophonie. Sometimes the adventures were enjoyed in the company of family members, such as my sister, Marie and her husband, John, my brother Peter and his wife, Pam and my cousins Helen, Molly, Frank and Richard; sometimes in the company of various friends including John, Leonie, Lorna, Marco, Paul, Peter and my gifted illustrator, Stewart; and sometimes they were enjoyed alone. I thank those friends and relations as well as the many strangers and new-found friends made while travelling for their companionship and support and I hope that these reminiscences might help them to relive happy times spent together.

The first tale, or chapter, is an account of a journey from Australia to Europe way back in 1956. In those days, nearly everyone who made such a trip did so by ship. The first passenger air service from Australia to Europe had been introduced by Qantas in 1939, the Kangaroo Route. The flight of 18,000 kilometres, with six hops or stops, took several days to cross Asia, the Middle East and the Mediterranean and involved hotel nights at several stops. It was first class only, and a one-way ticket cost the equivalent of a year's average Australian wage. The sea voyage of 20,000 kilometres via the Suez Canal took nearly a month, with numerous ports of call, and was available in both first and economy/second/tourist class, the tourist class fare being around two months average wage in 1956, i.e., one-sixth of the air fare. As air travel was, therefore, beyond the means of most, a trip to Europe for all but the very wealthy had to include a month's sea voyage in each direction. Such a trip could not be undertaken during one's annual leave of two or three weeks and could not even be squeezed into a schoolteacher's or university lecturer's summer holidays of six or seven weeks. A trip to Europe was, for most, a dream and, for a determined minority, it was a major, once-in-a-lifetime undertaking and involved being away from home and work for several months. The voyage itself was a major component of such trips and most post-war liners offered excellent accommodation, meals and entertainment, as well as a series of exotic ports of call along the way. Passengers from the Antipodes had the opportunity of mixing with fellow adventurers of various backgrounds and languages and of gradually easing into the heady cultural richness of Europe.

 France was then, and is now, the world's most visited tourist destination, some ninety million international visitors being received by its population of sixty-seven million in 2019. Seven million jostled to see the wonders of the royal palace of Versailles and over forty million visited Paris, making it the most popular international tourist city in the world[1]. These pages are intended to bring to life aspects of France that explain why it is such an alluring and loved destination. Hopefully, the stories will inspire some readers to turn off the telly, put down the book, lock up the house and hit the road, the iron road, the ocean waves or even the airways and to see this French world for themselves.

And if that is not possible, then I invite you to sit back in a comfortable armchair and, in your mind's eye, come with me!

John Fiennes
Brisbane

---

[1] Next in popularity came Spain, with 80 million visitors to a population of 47 million; USA with 75 million visitors to a population of 330 million; China, 63 million visitors to a population of 1400 million; Italy, 60 million visitors to a population also of 60 million: and the UK with 40 million visitors to a population of 67 million.

Chapter 1
Australia to Europe on The *Oceania*

A liner leaving Australia for Europe

Once upon a time, long, long ago, when I was a young man freshly out of university, the liner *Oceania* slowly pulled away from Station Pier in Melbourne on an August afternoon, the pale winter sun already low on the horizon, tugboats fore and aft straining to turn her, black smoke pouring from their short, fat funnels, white water churning above their hard-working stern propellers, several thousand well-wishers waving last goodbyes on the wharf, multi-coloured paper streamers unrolling and then breaking as the gap between the ship's side and the land grew wider and wider. Then, with three blasts from the ship's siren signalling "finished with tugs", the liner began to move under her own steam while the passengers lining the ship's rails watched their loved ones and "home sweet home" slowly fade into the dusk and into the distance. The month-long voyage to Europe had begun.

It took about two hours for the ship to steam down Port Phillip Bay and then out through the narrow opening known as "The Rip" linking the Bay to the open ocean and to the ocean swell, to the great winter rollers coming up from the Southern Ocean with their icy Antarctic waters. Once through the Heads, the liner slowed and then briefly stopped and the Port Phillip pilot, who had been in command of the ship all the way down the Bay and through the treacherous waters of the Rip, could be seen scrambling down a rope ladder on the leeward side midships and then leaping into a small launch bobbing up and down alongside the *Oceania*. Once he was safely on board, the launch headed back to the pilots' mother ship, the *Wyuna*, a handsome little steamer of 1,300 tonnes that had manoeuvred itself into position abreast of the *Oceania* and about a hundred metres away. The *Wyuna* patrolled the seas outside the Rip and was home to the harbour's pilots who lived on board, ready to steer ships between the open ocean and the wharves in Melbourne. It was almost dark by this time and I watched in awe at the skill of the seamen involved in the tricky operation. Along with a few others who had braved the cold wind and the rolling deck to watch, I joined in a round of applause and gave a grateful wave to the pilot and his mates as they pulled away from the ship's side. The *Oceania*'s engines then picked up speed again and we turned out to sea, leaving behind the *Wyuna*, the lights and lighthouse of Point Lonsdale and the safety and security of my homeland, heading into the open ocean, the darkness and the unknown future.

Dinner, our first meal on board, was served soon afterwards and many a passenger not yet accustomed to the rolling and pitching of the dining-room floor did not manage to stay at the table until the end of the meal to enjoy the excellent Italian cuisine being served. I was one of those who fled after the first course but, after a day or two I did get used to the movement and started to enjoy the meals and the company of the seven other English-speakers at my table, Australians and New Zealanders. Most of the passengers were Europeans, the majority of them Italian, and the dining-room had been organised in terms of the language spoken at each table of eight. There were, as I recall, four English tables, one French table, one Spanish, several Dutch, German, Greek and Slav ones, and a dozen or more Italian ones. The ship was not full, as it would have been on the voyage out from Italy when a thousand or so migrants would have boarded her in Naples and Messina; the return voyage, less than half full, was an opportunity for the hard-working crew to relax a little, to smile at and to chat with the passengers and for the chefs to show off a little, delighting passengers with special dishes a little too time-consuming or too expensive to be included in the menu on the outward voyage.

Four days out of Melbourne the ship arrived at our first port of call, Fremantle (the port of Perth in Western Australia), and it was a strange sensation to discover, on dry land once again, that the "sea legs" painfully acquired on board the ever-rolling ship now made walking along a footpath not as simple as it had previously been. I was fortunate in that family friends had come to meet the ship and drove me to the city to spend the day with them, visiting King's Park and the other major sights, finally delivering me back to the *Oceania* just in time for sailing. A number of new passengers had boarded in Fremantle including a youngish Dutchman who was allocated to share my tourist class cabin. He was a pleasant fellow, spoke good English as do most Dutch, and had an endless store of tales about his life in Indonesia, where he had been born in 1920 when that country had been the Dutch East Indies. Our next port of call was to be Djakarta, or Batavia as my cabinmate kept calling it. I was very much looking forward to visiting it as it would be my first experience of a foreign land and as, again, friends were planning to meet the ship and to show me the sights. My cabinmate, however, said that he would not be going ashore as he could not bear to see the decline and chaos of his hometown resulting from the 1948 declaration of independence and the departure of the Dutch after three hundred years of what he saw as benign colonisation.

The *Oceania* left Fremantle in the late afternoon and headed north, away from winter and towards the tropics. One evening after dinner, when the ship, having crossed the Tropic of Capricorn, was a little more than halfway between Fremantle and Djakarta and was gliding across calm seas, we passengers gathered on the deck to watch the approach of another liner. We had been told during the afternoon that if the weather continued to be favourable the two ships would pass very close to one another, ours on the way north to Europe and the other, the *Neptunia*, on its way south from Europe to Australia. At about nine p.m. the two ships were almost abreast of one another and to our surprise, when about five hundred metres apart, both vessels stopped and suddenly turned on their floodlights, brightly lighting up both ships and the flat stretch of water between them. To the further surprise of the passengers lining the rails, the *Oceania* lowered one of her lifeboats and, when it was afloat at the side of the ship, we saw that in addition to the four crew members on board there were four armed security officers and some eight other men wearing handcuffs. The lifeboat immediately moved away from the ship and headed off in the direction of the *Neptunia*. The moon was almost full, the seas flat calm, the tropical air warm and languid and we rather lazily watched the proceedings. The lifeboat pulled in alongside the *Neptunia* and the handcuffed men were rather roughly hustled on board. They were almost immediately replaced by TEN handcuffed men who were then transferred from the *Neptunia* to the *Oceania*. With the whole operation completed, the lifeboat hauled up and securely stowed on board and the ten strangers whisked out of sight below decks, the two ships saluted each other with a couple of deafening blasts on their sirens, the floodlights were extinguished, the engines began to throb again and both ships resumed their journeys.

Our friendly purser then broke official silence and explained that the two ships had simply been exchanging stowaways! Ten hopefuls, who had hidden on board the *Neptunia* when it had left Italy with a full load of migrants heading off to start a new life in Australia, had been swapped against eight disappointed souls who had found that Australia did not live up to expectations and who longed to return to Italy… for free, and had stowed away on the *Oceania*. This happened in those halcyon days before security checks became a requirement when boarding a plane, ship (or bus or train in some countries now). In those golden days the departure of passenger liners, at least from Australian ports, was quite a social event. Passengers were required to present their ticket and their passport to board the ship, but family and friends and members of the general public interested in inspecting the ship had merely to collect a visitor's pass from the shipping company's offices to be allowed to go on board on sailing day. "*Bon Voyage*" parties were held in the ship's public rooms, on the decks and in the larger cabins, and an hour before sailing time the ship's public address system would announce: "the ship is about to sail: all ashore who are going ashore". It was easy for a would-be stowaway to remain on board, harder no doubt to find somewhere to remain hidden during the voyage, especially once cold, hunger and the need for sleep became issues.

I think the passengers at my table felt rather sorry for these stowaways, especially for the group who had almost made it to Australia and were now on board the *Oceania* and heading back to Europe, all locked, it was reported, in the ship's brig for the remaining three weeks of the voyage.

The sea remained calm for the rest of the trip and three days after our moonlit rendezvous with the *Neptunia* we entered the Sunda Straits on our approach to Djakarta. We passed quite close to a string of islands, all palm-fringed and covered in lush tropical forest, save one, a small, rocky one which turned out to be Anak Krakatoa, the "Child of Krakatoa". It seemed to be little more than a pyramid-shaped cone of rock, with a wisp of white smoke lazily rising skywards from the top. It was in fact all that remains of the volcanic island of Krakatoa that had erupted in 1883 with such tremendous force that the bang had been heard in Australia, in Perth and Alice Springs; the resulting tsunami had damaged coastal villages and towns as far away as Singapore and Bali, over 30,000 people had been killed and the huge dust cloud thrown up had circled the earth for more than two years. But our approach to this first foreign port of call was idyllic, across flat calm seas, beneath bright blue skies and past a myriad of delightful-looking, lush blue-green islands.

The *Oceania* berthed in *Tanjung Priok*, the port of Djakarta and I was met and whisked, by chauffeur-driven car, to the home of Indonesian friends. The head of the household was a senior public servant who had recently spent some time in Melbourne on government business and I had been asked to help him "brush up" his English. His first language would, I guessed, have been *Bahasa Indonesia* and, as a senior public servant in the Dutch colonial administration, he would have spoken good Dutch but his English was, at best, rudimentary. I had invited him to the family home several times and had introduced him to an uncle who spoke fluent *Bahasa Indonesia*. In this way, we had been able to make him feel a little less lonely, than would otherwise have been the case, in between official duties and especially at weekends. I think he may have learnt more about the Australian way of life from my family than he did about good English from me, but he was happy with his experience of Melbourne and insisted that I should contact him when passing through Djakarta.

After three hundred years of colonial rule, the Dutch had begun to leave Indonesia only five years before I arrived and the country was still in a transitional stage. My erstwhile student had replaced the Dutch head of a civil service department and had been allocated a charming Dutch colonial house in the best part of Djakarta as his private residence. It was to his home, rather than to his ministry, that I was driven and there I met an extended family of more than twenty smiling souls gathered to meet his English teacher from Australia. The house was a typical white-painted, high-gabled Dutch building, set back from the street across a large, paved courtyard and surrounded by a high white masonry wall pierced by solid-looking timber gates reinforced by iron hinges and straps. Once through the gates and into the courtyard, one quickly saw that, unlike houses in Holland, this one had a ground floor that was largely open to the fresh air, with a colonnaded verandah front and back accessed through sliding glass doors and slatted timber shutters. For my visit, the family had laid out an incredible selection of dishes, rice presented in many different ways plus all sorts of meats, vegetables, fruits, nuts, creams and pastries... the sort of banquet the Java-Dutch colonials called a *rijsttafel* and which became almost a national dish in both the Netherlands and Indonesia. The lavishness of the meal and the generosity of my Indonesian hosts were overwhelming and more than three hours passed in sampling this and that delight and desperately trying to make polite conversation when neither party could really understand the other.

At last, my host proposed a quick look at the main sights of Djakarta on the way back to the ship and we managed to slip away. We drove to and past the elegant Merdeka Palace, now the residence of the president of the Indonesian Republic but built in the eighteenth century as the palace of the governors-general of the Dutch East Indies. We did not stop to take a photo as stopping in that area was, for security reasons, forbidden. My host explained that the new republic was still experiencing tensions between the dominant Muslim Nationalist movements and small Christian, Chinese, Indo-Dutch and other regional and "Western" groups. Apparently, a small minority had not wanted total independence from the Netherlands in January 1950 and had preferred some sort of federation of islands rather than a single national government. The province of West New Guinea had not been included in the new, Muslim republic and the Moluccas Islands had been included, against the wishes of its fifty per cent Christian people. More than 30,000 Moluccans had preferred to move to the (cold and damp) Netherlands rather than to live in the new Muslim republic. This unease was presumably the reason behind the profusion of fully armed police, soldiers and security guards all over the city, something I had never seen before, even in war-time Australia. We had to almost speed back to the port if I were not to miss the ship and my memories of the city were limited to the delightful lunch at my host's home, the handsome colonial buildings around Merdeka Square, the dusty green of the tree-lined streets, the neglected-looking and stagnant canals and the mostly dilapidated warehouses around the docks. Of course, the warmth of the welcome in that private home became the dominant memory of my first visit to Djakarta.

Our next port of call was Colombo and, once again, I was lucky enough to have a local contact to show me around. An Australian nurse and frequent visitor to our family home in Melbourne, Hilda had taken employment as "specialist nurse" to an elderly and childless Australian couple who had spent most of their working life as managers of a large, company-owned tea plantation in the hills about thirty kilometres out of Ceylon's second city and former capital, Kandy. When the *Oceania* arrived in Colombo the wife had died, the husband was in hospital in Colombo convalescing after a major stroke and serious attack of gout and Hilda, on hand to help him, was installed in the couple's townhouse in the leafy suburb of Cinnamon Gardens. There was no deep-water wharf available in Colombo in those days and the ship had anchored and was moored to two buoys in the inner harbour, passengers and luggage having to be ferried ashore in a fleet of barges and small boats. One of the first small boats to approach the *Oceania* was a very smart antique steam launch, gleaming black hull, cream superstructure with shiny brass and polished timber fittings, and a fine plume of black smoke curling up from its tall funnel. And there standing on the open after-deck stood our friend, Hilda, waving cheerily up to me!

Hilda was enjoying her role as (temporary) Lady of the Tea Plantation and had the use of the company's launch and chauffeur-driven car as well as of the fully staffed manager's townhouse. Having collected me from the ship she ordered the launch back to the jetty and the waiting car and we then set off to do a quick tour of the main city sights before heading off "up country", up to the tea plantation country. There would not be enough time to go as far as "her" plantation in Nuwala and so she had arranged for us to have an early lunch at the Queen's Hotel in Kandy, a quick look at the Temple of the Tooth, the main local sight, and then a fast drive back down to Colombo and "home" to *Cinnamon Gardens* for tiffin "with a few friends".

I gratefully accepted all this hospitality, of course, but it did not really turn out to be quite as pleasant as my day in Djakarta. Things started to go wrong as soon as we alighted from the launch and headed for the car which was parked about fifty metres away. We had to run the gauntlet of a crowd of emaciated beggars, some missing an arm or a leg or an eye, all clad in rags and all desperately crying out for help. The same sort of scene may have been commonplace in *Djakarta*, too, in the days of Dutch rule, but I had seen nothing like it there, perhaps because I was at all times in the hands of officials of the new government. Perhaps the new government in Indonesia had found homes and employment for Djakarta's beggars, perhaps they had simply been swept away from places where they might be seen by international visitors! In Ceylon, as it was still referred to by its British overlords (it became a "dominion" in 1948 and the independent Republic of Sri Lanka in 1972), I was in the company of the soon-to-be-expelled British plantation elite, fair game to the emerging nation's poor. To have these poor souls calling out "master, master" (not "mister" or even "sir", but the demeaning "master"), with hand outstretched and eyes pleading was really distressing, especially as I had literally to push them aside to get to the far side of the car, Hilda having unhesitatingly made her way to the near-side door. For a moment, I thought of yelling to the chauffeur for help but I quickly realised that, as a Ceylonese himself, he was probably disinclined to interfere. Hardening my heart I pushed my way around the car, opened the rear door and sank gratefully into the comfort of the beautifully maintained Daimler.

"Is it always like that?" I said to Hilda.

She rather testily replied, "Oh, you shouldn't let them worry you, they're not your responsibility". Then, with a smart rapping on the glass panel separating us from the driver and the front of the car, she gave the signal to drive off… and my tour of Ceylon began.

Colombo, the "Garden City of Asia" according to the tourist brochures, was an interesting place, a strange mixture of beauty and chaos, of wealthy-looking districts and dreadful slums, of old and new and of British, Dutch and Portuguese influences. The whole mix was partly hidden by masses of green and grey, the foliage and trunks of the hundreds of big, old banyan, fig, jacaranda and other trees: some colonial authority had decreed that these giant shade trees should be planted in the streets and open spaces of the city, Hilda explained. She added that Cinnamon Gardens, the inner suburb where the ruling class or "best people" lived, had originally been the plantation of cinnamon trees that, before the introduction of tea plants from China by the British, had made the fortune of the early Dutch colonists.

There were several traditional Dutch style buildings near the wharf, making that area reminiscent of the port area in Djakarta. Then we came to the centre of town, referred to as "the Fort", originally a fortress built by the Dutch when they ruled in Ceylon (1650–1800). The original fort had been replaced by a maze of rather narrow streets of commercial buildings which had more of a British look (Napoleonic France took over briefly from the Dutch and the British took over from the French in 1815), with the monumental parliament building probably being their principal contribution to Colombo's skyline. The contribution of the Portuguese (1505–1650) who had preceded the Dutch had probably been more cultural and genetic than architectural, with the Catholic religion gaining a firm foothold and intermarriage with the natives, always part of Portugal's colonial policy, resulting in a proliferation of Portuguese family names throughout the island. The grandiose Catholic cathedral, St Lucia's, looking like a scaled-down version of St Peter's in Rome, is the biggest church in Ceylon. The Dutch contribution here to religious architecture was the much smaller but very picturesque *Wolvendaal* Church, looking sadly neglected as we drove past (the Dutch policy, as with the British, was firmly opposed to interracial marriage and so there were not many mixed-race descendants to attend services of the Dutch Reformed Church, or of the nearby Presbyterian and Anglican churches!).

After this whirlwind tour of central Colombo, we set off for Kandy, a little over a hundred kilometres away in the hilly centre of the island. In the late nineteenth century, the British had built a railway up to Kandy and beyond to serve the many large tea plantations established on the steep, fertile slopes of the central mountain chain and the road followed the railway for much of the distance. After about twenty kilometres of fairly flat terrain and through the rather shabby sprawl of Colombo's poorer suburbs and shanty towns, both road and rail started to climb and entered the lush green valleys of the monsoon-visited western side of the island. Clearings in the rain forest saw lots of very small farms, rice-growing or cattle-raising seemingly the main occupations. All along the way there were villages, groups of whitewashed cement-faced houses, a police station, sometimes a small railway siding with a stationmaster's house and antique signal box, often a small Buddhist or Hindu temple, much less often a Christian church, an occasional shop or general store with a petrol pump outside and numerous small, rickety stalls cobbled together out of bits of timber, corrugated iron and palm thatch. These stalls, which appeared along the length of the road and not just in the villages, offered for sale all sorts of food and drink, fruit and vegetables and, less often, clothes and UMBRELLAS. That part of the country had a very high rainfall, particularly in the two monsoon seasons each year; my visit happened to have occurred in the middle of the southwest monsoon and heavy showers had indeed started soon after we had left Colombo. Fascinating as all this was, the most memorable feature of the drive up to Kandy was the narrowness of the winding road and the fact that we never seemed to get away from populated areas. There were people everywhere, working in the fields, buying and selling at the roadside stalls... and simply walking along the road in both directions and on both sides of the road, nearly always in single file, fortunately, as there was no footpath and pedestrians had to share the macadam of the road with the trucks, cars and bicycles using what must have been one of the busiest roads in the country, linking its two biggest cities. In my mind's eye, I can still see these files of people, often dressed in colourful sarongs or saris and sheltering under large black umbrellas, calmly walking along the edge of the road and I can still hear the blaring of the horn of our car as our driver whizzed past. I was sure he must have run over many a toe but Hilda laughed at my gasps of concern and assured me that he had never actually hit anyone!

And so, we made it to Kandy. When the British had taken over Colombo from the French, the central highlands were not part of the former Dutch colony and constituted the still-independent Kingdom of Kandy. A series of battles known as the Kandyan Wars ensued and was won, not without much difficulty, by the British who then extended their rule over the rest of the island, making Colombo the capital. The Kandyan kings had been strong upholders of the Buddhist religion and Kandy remained the religious centre of the island which is, to this day, perhaps eighty per cent Buddhist. In the sixteenth century, a relic of the Buddha, a single tooth, was brought to Kandy and enshrined in a temple built by the king. That temple, enlarged and embellished by subsequent kings, is the main attraction of Kandy today and, as we had arrived a little earlier than expected, Hilda and I decided to visit the temple before, rather than after, lunch.

The temple is within the compound of the former royal palace and, as the Queen's Hotel is almost next door, we left the Daimler at the hotel and walked along the lake edge to the palace compound. Kandy itself is built in the centre of a saucer-shaped depression in the high plateau, the walls of the depression being covered in a tropical forest. The centre of Kandy is an artificial lake, built in the early 1800s by the last king, with the royal compound on its tree-lined shore. The palace itself is a rather unimpressive single-storey building but there are other interesting buildings within the compound, most notably the Temple of the Tooth. The temple's building is protected by a crenelated wall and a moat (linked to the waters of the lake) and there is a monumental defensive gate leading into the temple grounds and shrine. It is all very picturesque and, going by the large number of respectful worshippers, of great religious significance to Buddhists. But to me, a non-believer, it was rather disappointing, of little architectural interest and very dilapidated and in need of much care, cleaning, painting and general refurbishment. I supposed that having just emerged from one hundred and fifty years of foreign occupation and rule the young dominion would soon make a start on righting those years of neglect.

And so, we adjourned to lunch at the Queen's Hotel, itself an interesting relic of colonial times and once the British governor's summer residence. When turned into an hotel, it had become, along with the golf club and the tennis club, one of the centres of social life for the many expatriate planters and their wives living "up in the hills" on the great tea plantations. Looking more like a white-painted version of a grey Hausmann-era building in Paris, the hotel welcomed guests in an entrance hall which still managed to project the British notions of refined opulence, respectability and tradition. Marble floors, mahogany panelling, chandeliers, potted palms and lines of bowing, sarong-clad servants abounded. The main dining-room, where we were served lunch, was strangely reminiscent of the first-class dining-room of P&O liners of the inter-war years, with timber shutters on the inside of the windows or portholes and rows of pillars dividing the room into three zones while supporting the deck or floor above. We had a set menu of chilled coconut soup, an excellent curry with rice, followed by the "Queen's dessert" of jelly and cream. Just getting jelly to set in that steamy tropical climate must have seemed a wonderful achievement to the planter families a century earlier but the arrival of a small serve of red jelly topped by a spoonful of cream was a bit of a disappointment to this diner, who expected a dessert fit for a queen to be a bit more elaborate. And there was something odd about the cream, which was not cream in colour but a watery white and was strangely tasteless. I said to Hilda that I had not seen any dairy herds on the drive up and asked her where the hotel would source its milk and cream.

"From the water buffaloes, of course", she laughed, "it's buffalo cream, and they don't add sugar or vanilla the way we do in Australia, that's why it seems strange."

Buffalo cream! Did I rudely say *yuck* or did I just think it?

After lunch, Hilda and I had a short walk along the lake shore while our driver brought the Daimler around to the front of the hotel. He presumably had had his lunch in the

"Downstairs" part of the hotel while we lunched more expansively Upstairs. Hilda rarely spoke to him, giving me the impression that he had already been told exactly what we would be doing, where and when the car would be needed, and indeed that he knew the routine of a quick tour of Colombo and of a visit to Kandy with lunch at the Queen's Hotel off by heart. After a few minutes of walking along under the trees, I noticed the Daimler approach and then slow to a crawl behind us until Hilda gave a wave and the car stopped beside us. We climbed aboard before the beggars outside the hotel across the road had time to besiege us and off we went back to Colombo.

We began the return trip with a short detour to Peradeniya and the very beautiful botanical gardens (more forest than gardens). The first cuttings of the tea plants brought from China by the British in the nineteenth century had been propagated there. By the late nineteenth century, the growing and processing of tea had displaced cinnamon and coffee, long the main crops cultivated by the Dutch, as Ceylon's major export industry. The cooler climate of the Central Highlands and the fertile soil of the steep hillsides suited tea growing and the panorama of terraced tea gardens in between surviving belts of tropical forest northwards from Peradeniya was truly breath-taking. From Peradeniya, we drove to Geragania, the nearest functioning tea plantation and factory to Kandy, but being short of time did not stop and tour the factory. Instead, we returned to the main road and hurried down to sea level and Colombo.

Cinnamon Gardens was the only part of Colombo that I saw that had been built according to some sort of town planning principles, with wide, tree-lined streets and with plenty of open spaces and eye-catching vistas to important buildings, such as the handsome city hall and national museum. The mansions of the city's elite and the townhouses of wealthy planters from the highlands were mostly located there and, as after 1948 the colonials were steadily being replaced in these exalted positions by the native-born, so the skin-colour of the residents of the Gardens was changing from white to brown. Hilda's "temporary townhouse" was actually a large, three-storey apartment, one of four in a white art deco building probably dating from the 1930s and hidden from the street by a couple of huge banyan trees, possibly the remnants of the garden of an earlier mansion on the site. There was a *porte-cochère* at the front entrance, a practical idea in a city with such a rainy climate, and the double front doors opened to a large vestibule from which a rather grand staircase swept up to the first floor and a long gallery running the width of the building. There were four apartment front doors opening to this gallery and Hilda's was the one at the right-hand end.

 The first thing that struck me, apart from the interesting architecture, was the number of servants on duty. As we had pulled in under the *porte-cochère*, the front doors had opened as if by magic and a grey-haired Ceylonese dressed in a colourful sarong and long-sleeved white shirt stepped forward to open the car door for Hilda and, with a slight bow, to usher her inside with me following in her wake. We walked up the stairs and as we turned towards the apartment door it too opened as if by magic and another white-shirted servant bowed us inside. While the elderly doorkeeper downstairs in charge of the front door and the vestibule was apparently shared by the four apartments, the middle-aged man who opened Hilda's door was the senior member of the staff of the townhouse, the "Head Boy", assisted by a much younger boy and a cook (whom I never actually saw). Hilda's front door opened into a square parquet-floored lobby from which stairs led up to three large en-suited bedrooms and down to the kitchen, garage and servants' quarters. Hilda led the way upstairs and invited me to freshen up in the guest bedroom next to her own. After a few minutes, we went downstairs and through double doors to a large and airy living-room which in turn opened out to a wide balcony overlooking the front garden and the big banyan trees. To my surprise, there was already a small group of people gathered there... Hilda's "few friends", all English or Scottish and in one way or another connected to the tea industry and to Hilda's hospitalised employer. They were all of Hilda's vintage, i.e., of my parents' age rather than my own, all of the *pukka sahib* type and, at the age of twenty-two, I felt a bit like a schoolboy being paraded before the school's board of governors. There were a few polite answers to my questions about tea and the plantations but once I had been given a few minutes of attention the topic of conversation turned to the way in which the British police or army (both withdrew from Ceylon and sailed to the UK not long after my visit) had recently sorted out Colombo's horrendous traffic problems, designing a system of roundabouts, one-way streets and traffic lights that, I was assured, the locals could never have thought up.

Tiffin, an expanded form of afternoon tea devised under the Raj in India and modestly copied in the nearby but slightly less imperial colony of Ceylon, was served on the balcony, the boys carrying out several small tables covered with white linen tablecloths on which they then placed a selection of scones, iced cakes and sandwiches. There was a beautiful silver tea service of a teapot, hot water jug, milk jug and sugar bowl and a tea set of fine bone China that looked awfully like my grandmother's prized Royal Albert tea set. Hilda presided from the table with the tea service and as she poured one of the boys would pass the cup, saucer and matching plate to the guests in turn, the other boy following along with a tray containing the milk jug and sugar bowl. When everybody had their cup of tea, the boys moved around offering the plates of food. Hilda apologised for the "simple tea" as she put it, adding that she and I had lunched rather well in Kandy and would have to set off again fairly soon for the harbour and the evening sailing of the *Oceania*. Everyone murmured agreement to Hilda's organisation of my one-day visit to Ceylon, someone adding that it was fortunate I had come before "we leave next year and the place goes to the dogs".

It was by then after four and time for me to leave. With only a little difficulty, I persuaded Hilda to remain with her guests and to allow me to head back to the ship in the care of her very reliable chauffeur. He was in fact the only servant whom she addressed by name (a *Sinhala-sounding* name I never quite picked up), the others being simply "Boy". It was something of a relief to leave the townhouse as the extent to which Hilda had settled into the role of a member of the ruling class, of living upstairs and ordering around the servant's downstairs, addressing quiet, grey-haired men as "Boy" in that peremptory tone of voice made me feel very uncomfortable. So, with many thanks for a wonderful day, I climbed back into the luxury and seclusion of the back seat of the Daimler and headed back to the port through the evening traffic, most of which was going in the opposite direction, allowing us to make it a quick trip. I was deposited at the port authority gates and was able to join the line of other *Oceania* passengers queueing at passport control and then at the jetty from which a ferry service shuttled passengers out to the ship. We were all on board by five thirty, as instructed before leaving in the morning, and soon after six the ship weighed anchor and sailed away, the lights of Colombo quickly disappearing into the darkness. In Colombo and Djakarta, being so close to the equator, there is no twilight and there were virtually no streetlights: night falls quite dramatically, black and silent.

The sea was calm, the air balmy, a waning moon in the sky and we steamed off across the Indian Ocean towards Aden, our next port of call. Most passengers opted for an early night after a busy day of sightseeing ashore but I happened to wake in the early hours of the morning and saw that the cabin seemed to be flooded with the light of the moon. Then the light disappeared and the cabin was in almost total darkness. Puzzled, I got out of bed and strode over to the open porthole and, as I did so, the bright light again filled the cabin. Looking out of the porthole I saw that we were passing very close to a tiny island[2] on which there was a tall lighthouse whose flashing beam was competing with the pale light of the crescent moon, creating a glittering curling top to the foam on the ship's bow wake as we glided silently along. The rest of the ship seemed to be asleep and I had the whole dream-like world to myself.

The seas remained calm but the temperatures rose steadily

---

[2] *Malaku*, the northernmost island/atoll of the Maldives.

as we approached Aden[3], the capital of the British protectorate of South Yemen and guarding the entrance to the Red Sea. We arrived off the Arabian coast early in the day and, as in Colombo, tied up to a buoy in lieu of berthing at a wharf. After breakfast, some of us went ashore by launch and walked up to the town centre, Steamer Point. On the highest point of the cliffs surrounding the harbour was a battlemented fort, with a Union Jack hanging limply and still. There was a straggle of shops around the waterfront mostly staffed, I think, by wary-looking Indians and offering a meagre assortment of goods for sale to tourists: watches and cameras, Panama hats, strings of beads made from date pits or coral, packs of coffee beans (the old port of Mocha was not far along the coast), fly whisks and bottles of unidentified brightly coloured soft drink. There were almost as many police and British army chaps around as there were civilians, the latter mostly clad in grubby-looking flowing Arab dress and headgear. Our stroll around the town took less than an hour, the sun was getting high in the heavens even by ten a.m. and we were soon back at the jetty waiting for the shuttle launch to take us back to the shady decks of the ship... and lunch in the dining-room, the only part of tourist class accommodation on the *Oceania* that was air-conditioned.

We left Aden in the afternoon and by the next morning

---

[3] On a later voyage between Australia and Europe via Suez my ship had called at Djibouti, on the opposite or western and African side of the entrance to the Red Sea. Djibouti was even dustier and grittier than Aden and had even less to offer in the line of sightseeing. It was the "capital" of the then colony of French Somaliland, its main claim to fame being that it was the port for land-locked Ethiopia and was linked to Addis Ababa in 1897 by the French-built metre-gauge railway. In 2015, that line was replaced by an electrified standard-gauge railway built and funded by China.

were making our way up the Red Sea towards the Suez Canal. It was hot, there was no breeze other than that made by the forward movement of the ship itself and the swimming pool and the dining-room were the only popular places during the day. At night, many passengers tried sleeping on deck rather than in inside cabins, where the only air supply was from the punkah-louvre system, which seemed to supply warm rather than fresh air and which was often very noisy. We had three nights in the Red Sea and on the second the evening's entertainment was announced as a filmed version of Verdi's *Tosca*, to be shown under the stars on the top deck, where a hundred or so chairs had been lined up for us. We were aboard an Italian liner: the crew and probably half of the passengers were Italian, so the choice of film was understandable and, as I was already a Verdi fan, very welcome. What better setting could there be to listen to the aria: "The stars were brightly shining" than the open top deck of an Italian liner gliding along in the moonlight? Tosca, you remember, is a famous diva who near the end of the opera stabs to death the villain, Baron Scarpia, and ends up committing suicide to escape arrest. Not long before the stabbing scene, a chap sitting two rows in front of me suddenly stood, leant forwards and stabbed the man in front of him! Uproar ensued! Women screamed, other passengers leapt up, some to grab the assailant, others to help the victim, ship's officers resplendent in their white, blue and gold uniforms tried to bring calm to the scene. The film stopped, of course, and we English-speaking onlookers adjourned to the poolside bar for a stiff pick-me-up and to discuss the evening's entertainment. In due course, one of the officers joined us and let it be known that the victim had not been seriously injured and had been allowed to leave the ship's hospital with the shoulder wound dressed and his arm in a sling. His assailant, on the other hand, was "under ship's arrest", whatever that meant. The incident, our friendly officer explained, with a shrug of the shoulders, was pretty trivial: two chaps vying for the attention of the same woman, a matter of "That's *amore*", as Dean Martin was singing on the Hit Parade. And so, the evening came to an unusual end. In the morning, when I emerged from my cabin (on the lowest, cheapest deck), I was surprised to find a sailor sitting on a stool outside the door of the cabin next door. To my "*Buongiorno,*" he replied "*Signore*" and I went on to the dining-room for breakfast.

On the way back, I met our friend the purser and asked him about the sailor on the stool. "Oh", he said with his usual shrug, "he is there because the ship's prison is full up, with the stowaways from the *Neptunia*, and so we had to put last night's assailant in an empty cabin... the one next to yours. Don't worry, they would have locked the communicating door with your cabin first."

I hoped so!

We spent the morning around the pool reliving the excitement of the previous night while the afternoon was given to discussing plans for a shore excursion in Egypt. By the time I went down to my cabin to shower and change for dinner, the door of the cabin next to mine was open, the stool was in the middle of the opening and the crewman was smoking and chatting with the prisoner who was sitting on a stool just inside. By the following evening, the prisoner had apparently been reclassified as not dangerous and the guard was no longer posted. I never saw the occupant of the cabin again. Had he been squeezed into the crowded ship's brig? Perhaps another prisoner had died from the heat during the passage of the Red

Sea and been buried at sea, thus creating a vacancy? Had he been acquitted by the captain and let back to mingle with the other passengers? Had he been put ashore and handed over to the Egyptian police, as by next morning we had arrived in Port Suez? I never did find an answer to these questions and must admit that I forgot all about them, so interesting did our day in Egypt prove to be.

The ship had arrived in Port Suez very early in the morning and, by five a.m., a small group of passengers including myself was ferried ashore where we piled into two large cars and set off across the desert towards Cairo. Eight of us had opted to do *"Le Quick Trip to Cairo"* organised by Thomas Cook and Company. This required us to leave the ship at the southern end of the Canal and, while the *Oceania* transited the Canal, we would speed off to Cairo and its sights and then would re-join the ship in Port Said at around midnight when it would emerge at the northern end of the Canal and embark its adventurous passengers. It was quite chilly on the wharf in Port Suez, and we were all glad of a bit of animal warmth once we were in the cars and had closed the doors and windows. Fortunately, within half an hour the sun started to rise and to turn the desert a deep purple then a pale pink and finally the sandy, ochre colour we had expected. After about an hour, we arrived in the outskirts of Cairo, an area which our guide said was the "Garden Suburb of Heliopolis". The car pulled up in front of a huge Arabian Nights sort of building, the Heliopolis Palace Hotel[4].

A tall, bearded man, magnificently dressed in multi-

---

[4] In the 1980s, the building was refurbished and became, as it still is, the Heliopolis Palace, official residence of the President of Egypt.

coloured flowing robes and carrying in his right hand a long, silver-tipped staff of office, strode down the monumental front steps. Gesturing towards the hotel entrance the Major Domo intoned: "Welcome, welcome, S.S. *Oceania*, to the quick breakfast," and we all piled out of the cars, up the steps and into the palatial hotel. Our way across the vast lobby and into the magnificent domed dining-room was marked out by a long, red carpet lined on either side by a row of young men dressed in voluminous white trousers, red sash, white shirt, black jacket and red tarboosh, the same uniform being worn by the waiters in the dining room, one stationed behind each of our chairs at the large table reserved for our small group. We were served a splendid if slightly strange breakfast, presumably one the Egyptian staff believed their former British masters (and Antipodean British offspring) would appreciate: platters of bacon, fried eggs, chipolata sausages and grilled tomatoes, all kept warm on spirit stoves on a nearby sideboard; toast made to order by the chap standing behind your chair; bowls of rice cooked in milk and garnished with sliced tinned peaches; and then there were thick slices of a very rich fruit cake, all to be washed down by a limitless supply of tea, with a choice between Twinings English Breakfast Tea or the locally-favoured mint tea.

Suitably fortified, we returned to the cars and set off into Cairo proper and our day's work: a visit to the Egyptian Museum in the city centre followed by a trip out to the pyramids at Giza, with lunch at the Mina House Hotel, then back to the city centre to visit Saladin's citadel, the grand mosque and Abu Serga, the church of St Sergius, the oldest

Coptic church in Egypt[5]. Then we were to have tea at a leading hotel (a replacement in the itinerary for the long-established Shepheard's Hotel, favourite haunt of the British expatriates, which had been fire-bombed by Egyptian nationalists), and then we were to set off to Port Said to re-join the *Oceania*. The whole tour ran smoothly and was the beginning of my personal lifelong love affair with Egypt. The pyramids and Great Sphinx out at Giza, enigmatic, mysterious, timeless, were absolutely stunning and the visit to the Egyptian Museum and the treasures of the pharaohs' tombs, although so rushed, convinced me that I had to return to Egypt and spend weeks or months, not days, there.

We made it to Port Said with an hour or so to spare, just enough time for a quick look at the famous Art Deco emporium of Simon Arzt, in front of which the *Oceania* had berthed. Ever since the opening of the Canal in 1869 by Empress Eugénie of France, passengers transiting the Canal have been able to buy their mementoes of Egypt, large or small, from the Arzt family. Next door was the office of Thomas Cook, another century-old family company and a bit further still, at the actual northern entrance to the Canal, was a tall bronze statue of Ferdinand de Lesseps, the French engineer who had designed and built the Canal, his right arm outstretched and pointing the way southwards, to India, Asia and Australasia via his short cut. We staggered up the gangway of the *Oceania* and collapsed in our cabins after a very long but unforgettably wonderful day. I was already asleep when

---

[5] Dating from the fifth century and built, we were assured, on the very spot where Joseph, Mary and their child Jesus had lived for twelve years while sheltering in Egypt from the wrath of King Herod.

the ship sailed a little later and I woke late the next morning to see through the porthole the sun shining on the blue waters of what must have been the Mediterranean Sea.

Our first sighting of the European mainland occurred two or three days later when we passed on the starboard side the mountainous coast of the "toe" of the long-legged Italian "boot". A few hours later, the coast of Sicily came in to view on the port side, with cloud-capped and somnolent Mount Etna seeming to smother the towns along the Sicilian coast, Catania, Taormina and Messina. The passage through the Straits of Messina around midday was very exciting, although we did not stop and caught no sight of either Scylla or Charybdis, monsters who Homer avowed dwelt there. What we did see was the constant movement of ships of all sizes, from fishing boats to ferries, from cargo ships to passenger liners, some travelling north-south like us, but the majority travelling east-west between the mainland and Sicily. We passed a large double-decked ferry carrying passengers, cars, trucks and the eight carriages of a train, its passengers gazing out of their windows at us just as we stared at them. That was when I first learnt that in Europe there were several stretches of water too wide for a railway bridge to be built and where the trains were carefully rolled onto tracks fixed to ferry decks, transported across the water, and then, with the ferry's tracks carefully aligned with the railway lines on the shore, able to be attached to a waiting locomotive and to speed off on their journey. The train we saw was travelling from Palermo in Sicily to Rome and just here it was crossing the Straits between Messina on the island of Sicily and Villa San Giovanni in Calabria on the mainland. Similar arrangements exist between Dover and Dunkirk to enable the Night Ferry train to travel from London directly to Paris while its passenger's slumber undisturbed in its sleeping cars. Trains also cross the sea like this between Copenhagen and Stockholm[6] and illustrate the extent to which the vast railway network in Europe makes travel so easy for tourists.

Once through the Straits of Messina we headed north-east towards the Aeolian Islands, another haunt of mythical creatures and that evening Vulcan, Aeolus and a collection of other gods and monsters from the earth's centre gave us a spectacular greeting, with the island of Stromboli erupting violently as we sailed by. This firework display lighting up the night sky was a great finale to the month-long voyage on the *Oceania*. To some extent, it tempered the sadness of leaving the ship a day later when we berthed in Genoa, a ship that had become almost a second home to many of us. I began to feel rather apprehensive about parting from the crew and passengers, many of whom had become real friends, and set off on my own.

But, I reminded myself, this is just the beginning: you are on your way to France and so, after lingering for a couple of days in Genoa with my shipboard friends, spending a day at the beach with them in beautiful Portofino and then plucking up courage and setting off alone, I began my train journey to Paris.

---

[6] The night ferry service between London and Paris ended in 1980. Direct daylight trains, the Eurostar service, started in 1994 with completion of the Eurotunnel between Dover and Calais. Ferries still operate for cars, trucks and foot passengers. As of 2020, the Stockholm-Copenhagen trains use the sixteen-kilometre-long Oresund bridge and tunnel, opened for both road and rail traffic in 2000 and the ferries no longer operate. The train ferry across the Straits of Messina is still operating in 2020.

Chapter 2
Italy to Aquitaine

(i) Passing through Paris

The first leg of the trip from the ship to my future place of employment as a teacher and as a postgraduate student was a short one of just two hours, by train to Milan, where the family of a friend from my university days in Melbourne lived. My friend was by then working in England but his parents had kindly invited me to make an overnight stop in Milan and met me at the station. Milan's Central Station had been built by Mussolini in the 1930s on a scale and in an architectural style that in a way made it look like one of the engineering feats of ancient Rome. The high vaulted roofs over the various galleries and platforms were said to be inspired by the Baths of Caracalla in Rome and for someone like me who had never grown out of a boyhood love of playing trains, *Milano Centrale* was quite breathtaking. Of course, there were many other wonders there to see, the nearby cathedral probably being the city's greatest treasure. My friend's family lived in a beautiful apartment on the top floor of an Art Deco building quite near the station and, from their roof garden, there was a fine view of the upper part of the cathedral and of the *Madonnina* (a statue of the Virgin Mary) on the top of the tallest pinnacle. With his parents, an Australian married to an

Italian, my friend had lived through the Second World War in that apartment, when the station and its vast railway yards had been a favourite target for Allied bombers. Inevitably, the nearby cathedral and opera house (*La Scala*) and much of the historic centre of the city had been hit, reduced to rubble and burnt (many raids had seen incendiary bombs rather than high explosive bombs dropped on the city). The view from the roof garden would have been horribly different then!

During that very pleasant dinner, bed and breakfast *en famille* I learnt that my hosts had met while postgraduate students in Paris and they were happy to talk late into the night about student life in France, which I was about to experience. They knew the European rail system very well and advised me not to take the direct train from Milan to Paris as it travelled overnight and so deprived travellers of the spectacular scenery along the way. I therefore next day took a late morning train to Lausanne, stayed the night there, and continued on in the morning to Paris. The trip from Milan to Lausanne was truly extraordinary. Within half an hour of leaving the city, we were racing along the shores of Lake Maggiore, through Stresa and Arona and climbing up into the mountains and looking back down to the lakes and villas and gardens. *Isola Bella* and the summer palace of the Borromeo family came in to view and then, with the train climbing, climbing, always climbing, ….Domodossola station and the approaches to the Simplon Tunnel. Eight miles long through the Alps in darkness and then we suddenly emerged into the sunshine and Switzerland. Down, down the train raced, following mountain streams, through Brig and Sion and the junction of the line to the Matterhorn, then past Martigny and the rack railway up to Mont Blanc and Chamonix. Then we were racing along beside the icy, green headwaters of the *Rhône River* and of *Lake Léman* itself. The railway line runs along the very edge of the lake and on the outskirts of Montreux, it passes just a few metres from the famous *Château de Chillon* on its little lakeside islet. It was the most scenic railway trip of my life and I was a little reluctant to leave the train when, in the late afternoon, we arrived in Lausanne on the steep northern side of *Lake Léman*.

After a very pleasant stop for dinner, bed and breakfast in the charming old Hôtel Byron near the station, I boarded the gleaming, new, stainless-steel *"Paris-Éclair"*, a *rapide avec supplément*, for Paris. (An *"éclair"* is, in French, a flash of lightning as well as a creamy *pâtisserie* and so the train's name in English might well be translated as the *"Paris Flash"*). An ignorant beginner as far as European train travel was concerned, I had chosen that train as it was scheduled to leave at a convenient hour (about nine a.m.) and I had not yet learnt that convenience and speed would mean an increased cost, the *supplément de Vitesse* and *supplément de luxe*. But I was already at the station with my luggage, the train was about to depart and so I paid up and jumped on board. It turned out to be a one-class train, all first class, with all seating in compartments of six seats, a corridor along one side of the carriage and a folding seat at the end of the corridor for the train attendant. I found a compartment where five seats were already occupied: the two window seats by an aristocratic-looking Swiss grandmother and her six- or seven-year-old granddaughter, the two corridor seats by two more well-dressed and haughty-looking ladies, and the middle seat facing the engine was occupied by the French poodle of one of the ladies. I rather hesitatingly took the one empty seat, my *bonjour mesdames* being ignored by all as the train glided out of Lausanne and quickly gathered speed. Only two stops were scheduled, one at Vallorbe at the Swiss-French frontier where passports would be checked by the frontier police and one in Dijon. At Vallorbe, another well-dressed and be-ringed matron arrived at the compartment door, the conductor following her with her luggage. Pointing at me and waving a piece of paper, which proved to be her seat reservation, she turned to the conductor and said (I guessed, I could not quite understand her rapid and angry speech) something like, "Get rid of that fellow".

The conductor asked to see my ticket and, when I showed it to him, he sighed and said: "Alas, monsieur, this is indeed a ticket, but it is not a reservation. The train is fully booked and you are sitting in the seat this lady has reserved."

Of course, I hurriedly collected my things and stepped out in to the corridor and the lady took her place. The other passengers and the dog watched on in silence, no doubt unsurprised at the uncouth behaviour of the foreigner. I asked the conductor where I should sit and suggested that if the dog were to sit on its owner's lap or at her feet there would be a seat available for me in the compartment. Clearly shocked, he said that was out of the question as the owner had paid for the dog's ticket. The best he could do was to offer me his own folding seat at the end of the corridor, saying that he did not have much time to sit down anyway and could, if need be, find a seat with his colleague in the luggage van. And so that is how I arrived in *Douce France* and my dream city of Paris... disgruntled and disappointed.

Once the train had pulled into the *Gare de Lyon* in Paris, however, things improved. One of the silent "corridor seat" ladies from the compartment caught up with me as we walked along the platform. She was American. Her silence had been largely the result of her inability to speak French. She had seen my Australian passport when it was being checked at Vallorbe and began by apologising for not having spoken up at my shabby treatment by "those snooty women" over the reservation matter. She declared that sending a passenger out to the corridor while that yappy poodle and that spoilt little girl took up a whole seat each was ridiculous. I agreed, of course, even though their seats had indeed been paid for AND reserved, unlike mine... and felt much comforted by the motherly American matron. She continued chatting as we walked through the main station concourse with our luggage and then insisted that I join her in a taxi to the hotel. "I always stay at the Hotel Normandy at the bottom of the Avenue", she said, "What about you?"

I happened to have reserved a room in a much humbler hotel in a side street off the Avenue de l'Opéra, and so I accepted gratefully. My first ride in a Paris taxi... a Citroën, horn honking as we swept away from the station and along the rue de Lyon to the *Place de la Bastille* and into the rue du Faubourg Saint Antoine, which became the rue de Rivoli, then under the canopy of chestnut-trees, across the *Place de la Comédie Française* and into the *Avenue de l'Opéra*... and it was free and fabulous! I was dropped off at the corner of the rue Sainte Anne, waved "goodbye" to my fairy godmother and walked along to my little hotel, anxious to settle into my room and then to set off on my first day of exploring Paris.

My first stop once I had left the hotel was the central office of the CNEP, the *Comptoir National d'Escompte de Paris*, the French bank (which later became the BNP) with which I had opened an account in Australia. The bank was holding mail for me and I would be dealing with it during my couple of years at university in France. The CNEP was housed in a handsome neo-classical building quite close by and I arrived just a few minutes after it had reopened following its two-hour closure for lunch. The interior of the building was even more opulent than the exterior, which I suppose was understandable as it was after all the bank's head office, but it was a bit intimidating! Even more disconcerting was the almost church-like silence of the place. Although there was a trickle of customers coming and going all the time, they somehow made little noise even on the marble floors, while the bank clerks and officers moving about behind the iron grilles and glass screens made even less. I was greeted by a very polite young man at the *Renseignements* desk just inside the entrance and was then escorted up one flight of marble stairs to the waiting area of the section handling *Etrangers*.

After a short wait an elderly, white-haired man emerged and came towards me beaming, both hands outstretched: *"Cher Monsieur, vous êtes enfin arrivé! Que c'est loin, l'Australie! Vous avez fait un beau voyage?"* and so on.

I found it hard to understand that a poor student from far away would receive such courteous attention, but I quickly discovered that that was to be the way I was generally received throughout my stay in France. I think that the French did then, and still do, regard politeness as important in life, as something that costs little and makes life easier for everyone. And I suspected then, and still do, that they make an extra effort to be polite and even friendly when foreigners make an effort, even a very slight effort, to speak French and not to shout loudly in their own foreign tongue, English or German or Chinese or whatever their own language might be. So my first day in France, which had begun rather unhappily on the *"Paris-Éclair"*, ended very happily at the hands of the staff of the CNEP. But of course, the *"Paris-Éclair"* had started in

Switzerland, and even the French-speaking cantons of Switzerland are not quite France!

The next day, I made my way to the branch of the education ministry that was responsible for foreign students and their scholarships. It was housed in another grand building not quite as opulent as the bank's head office but inhabited by a team of civil servants just as polite and helpful as had been the bank staff. Another elderly gentleman, the officer in charge of the section, seemed delighted to have a student from far away Australia come all the way to France to study French. On completing all the paperwork involved (and there was a great deal of it: the French seemed to have invented both bureaucracy and casefiles (*bureau* and *dossier* are indeed French words), he plied me with advice on how to adjust to student life in France and promised me that I would like Bordeaux, where I was to take up my scholarship. It was, he said, with some exaggeration, almost as interesting as Paris. "*Vous allez voir les Allées de Tourny*", he said as we parted, and I was indeed to learn that the citizens of Bordeaux believed that handsome *promenade* to equal if not to surpass the *Champs Elysées*, which Parisians all believe is the most beautiful boulevard in the world!

(ii) A student in Bordeaux

I had come to France and had enrolled at the University of Bordeaux to prepare a postgraduate degree in French Literature. An impecunious twenty-two-year-old student from abroad, I had had the good fortune of having been awarded a position of *Assistant d'Anglais*, or English Assistant, in the most prestigious secondary school in the city, a position which would see me housed and fed in the school for the duration of the academic year in return for twelve hours of work a week as an assistant to the full-time local English master. After a few weeks in Paris, during which I worked hard at lifting my Australian French to a level of proficiency sufficient for me to handle a classroom of lively French teenagers, I had boarded the train and set off for the south-west, for Aquitaine.

Bordeaux is just under six hundred kilometres from Paris, the main stops along the way being in Orléans, Tours, Poitiers and Angoulême. In my student days the *Trains Rapides* did the trip in five hours, the *Trains Express* taking about six hours and the *Trains Omnibus*, which stopped at all stations, even longer. There was one train a day in each direction, which did the trip in four hours, non-stop, "*Le Drapeau*" first class with a supplement for speed (like the "*Paris-Éclair*)" so I never travelled on that one! Since then, a new, high-speed line has been built and the TGVs, carrying both first and economy class passengers in great comfort, now do the whole trip non-stop in two hours and ten minutes!

Bordeaux is built on the southern bank of the Garonne River, just upstream from its junction with the Dordogne, where the combined waters are very wide and deep and form an estuary known as the *Gironde*. While the area had been lived in by the Celts and earlier races, the city itself was founded in 56BC by Publius Crassus, one of Julius Caesar's lieutenants, the settlement being known then as Burdigala. Not much remains of the Roman city other than a section of a 15,000-seat stadium, the *Palais Gallien*, but the social centre of the modern city, the *Place de la Comédie*, is more or less on the site of the forum of Roman Burdigala, which extended from there right to the banks of the Garonne. About ninety kilometres downstream from the city, the Gironde estuary opens out to the Atlantic Ocean.

Approaching Bordeaux from Paris, whether by road or by rail, one arrives at a spot on the northern bank of the great river with a clear view of the spires and towers of the city on the other side. A great suspension bridge, the *Pont d'Aquitaine*, built in 1965, now carries the motorway across the river and around the western edge of the city. A kilometre further upstream is the *Pont Chaban-Delmas*, a state-of-the-art vertical lift bridge built in 2012: when its central span is raised quite big ocean liners can continue upstream and berth at the *Port de la Lune* on the south bank of the river, a few hundred metres from the CBD. A short distance further upstream yet is the handsome stone and brick *Pont de Pierre,* commissioned by Napoleon I but not finally completed until 1822. The river is over five hundred metres wide here where it sweeps past Bordeaux, very deep and with strong currents. It is tidal and salty despite being so far inland, and bridge-building posed extreme technical difficulties which even the Romans could not overcome. Napoleon's was not only the first bridge ever built across the Garonne between the sea and the city but it was the only road bridge across the river in Bordeaux until the construction of the *Pont St Jean* a little further upstream again in 1965; the iron railway bridge built in 1860, and still in use, was the first of many engineering marvels to be designed by the young Gustave Eiffel.

The quays along the edge of the Bordeaux CBD have been the main port of Aquitaine for more than a thousand years: from here the young Duchess Eleanor of Aquitaine left for Paris as the bride of Louis VII of France in 1137; here Richard the Lionheart, her son, landed to claim the city and duchy inherited from his mother; here the English kings landed their troops and supplies throughout the three hundred years of English rule in Aquitaine and Gascony (1152–1453); here in 1453, ending the Hundred Years' War just twenty-two years after the burning of Joan of Arc in Rouen, Charles VII besieged and captured the English stronghold and reduced their occupation of French soil to just the port of Calais in the north, a toehold eventually lost in 1558. Bordeaux is a city steeped in history and full of fascinating architectural reminders of its past.

The *Lycée Montaigne* in which I taught and lived was open only to boys[7] in the final two years of secondary school or in the first year of tertiary study (preparing to sit entrance exams for the elite *écoles supérieures* in Paris). The Lycée, like the university nearby, was housed in grand seventeenth- and eighteenth-century buildings which opened directly to the crowded streets of the inner city. Students had no gardens or playing fields where they could meet and relax, just large, asphalted courtyards where, between classes, they stood around talking and smoking under the plane trees. School uniforms were non-existent in the *lycées,* corporal punishment in schools had been abolished before the Second World War, and many secondary school students on arriving at school in the morning, every morning, would walk up to their teachers and shake hands with a *"Bonjour, monsieur"*. Many students shook hands with one another every morning. It seemed to me so strangely formal and old-fashioned and yet almost aggressively democratic and egalitarian. So, student life

---

[7] There was a comparable elite secondary school for girls on the other side of the inner city, the *Lycée Camille Jullian.*

differed greatly from what I had known in Australia, with far more emphasis on study and discussion and almost no emphasis on sport. This had suited me well as I had never really been interested in sport and quickly came to enjoy Bordeaux's café life and endless debates and discussions about politics and world affairs.

Even the teachers and university lecturers adjourned to the nearby cafés and small parks or squares for relaxation. Across the road from my *Lycée* was the Café Montaigne and it was there that staff tended to gather for a coffee and a cigarette during the day and at night for a glass of wine, a game of cards and endless chat, reviewing and resolving the world's problems. The dozen or so university students I frequented were all doing postgraduate studies of one sort or another... master or doctoral degrees, teaching diplomas and so on. They were a bit boisterous at times but in a sophisticated way. On winter evenings we would gather in a corner of the large dining-room lined with mirrors and red velvet banquettes. Two or three waiters in black trousers, white jackets and black bow ties flittered about and the whole scene was presided over by *Monsieur le patron* who sat at the cash desk on a raised dais in the centre of the room. The waiters handed up to him the little Bakelite saucers with the accounts and cash payments and he handed back the saucers with the receipts and change, which the waiters then brought back to the customers who would take the receipt and check to see that the change covered the customary ten per cent tip for the staff.

One evening, our group, for reasons that now escape me, "stole" the high-heeled shoe of Annette, one of the education students, and passed it around the tables and along the banquette, with poor Annette laughingly chasing it and never quite catching it before it disappeared under a table or behind the hat stand or a potted palm. Eventually the joke wore thin, and Annette gave up and went back to her chair and an uncomfortable silence descended on us all, like a group of naughty children who had been told to sit down and behave properly. And then quite magically, normalcy returned: one of the waiters appeared from nowhere bearing aloft a silver tray with the missing shoe sitting in upright splendour. He approached Annette's table and with a bow and a flourish presented the shoe as if it were Cinderella's glass slipper, saying: *"le soulier de Mademoiselle est avancé."*

Bordeaux is the only big city in France (population 600,000 in 2020) where snow is almost unknown in winter, but it nonetheless does get very cold, especially by Australian standards. One evening, close to Christmas, we were all there in the Café Montaigne, sipping *un grog* (a hot toddy), when I produced a little bit of Australian sunshine for my colleagues. My mother had sent me a traditional Christmas cake, which she would have made with flour, butter, sugar, eggs, spices, almonds, and mixed dried fruit soaked overnight in cognac. Everyone in the house would have helped with the chopping and stirring of the rich and heavy mixture before it was baked, sealed into an airtight tin, wrapped in a tight calico cover, carefully addressed to a far away son and despatched on its long journey by ship to distant France and the absent family member. It arrived just before Christmas and as I unwrapped it and opened the airtight container the sight of the cake's shiny glazed surface and the smell of the spices and brandy instantly carried me across the miles to my Home Sweet Home… it was almost like a scene from Dickens's *A Christmas Carol*.

I took the cake in its tin across to the Café Montaigne and passed it to our favourite waiter, asking him to cut it in to "fingers" and to bring it to the table once all of our group had arrived and had been served a drink. Annette had spent a year or two in England studying English and was able to tell the others something of the traditions of an English Christmas – including that of the Christmas cake which enriched many an afternoon tea once Christmas Day had passed. The others were all amazed that a cake could supposedly remain fresh and edible after the long voyage from Australia and when the waiter arrived and started passing around the slices there were a few in the group who rather gingerly accepted their share. English and British cuisine have a very poor reputation in France! My mother's Christmas cake, however, turned out to be a great hit with everybody wanting more until, fortunately, somebody called out that I should get a second slice before it was all gone!

Across the road from the *lycée* was the medieval heart of the city, entered through the thirteenth century *Porte de la Grosse Cloche* where the southern walls once stood. The gate and walls on the northern side of the medieval centre were replaced in the seventeenth and eighteenth centuries by wide streets such as the *Cours Alsace et Lorraine* and *the Cours de l'Intendance*. The long, straight and narrow rue Sainte Catherine had bisected the city from medieval times and had always been a busy shopping street, as it still is. At its northern end, it opens into a fine square, originally the forum of the Roman city of Burdigala, with on one side the really

Le Grand Théâtre

superb *Grand Théâtre* and on the other side the handsome *Allées de Tourny.*

On the riverside, behind the *Grand Théâtre*, are the fifteenth century *Porte du Palais*, the semi-circular *Place de la Bourse* and the long curve of eighteenth-century mansions and warehouses facing the river. The cathedral, on the southern edge of the medieval centre, is a strange hodge-podge of Romanesque, Gothic and late Renaissance architecture, the detached bell tower, the *Tour Pey Berland*, being perhaps the most interesting part of it architecturally. Duchess Eleanor of Aquitaine married the young King Louis VII of France in this cathedral in 1137 and fifteen years later managed to have the marriage annulled. Almost immediately afterwards, she married Henry Plantagenet, Count of Anjou and Duke of Normandy, who two years later became King of England. On her death in 1204, Eleanor's duchy of Aquitaine passed to her son, Richard the Lionheart, by then Duke of Normandy and this south-western third of France passed under English rule. I never tired of walking around the city poking into the byways of history, admiring the buildings and chatting with the locals… the possibilities were endless.

Then one day I was summoned to the concierge's lodge at the *Lycée* and handed a note: my father's cousin and her husband were touring Europe, had made a detour to Bordeaux to visit me, and would be calling at six p.m. to take me out to dinner. Frank and Molly were a lovely couple, recently retired and comfortably off. In addition to looking up stray relatives such as me, they were interested in regional food and wine, they were willing to visit places of pilgrimage, such as Lourdes and Compostela (probably why they were in south-west France) and of course, as they were from Australia which is rather short on ancient monuments, they were interested in castles and cathedrals. Over a wonderful meal in a restaurant that I could never have afforded to visit, we discussed what they might do in the two or three days they thought of spending in Bordeaux. With input from some of my Café Montaigne friends, it was agreed that one day should be spent sightseeing in the city itself, one day on a couple of *circuits de vin* and one day on a visit to a château other than the ones associated with particular vineyards. As my cousins were particularly interested in dessert wines not widely known in Australia, we opted to do a tour of the Sauternes-Bazardais area which would include a look at, if not a visit to, the fabled *Château d'Yquem* near the village of Sauternes. As it was close by, we would also visit on that day the *Château of La Brède*, the home of the eighteenth-century Bordeaux writer, Montesquieu. We would then cross the river at Langon and return to Bordeaux via Cadillac with its château built by the Duc d'Epernon, a favourite of King Henri IV. On the following day, we would do a tour of the *Médoc* region including the great *Château Margaux* vineyards and have a seafood lunch at Arcachon. Both of these tours were expertly organised for us by the *Maison des Vins* near the *Grand Théâtre* and I offered my own services as guide for the city tour, including as a highlight our attendance at a symphony concert in the *Grand Théâtre* in the evening. The *Grand Théâtre* is Bordeaux's opera house, was completed in 1780 to what the proud locals call a "*grandiose et élégant*" design which was subsequently reproduced, usually with less success, in Paris and in many European capitals. My plan to showcase the city to my cousins went off very well: they were vastly impressed by Bordeaux, by the stunningly beautiful *Grand Théâtre* and by the surrounding countryside, a panoply of beautifully kept vineyards and of historic châteaux and churches. In this way, my *Bordelais* friends met two more Australians and found them surprisingly civilised and I had the most marvellous mid-term break (and a surfeit of fine food and wine) that any student could hope for.

My cousins left Bordeaux in the direction of Lourdes, travelling by way of Agen, Toulouse and Tarbes, intending to continue on by train from Lourdes to Dax, Biarritz and the Spanish frontier. Forty or so years later, I was back in France revisiting my old haunts and planning to relive those pleasant few days. From Paris, I set off by train on a round trip, with stops in Limoges and Toulouse, to spend some time in Gascony before reaching Bordeaux and then zipping back to Paris on the newest, fastest TGV. So, I set off for Gascony, land of musketeers, *foie gras*, fine wines and ancient towns such as Auch and Condom. Did I say Condom? Yes, and to add a touch of spirit, *Condom-en-Armagnac*!

Chapter 3
Condom-En-Armagnac

Getting to Condom was almost as difficult as getting a condom on can be, both requiring rock-hard purpose and determination. The railway linking Condom to the main Bordeaux-Toulouse-Narbonne line is now closed to passenger trains and the only means of approach by public transport is by bus, with rather infrequent services available from the railway stations in Agen, Auch and Mont-de-Marsan, each being forty or more kilometres away. I made my way to Condom via Agen on the connecting bus which meandered its way south to Condom and eventually on to Auch, the ancient capital and cathedral city of Gascony, on the banks of the river Gers. I had already visited Auch and had attended a symphony concert in the beautiful cathedral and I have great memories of a superb Sunday dinner there, *Le Tout Canard*[8] at the fabulous *Le France Bar* et *Brasserie* facing the cathedral. Auch is a really fascinating old town, slumbering through the twentieth century and dreaming of its glory days. Nowadays, since

---

[8] *Le Tout Canard*, or Duck All Ways, was a platter of choice pieces of duck cooked in various ways: breast, drumsticks, wings etc. roasted, sautéed, poached in wine, or presented in a *ballotine*, mousse or *pâté*. The garnish included a tiny pot of orange sauce, olives stuffed with artichoke heart, finely sliced ham, green beans and shredded lettuce. It was a gastronomic and artistic creation from the chef... and an amazing delight for the diner!

Napoleon I's abolition of the provinces and provincial governors, (replacing them by *départments*, smaller geographical areas supervised by a *Préfet* or Prefect rather than a governor), Auch is the *préfecture* or seat of the Prefect, the Paris-appointed official who supervises the way the locally-elected mayors and councillors run the *départment* of Gers. Much of the department of Gers is the ancient county of Armagnac, centred on the county town of Lectoure where a large part of the château of the counts of Armagnac still stands.

Condom, somewhat smaller than Auch (who worries about size, even in this context?) but a little larger than Lectoure, about twenty kilometres to the west, is well and truly *en Armagnac* geographically and even spiritually, as Condom boasts a very interesting *Musée de l'Armagnac,* so appropriately housed in part of the former palace of the bishops of Condom, the lords spiritual of the diocese. No longer an episcopal city, Condom is a rather sleepy market town halfway between the plum-tree orchards and prune production around Agen and the geese- and duck-raising farms around Auch. It is a pretty little place with a population of about 8,000 nestled in the valley of the river Baïse and dominated by the tall square tower of the former abbey-cathedral, now a mere parish church, of St Pierre. In the early 1800s, the river was made navigable all the way down to its junction with the Garonne and then on to Bordeaux and the sea and so Condom became the main point of despatch for the barrels and bottles of Armagnac produced in Gascony and exported to appreciative drinkers throughout the world.

There had been people living here in the Bronze Age. In the first century BC, the Romans arrived as part of the conquest of Gaul by Julius Caesar. Roman engineers bridged the river and built a fort or *castrum* to protect both the river crossing and travellers on the roads from Toulouse to the Atlantic coast and to the high mountain pass through the Pyrenees to Spain. The *castrum* grew with the arrival of Roman settlers, farmers and merchants and in the seventh century AD a monastery was founded. In the early eleventh century, Pope Benedict VIII approved the establishment of the Abbey of Condom and in 1317 Condom was raised to the status of a bishopric, subject to the archbishopric of Bordeaux. The abbey church became *ipso facto* the Condom cathedral and the last abbot, Dom Raymond de Galard, became the first Bishop of Condom. (The best-known holder of the bishopric was Jacques-Bénigne Bossuet, a famous theologian and orator at the court of Louis XIV). Another famous local was Count Charles d'Artagnan, a real-life captain of musketeers in the royal guard of Louis XIV. His adventurous life, much embroidered, formed the basis of the tales of *The Three Musketeers* written by Alexandre Dumas and of several film and television versions of his life. D'Artagnan's birthplace, the *Château de Castelmore,* is about twenty kilometres away to the south-west near the village of Lupiac.

The Roman Road had become one of the four ways through France for pilgrims heading to the great shrine of St James in Compostela in north-west Spain. Catering for the pilgrims required the construction of hospices, convents and monasteries, the development of farmers' markets, shops and taverns... and the organisation of civil authorities and even courts and castles to control the crowds. The dukes of Gascony ruled here when the area was not being attacked or occupied by the English as it was, after all, part of the great dowry of Aquitaine brought to Henry II of England on his marriage with Eleanor of Aquitaine.

Baïse, the name of the river, seems to anglophones (but not to francophones) an extraordinarily appropriate name for a river on whose banks the town of Condom stands... as the English translation of Baïse (minus the diaresis) is that four-letter word beginning with "f" which dares not be printed here. The name of the town on the banks of the aforenamed river derives not from the name of the river or from the actions of the people cavorting or living on its banks but simply from the fact that the town grew up at the junction, or confluence, of two rivers, the Baïse and the smaller Gélé. "Condomagos" was the place-name used by the Gauls and meant the river junction market. And the shortened form of that word was accepted by the Romans and then by medieval France as the name of the emerging town.

Though steeped in history, Condom would probably have slumbered on, unknown outside of France, had it not been for the actions of those troublesome neighbours across the Channel, the English. In the early eighteenth century, doing a grand tour of Europe became a fashionable, if not essential, part of the education of young gentlemen of the English wealthy classes. Amorous adventures with hot-blooded Continental ladies often formed part of that education. Since the time of ancient Egypt, men and women had used various types of prophylactics to avoid contracting venereal disease and to discourage conception: sheaths made of animal tissue such as sheep intestine, or linen and silk, were common in sixteenth- and seventeenth-century Europe. In England, a phrase commonly used was "to enter in

Condom

armour" but by the early 1700s, the word "condum" was beginning to predominate. Just why is not really known.

The word is thought to perhaps have come from the Latin *condere,* meaning to protect or to cover. An ambitious colonel in King Charles II's soldiery was said to have delighted the Merry Monarch by introducing improved versions of "armour" to his king and a century later a savvy London doctor by the name of Condon was, for some time, given the credit of designing an even more satisfactory version of the sheath. Dr Condon has, however, proved to be a mythical rather than an historical figure, as has Charles II's helpful colonel. In German, the term *kondom* appeared in the early eighteenth century, possibly traceable to the same mythical English doctor, as cultural links with England had been hugely strengthened by the accession to the English throne in 1714 of King George I of the German-speaking House of Hanover. In France and Italy, the term *redingote anglaise,* or "English overcoat" was in vogue and was used by that well-known ladies' man, Casanova. The terms *condom* and *kondom* were both in use in Utrecht in the Netherlands in 1712 to advertise sales of safe sex in the brothels of that city, choc-a-bloc with soldiers, diplomats and civil servants drawing up the Treaty of Utrecht which ended the long War of the Spanish Succession. In 1725, there were shops in London selling fashionable condoms, washable and re-useable ones, often embellished with gay ribbons "for fastening in place" ... Nobody seems to have consulted the poor citizens of far-away Condom on the matter. In eighteenth-century France, polite circles of society used the term *préservatif,* leaving the more vulgar *condom* to the English. When in nineteenth-century England, the term "French Letter" began to be used the French responded with

Capote Anglaise (an English cap or hood: the bonnet of a car is, in French, the *capote*). While in twenty-first-century English, the terms raincoat (of no particular nationality), rubber, and French Letter or franger are still in use, condom remains king and is indeed almost universally used... except perhaps in Condom, where the pharmacies and vending machines offer only *préservatifs*!

Scoring points off one another is, of course, an old tradition in Anglo-French relationships. The Battle of Fontenoy in 1745 is said to have been won by the French after a French officer, courteously approached by his opposite number from the English army facing him and invited to open fire, is said to have politely replied "*Messieurs les Anglais, tirez les premiers*", or "After you". The English accepted the offer, fired first and, while they were reloading their muskets, were mown down by the French survivors of the initial fusillade.

In the middle of the nineteenth century, rubber condoms began to be widely used and by the early 1900s latex had become the most favoured material in their manufacture, which by then was mechanised and on an industrial scale worldwide. In the 1990s, the mayor of Condom decided that his municipality should somehow be able to benefit from having its ancient name used worldwide in the interests of pleasure and safety. After attending various conferences in the USA, he envisaged establishing Condom as a major centre for research in to contraception and AIDS, but eventually had to settle for a small *Musée du Préservatif* which opened in 2004. The museum and the many signs around the town incorporating the name "Condom" are a great attraction with camera-toting tourists but are still the cause of some unease among the local citizenry who do not quite see the joke.

A little further north-east of Agen than Condom is to the south-west, lies the quaint village of Montcuq, where the inhabitants have also had to deal with a linguistic curiosity. A final "q" is not normally pronounced in French but its silence in this case would result in the village name being pronounced in the same way as *mon cul*, where the l is silent: *mon cul* = my arse. Passengers travelling by bus from the nearby big town, Cahors, would if they wished to alight in Montcuq need to ask the driver for "*L'arrêt de Montcuq, s'il vous plaît*". As *l'arrêt*, the stop, is pronounced in exactly the same way as *la raie*, the parting (of a gentleman's hair) or a crack, they would, if the final q were left silent, be asking for "the crack of my arse, please" ...a disconcerting thing to say to any bus driver. Some understanding of local vocabulary and history, as well as of rules of pronunciation, would be helpful for tourists travelling to villages such as La Fion (the fanny in Savoy) or to Anus and nearby Orgy (yes, the same meanings in French and English) both being hamlets in Burgundy. The reasoning behind these choices of names is in most cases as little understood as that of the English translation of *un préservatif*! These village names would, of course, be no more surprising to English-speaking travellers in Burgundy and Savoy than would have been the large red electric sign atop the then tallest building in Canberra which so surprised a friend of mine, newly-arrived from Portugal. The sign was advertising the Commercial and General Assurance Company and simply said "CAGA", which in Portuguese means "shit"!

I spent a very pleasant few days in Condom, staying in a comfortable, modern little hotel, Le Logis des Cordeliers, discreetly hidden behind a high stone wall and a screen of olive trees so as not to spoil the *olde worlde* appearance of the surroundings. I could not afford the refinements of the elegant Hôtel Les Trois Lys but did splurge on a wonderful meal at *Le Balcon* restaurant on the *Place St Pierre* and on another at the equally charming restaurant *La Table des Cordeliers*. (The *Cordeliers* were the Franciscan friars, so named because of the white cord or rope they wear around the waist over their brown habits). Curiously, I discovered that the motel in which I was staying had been built on the site of the graveyard of the Franciscan monastery. The monastery had been closed down at the time of the Revolution and the parts of the old building that had survived were now functioning as the very atmospheric *Cordeliers* restaurant. Similar snippets of history revealed that the handsome eighteenth-century building in the main street and now used as a school had been built as the town house of the de Polignac family. The Duchesse de Polignac was Queen Marie Antoinette's closest friend and lady-in-waiting. Those very attractive old buildings on the edge of town and now serving as a community centre, retirement home, pilgrim refuge and backpackers' hostel, dated from 1283 and were originally a Dominican convent, founded by St Dominic himself. The convent had been closed at the Revolution and the buildings had been turned into an army barracks, housing four hundred men and four hundred horses! In 1892, the soldiers left and the property became a convent once again, this time housing Carmelite nuns. After a hundred years or so, the Carmelite convent closed and in 2010 the municipality of Condom purchased the buildings and, after refurbishment, the property reopened as the community centre and hostel it now is. If I had known in time I could have slept with the ghosts of the Dominican and Carmelite nuns instead of with those of the Franciscan friars!

Chapter 4
Zig-Zagging Through France

(i) Cherbourg to Conques

One year, my cousin Helen and I spent four weeks of the early European summer on a zig-zagging tour of the French countryside. We had worked out an itinerary that suited us both, catering for Helen's interest in medieval studies and monasticism, mine in history and architecture, and a shared interest in French culture, food and life. Where possible, the itinerary took in parts of the pilgrim road to Compostela in Spain and, like Chaucer's pilgrims on the way to Canterbury, we did the journey in easy stages and were attentive to both physical and spiritual needs along the way. I had travelled to France by flying from Brisbane to the USA, taking a ship from Galveston to Lisbon and travelling by train from Lisbon to Paris and on to Cherbourg in Normandy. Helen had flown from Melbourne to London and then travelled by train to Wales where she attended a summer school in medieval studies run by the University of Wales. On completing the course, she went to visit relatives in Bath and then on to Portsmouth where she boarded the Brittany Ferries *Normandie Express* fast catamaran (it does forty-two knots) to Cherbourg. I had arrived in Cherbourg the evening before and one May morning I picked up the car which we had arranged to hire for the month and drove, albeit a little gingerly at first and on the "wrong" side of the road (to Australian, British and a few other idiosyncratic drivers), to the harbour.

The *Normandie Express* arrived in Cherbourg on schedule at noon, berthing where the transatlantic liners (including the *Titanic*, *Queen Mary* and *Normandie*) used to arrive and were met by the boat trains to whisk their passengers to and from Paris. The old terminal has been turned into a maritime museum, the train tracks torn up and today's passengers are bussed a kilometre or so to a new ferry passenger terminal, which they enter from the harbour security zone and walk through to be met by friends, relatives and taxi drivers beyond the security barriers. Helen seemed none the worse for the three-hour, high-speed crossing from Portsmouth and so we climbed into our smart new green Citroën 3 and were soon on our way, Helen navigating and me driving. We decided to defer lunch for an hour or so, to give Helen time to get her land legs and to give us the opportunity of finding a town smaller than Cherbourg in which to find a nice little café where we could start our study of French regional cuisine.

Our first challenge was to get out of Cherbourg which, like most towns in France, consists of an ancient town centre, of mostly narrow, winding and often one-way streets, surrounded by newer areas where boulevards, roundabouts and speeding motorists abound. We quickly learnt that road signs in France often differ from those in Australia. We were nonplussed at first, on coming to an intersection where there were four roads meeting, to find each road signed with a possible destination (such as Mont Saint-Michel and Saint-Malo or Rouen) and the fourth road bearing the sign *Toutes Directions* i.e. "to everywhere". Which sign did you believe?

We learnt to solve this problem by driving round and round the roundabout reading the signs and gradually working out their hidden (to us) meanings. Onlookers and other motorists were no doubt amused or annoyed by this tactic, but it served us well!

We got away from Cherbourg with only a few wrong turns and headed off towards Caen, our first overnight stop. By half past one we were in Valonges, a small market town, and we decided to make this place our lunch stop. We parked under the plane trees in the main square and rather hurriedly found a little restaurant where we seemed to be the last to arrive for lunch and the only ones to sit outside on the terrace (it was a bit cool and cloudy). We started our regular practice of having the economical *plat du jour* (if not the whole three courses of the *menu du jour*) and a glass of wine, with the good intention of having only a light meal in the evening (when the daily special is not usually available). I was careful to see if my driving was affected by the glass of wine and can happily report that such did not seem to be the case. I had no collisions with kerb or cow, pedestrian or policeman, in the whole 4,000 kilometres covered in the C3... although Helen did, I think, have one or two heart-stopping moments in the passenger seat when, emboldened by a glass of rosé, I overtook slow-moving vehicles on winding country roads and just managed to get back to safety before the double lines, or oncoming traffic, appeared!

After lunch, as it was already three o'clock, we decided to head off to Caen, where we arrived around five p.m., just in time for the evening peak hour traffic. Our hotel, the Hôtel de la Fontaine was, we knew, near the *Place de la République* and, even without a map, we guessed that that meant we should follow the signs saying *Centre Ville*, which we did, and lo and behold we were soon in the *Place de la République* and found a spot in the underground car park there. We quickly checked in at the hotel, a good little two-star place run by a friendly young couple and headed off for a bit of sightseeing. The castle was close by and we were soon up on the ramparts and looking out over the city. Although Rouen has displaced Caen as the capital of Normandy, Caen was William the Conqueror's capital and he and his father built much of the castle, a huge fortress dominating the city and the port (on the river). To consolidate his position, William, who was the duke's bastard but only son, had married his cousin, the very legitimate and wealthy heiress Matilda, and in middle age William decided to repent of his many transgressions. To expiate the slaughter of the English at the Battle of Hastings, he had an abbey[9] built on the site of the battle and he provided a large endowment so that Mass would continually be said for the souls of those killed. To expiate his flouting of church law in marrying his first cousin, he provided the funds to establish two great abbeys in Caen, the *Abbaye aux Dames,* where Queen Matilda was buried in 1083, and the *Abbaye aux Hommes*, where William was buried on his death in Rouen four years later[10]. The two abbeys and the many church spires dominate the view of the city from the castle and we hurried down to the *Abbaye aux Dames*, the closer of the two, as the light began to fade. We

---

[9] Battle Abbey, in Sussex, a Benedictine abbey established in 1071 with sixty monks from Marmoutier Abbey in Tours, France. It was closed and largely demolished by Henry VIII in 1538.

[10] William the Conqueror's eldest son, Robert, succeeded him as Duke of Normandy while his second son, William, received the apparently lesser inheritance of the kingdom of England.

got there in time to slip inside and catch the last strains of Benediction and saw a small group of earnest young people around the high altar begin to disperse as we walked in. The young priest looked us over as we approached but civilly acknowledged our respectful "*Bonsoir, mon père,*" before disappearing into the shadows. A local cell of *Opus Dei*?! The abbey church is very large, pure Romanesque, simple and sober in its decoration, faithfully restored after the devastation of the Second World War bombing and very impressive.

By this time, it was after seven and so we decided to give up on sightseeing and head for dinner. We read the menus outside a few places and opted for one near the marina, recommended by the people at our hotel. Helen was determined to try regional fare and so ordered *Tripes à la Mode de Caen*. I had tried the dish years earlier, had found it unpleasant and told Helen so. After a few mouthfuls, she agreed and had to content herself with a few vegetables from my order (supplemented, naturally, by a substantial entrée and a good dessert!). We could not, of course, stick to our policy of having only a light meal in the evening as the weather had turned a bit chilly and we didn't want to go to bed cold and hungry in a strange place, so we sort of forced ourselves to manage the three courses!

In the morning we had a quick look at the CBD (discovering that *Galeries Lafayette*[11] and all its temptations was just around the corner from the hotel!) and then set off for Mont-Saint-Michel, our lunch stop, and Saint-Malo, our overnight stop. We made fairly good time, despite our late start, and came within sight of the mount on its island by noon.

---

[11] Galeries Lafayette, the biggest department store in Paris, has branches in Caen and many provincial cities as well as abroad.

The approach across the causeway is very impressive and will be even more so when the recently announced project (to move the tourist car park and bus station back to the mainland and to replace the causeway with a bridge which will allow the sea to ebb and flow naturally between the island and the mainland) is completed.

At sea level the island and abbey are surrounded by

Mont-Saint-Michel

massive fortifications pierced by, I think, just one great gateway, *La Porte du Roy*, set between twin towers and protected by drawbridge and portcullis. Once inside the gates, the visitor walks up a winding narrow street lined with souvenir shops, restaurants and small hotels and ending at the gateway to the abbey proper, the *Grand Degré*. This is where the real climb begins, a seemingly endless series of stone staircases and ramps twisting and turning ever upwards until one emerges, pretty breathless, on the square in front of the abbey church.

I looked over the parapet at the rooftops, tourists and sea below and estimated that we were at least twenty stories above sea level, and we had not yet entered the church or climbed to its roof or central tower. Just how the monks found the patience, the skills and the materials to build the place is really amazing. Of course, the abbey had a great business going in the Middle Ages in that it housed a piece of red cloth said to be part of the Archangel Michael's cloak, plus a block of marble on which the archangel had stepped and left a footprint! Pilgrims flocked there to venerate the saint possibly in even greater numbers than the crowds of tourists and souvenir hunters of today. But the grandeur and beauty of the engineering and architectural achievements of a thousand years really are compelling, and the overall result of this strange mixture of Romanesque, Gothic and eighteenth-century Neo-Classical is one of beauty and harmony. We prefaced our visit to the abbey with a visit to the famous restaurant of *Mère Poulard* who, a century or so ago, was suddenly invaded by a large number of people wanting lunch: all she had on hand was a good supply of eggs, bread and butter. So she whipped up an omelette, three eggs per person, and kept on whipping and whipping until the egg mixture was well on the way to becoming a soufflé. She then cooked it as an omelette in a frying pan with lots of melted butter and *voilà, Omelette à la Mère Poulard*! The restaurant *À la Mère Poulard* has been a roaring success ever since!

Helen and I washed the omelette down with a jug of cider (we were still in Normandy, where cider rather than wine is the national drink). As a result, frequent pauses to catch the breath and a few Zs were needed as we shortly thereafter climbed the hundreds of steps up through the *Merveille* to the abbey church and cloisters. The climb, and the brisk sea breeze at the top, probably sobered us up enough too to later on collapse into the trusty Citroën for the drive on to Saint-Malo, across the border in Brittany.

We reached Saint-Malo around six p.m., checked in to our

little two-star Hôtel de l'Europe and had a pleasant evening meal in the hotel dining-room. After the meal, we drove the kilometre or so into the old town, the *Vieille Ville*, a fortified stronghold with great granite ramparts facing the ocean and the English[12]. We walked along part of the sea wall watching the Atlantic surf crashing and foaming on the rocks below, poked around a little in the rather touristy picturesque streets lined with expensive boutiques and bistros, and then headed back to the Hôtel de l'Europe and bed. In the morning, we had an early *café au lait* and set off for our next overnight destination, the twelfth century Cistercian *Abbaye de N-D de Melleray*.

Our route took us through Dol-de-Bretagne, once an important ecclesiastical centre and market town. It is full of half-timbered houses and flower boxes and is quite picturesque but is now little more than a rather sleepy minor railway junction. The main building material other than the timber and render of the quaint façades in the main street seems to be the local charcoal grey stone which gives the town a rather sombre appearance. Dol is dominated by its cathedral, dedicated to St Samson (having no known connection with Delilah) who, like St Patrick, is said to have come from Wales and to have Christianised the local pagans! There was a cold wind blowing when we were in Dol and the odd spit of rain encouraged us to take shelter in a little patisserie which just happened to have a *salon de thé* adjoining, so we warmed ourselves up with a little indulgence of coffee and cake before

---

[12] Saint-Malo is the setting of Anthony Doerr's marvellously evocative novel *All the Light We Cannot See*, the story of a blind girl living in Saint-Malo during the German occupation in the 1940s. Read the book and then visit the ramparts!

hitting the road again. Our next stop was in Châteaubriant, a livelier market town and not far from our destination, the abbey at Melleray.[13] The wind had stopped but there was still a bit of drizzle around so we again retreated to a little café and this time had a *croque monsieur* and a glass of wine, just in case the monks offered us not much more than bread and water for the evening meal.

We reached Melleray at about five o'clock. There is no village, just the abbey buildings in a clearing in the woods: the Cistercians were much keener on seclusion and *le désert* than were the Benedictines, whose monasteries often grew into large towns. Melleray had been one of the earliest daughter houses of Cîteaux and the abbey church, consecrated in 1154, is pure Romanesque, just a nave and apse, no transepts, no tower, simple and uncluttered. The monastic buildings stand at the edge of a small lake (actually a large fishpond built by the monks centuries ago), with poplars and ancient elms lining the banks and surrounding the whole in a shimmering screen of green and gold. The main monastery buildings date from the seventeenth century and a new guest house, harmonising with the earlier buildings, had been put up in 1990. The guest-master welcomed us and showed us to our very pleasant en-suite rooms, and we then explored the grounds a little before heading to Vespers and the evening meal (a delicious vegetable soup followed by fish and fruit, with plenty of excellent bread and a bottle of good wine, so we had not, after all, needed to

---

[13] Welcoming guests has been a monastic tradition for over a thousand years and we found that a short stay in the peaceful setting of a convent or monastery can be both interesting and calming as well as economical, as most set their tariff well below those of even modest hotels. A useful guide can be found at: www.guidestchristophe.com. Also see Footnote 17.

make the stop in Châteaubriant!). After the meal, we had another walk, went to Compline and then to bed. In the morning, after Mass and breakfast, we left this rather atypical B&B and set off for the Loire Valley, where we were to stay with Mary G, a schoolmate of Helen's who had a property near Loches and had offered us the use of one of her guest cottages. Our lunch stop was to be in Solesmes, on the river Sarthe, where we planned to visit the great Benedictine abbey entrusted with preserving the tradition of Gregorian chant once Vatican II allowed the use of "modern" music in the 1960s.

We got to Solesmes around midday, just missing the Office of *Sext* (sung at the sixth hour after sunrise, i.e., noon) and so had to wait around for a couple of hours for the next Office, at about two p.m. We filled in the time by having lunch and by visiting the abbey church. There had been a Benedictine priory there for many centuries but it had been closed and destroyed during the French Revolution. In 1833, rebuilding commenced and by 1875 the place was a great monastic complex again, with over a hundred monks and a vast Neo-Gothic abbey church. Solesmes is still thriving and has sent groups of its monks to set up daughter monasteries in many parts of France and abroad. *None*, the Office which we in due course attended, is a very short service (ten minutes) and so we didn't really have an opportunity to appreciate much Gregorian chant, but we were to make up this deficiency in one of Solesmes's daughter abbeys[14] later in our travels!

We drove on from Solesmes to Tours where, in trying to avoid the city centre while still intent on crossing the Loire by one of the city's bridges, we got hopelessly lost! We had no

---

[14] The Abbey of Fontgombault.

detailed map of the city and the locals I asked gave such strange answers that it took several stops and about-turns to cross the river. In retrospect, I think that it was probably my question that was strange (how to cross the river without going into the centre of town). Only crazy foreigners could want to come to Tours and cross the river without wanting to have a look at their beautiful city! But we were pressed for time: it was Saturday and already nearly four o'clock and we needed to do some shopping in Loches before the shops closed as we would be doing our own housekeeping for the week in the cottage, and the cottage was nine kilometres away from Loches and the shops.

As it turned out, we finally got through Tours, crossed the river and reached Loches in time to stock up with bread, cheese, *pâté de campagne,* fresh asparagus, eggs, mushrooms, wine and enough other basic necessities of life to last at least over the weekend. We reached the village of Verneuil-sur-Indre soon after five o'clock and although Verneuil turned out to be a very small village, built in the lee of a handsome Loire Valley château complete with round towers, candle snuffer turrets, tall chimneys and Renaissance windows, we had a lot of trouble finding the right cottage and it was not until I had knocked on a few doors and asked for "*les Australiens*" that we eventually found the right place. Mary and her husband were charming hosts, insisting that we have dinner with them in the main house that first night, and subsequently, regaling us with food and drink, wine and song and companionship and had me humming if not singing that old French drinking song "*Vive la compagnie!*" Pure chance had brought our hosts from Australia to Verneuil a few years earlier and only after buying the property did they discover that the neighbouring vineyard belonged, and had belonged for centuries, to Mary's extended family. Mary had not known that her grandfather had come to Australia from that part of Touraine, and she now finds herself spending several months of each year back among the vineyards of her forefathers!

We used Verneuil as a base to tour the surrounding district, but on our first weekend we took the advice of Mary and John and went to Mass at Fontgombault, a thirty-minute drive away. The abbey at Fontgombault had been founded in the eleventh century, had prospered, then declined, and had been closed and wrecked during the French Revolution. About a hundred years ago, it had been reopened by a group of monks from Solesmes and is now another thriving Benedictine community able to make daughter foundations itself. The Romanesque abbey church dates from the twelfth century and has now been completely restored. Although tucked away in a forest, the place was really busy when we were there, the ten a.m. Sunday Mass being packed out, with a troop of Boy Scouts and Girl Guides in the front rows for some ceremony of which we had not been forewarned. We counted eighty-eight monks in the choir stalls, the majority of them looking to be under fifty years old. What John and Mary had NOT told us was that we were in for Solemn Pontifical High Mass, according to the Tridentine Rite, with all the trimmings including a solemn Asperges and the Office of Sext at the beginning. There were clouds of incense; the old, familiar Gregorian chant "*Credo in Unum Deum*" was very moving, the attention of the congregation impressive, and the devotion of the monks exemplary… but two- and a-bit hours in a chilly abbey church was a touch long!

There was another surprise in store for us that day. Once

the scouts and guides had been blessed and the Mass had got under way and the Nicene Creed had been recited, the proceedings suddenly stopped. A couple of monks came down into the nave from the choirstalls and shepherded all the scouts and guides outside. Then all the monks trooped out, two by two until only the abbot, bringing up the rear of the procession, remained in the church. He turned away from the door and took up a position facing the lay congregation and, standing at the top of the steps from the nave to the choir, launched into a sermon, or rather an exhortation! He held in his hand a pastoral letter from the local bishop and explained that the bishop had directed that in every church of the diocese that Sunday the congregation should be urged to boycott and condemn the recently published the *da Vinci Code* by Dan Brown. This pastoral letter had been issued on the direct instructions of the Pope, John-Paul II, and its promulgation in every church that Sunday was apparently unprecedented in modern-day France. I tried to quietly translate the abbot's words, which were of course in French, to Helen and may well have missed a few things and misunderstood others, but I ended up with the impression that the abbot was reluctantly doing what he had been told to do. The congregation seemed stunned by the directive: I won't say there were titters of laughter because the abbot was obviously very respected but as we filed out of the church after Mass and listened to the comments of the locals, I received the impression that the French thought the old man (John-Paul II) "had lost it" and had not realised that his condemnation of the book was the best bit of publicity the author could have hoped for in the modern, free-thinking world. I had already read the book and had thought it a jolly good yarn and page-turner, but historically nonsense. I wouldn't bother going to see the film and had assumed Dan Brown's motive was the perfectly legitimate one of making money rather than of attacking the church! But the Abbot's words served to wake us all up and pay attention to the rest of the Mass: what other surprises might there be in store?

After Mass Helen and I drove around the countryside looking for somewhere pleasant to have Sunday dinner. Everyone else seemed to have had the same idea and business was brisk at the small hotels and restaurants we found. We eventually found one a little way beyond the village of Lingé, an inn or *auberge*, which offered both rooms and a restaurant. *La Gabrière* was situated at the edge of a pretty lake and the obliging owners agreed to squeeze us in at the last table on the terrace, inside being already full, and we had a truly delightful meal, warming ourselves in the sunshine after the two hours of chill in the abbey church. As we had been the last table to start, many of the others were leaving as we finished our dessert and so we were able to watch an interesting display of life in the country as the different groups left the restaurant and headed for their cars. At a large table near us, there had been an extended family which turned out to include a sixtyish Englishman and his son, the latter married to a local French girl. The father spoke to us and said that he had moved to France to live nearly twenty years ago: he was a keen huntsman and angler and waxed quite lyrical about the way the local woods abounded in game and the streams and lakes in fish. He was very happy and had no regrets about leaving his motherland. Then there was another extended family, which emerged from inside the restaurant, apparently after a birthday dinner for Grandma, a little old lady beautifully dressed and groomed, carrying a large bunch of long-stemmed roses and surrounded by solicitous children and fidgeting grandchildren. There were young and middle-aged couples rather more smartly dressed than you would expect to see at a country pub in Australia and we began to develop some expertise (so we thought) in detecting which couples were enjoying a secret and perhaps illicit tryst rather than a Sunday *en famille*. The over-attentive well-dressed male, giving in on every decision to the particularly difficult and demanding female, was easily identified and quickly suspected. The immaculately turned-out female enjoying a *tête-à-tête* with her handsome toy-boy was also at times noted, though this was more often observed in the large towns than out in the countryside after Sunday Mass.

While there were many similarities in the social behaviour of these country French people with that familiar to us back in Australia, I formed the view, and I think that Helen came to share it, that the French were somehow much more relaxed and at ease with themselves and with life than we are in Australia. I attribute some of this difference to the difference between the WASP background of Australian life and the catholic background of the French and indeed of the Mediterranean world. I have written "catholic" with a small "c" because I am not using the word in the sense of "Catholic Church" but of "general" or "all-embracing". The social world of the Mediterranean that I see as contrasting with the WASP world is not necessarily Catholic. The gardens of the Alhambra, the Pont du Gard, the Parthenon in Athens, the Topkapi Palace, the Library of Alexandria and the cultures that built them were not Catholic or even Christian. They seem to me to have emerged from communities favoured by climate and environment, where daily life did not have to be an endless struggle to find food and shelter (as it is north of the Alps and of the Rhine in Europe). A community needs spare time, leisure time, if it is going to develop culture, a philosophy of life! I'm convinced that the poor old northerners in Europe (read "WASPs") have focussed too long on food and shelter, on material things, though they may by now have caught up. The tunnel vision focussed on prosperity is now best seen in the lifestyle of the USA, where greed, self and hypocrisy seem to be the most outstanding features. The New World, or at least the USA, has not yet learnt the Mediterranean art of enjoying life. I think of the outrage in the USA over President Bill Clinton's affair with a research assistant and contrast that with the way in which, in the very same year, nobody in France batted an eyelid when President Mitterrand's funeral was held with his widow, his mistress, his legitimate and his illegitimate children in the places of honour! There seems to be much more tolerance and much less Puritanism in France than in Australia and the Anglo-Saxon world, and both Helen and I (each with individual views on life) felt very comfortable in France whether in church, café, countryside or crowded street! I grew hopeful that in Australia, where food and shelter are not all-consuming considerations and where from the 1850s the idea of the eight-hour (and no longer) working day received government approval, a culture more focussed on individual happiness than on corporate profits, would prevail.

Enough of these ruminations! We made our way back to Verneuil-sur-Indre late in the afternoon and then spent the rest of the week doing day trips from the village and taking in the châteaux of Amboise (we had lunch in a café on the banks of the Loire); Azay-le-Rideau, mirrored in its lake; fantastic Chambord (just an ice cream there at a kiosk in the grounds); Chaumont and its wonderful terrace overlooking the river;

Cheverny, only looked at through the gilded wrought iron gates; the incomparable Chenonceau, beautifully furnished and decorated with masses of flowers from the gardens; Chinon high on its hill (with the shades of Eleanor of Aquitaine, Henry Plantagenet, Richard the Lionheart and Joan of Arc supervising the long-overdue restoration: perhaps the shade of Cardinal Richelieu is there too, protesting, as it was he who had ordered the demolition of much of the fortress in the seventeenth century!); and Villandry, furnished, and still lived in by the owners, with its wonderful gardens and *parterres* which you admire from the terraces and upper stories.

Loches, our town for shopping, was itself a charming place. There remain over a kilometre of its medieval walls and gates, a great keep or fortress high on the hill, a less bellicose *Logis Royal* or Royal Residence halfway down the hill and a strange cathedral, *St Ours*, in between. Well, it is not really a cathedral but a *collégiale*, a large church built and endowed by early kings where a group or "college" of Canons read or chanted the Divine Office each day (without actually being monks living in a monastery). St Ours is a very strange building, Romanesque, dating from the eleventh century, but with a roof consisting of the most unusual stone "pyramids" where you would expect to see vaults or domes. We went to Mass there on Ascension Thursday: the place was ablaze with candles and electric lights illuminating the high roof, the altar decked with flowers, the organ thundering and rumbling and the packed congregation singing along with gusto conducted by a lively young woman who seemed to be choir mistress, MC and General Factotum for the elderly parish priest. There were no altar boys, but she and other members of the congregation read lessons and were otherwise quite involved in proceedings. At the end of Mass, the priest read out a few parish announcements, including one about special buses being organised to transport parishioners to the cathedral in Tours on Sunday to take part in the ordination of a young man from the Loches area. A parish picnic lunch was being organised in conjunction with the ceremony and the buzz of conversation that greeted this announcement seemed to indicate great interest in the trip, affection for the ordinand and enthusiasm for parish outings. As Helen and I left the church, we found that the priest wanted to shake our hands, as he did those of the rest of the congregation, and we were quite caught up in the excitement and, dare I say it, the happiness of the people spilling out into the sunshine!

We had a very good lunch in Loches a couple of times, on the second occasion falling into conversation with a young couple at the table next to ours on the terrace. She was a really beautiful, sweet, blonde and he was a tall, dark and handsome fellow. They had two small children to whom they seemed to speak alternately in French and in English! He turned out to be an Australian, from Melbourne, and she a local Loches girl who had lived in and gone to school in England and in Singapore and spoke impeccable English. Husband and wife had met and married in Paris and had recently moved to Loches where the chap had set up his own business (in "graphics", whatever that really means). We had a lovely lunchtime chat with them and, as we were leaving and mentioned that we were planning to visit the nearby *château de Montrésor* on our travels, she said something like: "Oh well, it is not open to the public at present but just tell my grandmother about meeting us and I'm sure she will be happy to show you around!"

We did climb to the top of the keep in Loches and did go in to the *Logis Royal*. The keep is huge and high and grim and was used by the Germans during the Second World War as a prison and Gestapo interrogation centre. It was very cold inside and when we had climbed the umpteen stairs to the top and emerged onto the flat roof we were nearly blown off by the force of the wind. Much warmer and pleasanter was the royal residence (I suppose it is not big enough to be called a palace and as it is a lovely Renaissance-style house rather than any sort of fortification maybe that is why it is never referred to as a castle or château). Charles VII lived there as Dauphin and from there was persuaded by Joan of Arc to go with her to Rheims to be crowned king. Charles VIII also spent time there, with his mistress Agnes Sorel (who is buried in the *collégiale de St Ours*) and with his queen, Anne de Bretagne. Poor Anne was the only child of the last Duke of (an independent) Brittany and her marriage to Charles VIII brought Brittany into the kingdom of France. Anne seems to have been a kind, intelligent and devout soul and she had a lot to put up with in Charles VIII. And then when he died the poor thing was constrained to marry his nephew and heir, Louis XII, to keep Brittany as part of France. No wonder Anne became an enthusiastic needlewoman and gardener!

Another outing from Verneuil took us through Chinon and Descartes to Fontevraud, near Saumur. The Royal Abbey of Fontevraud had, like so many other monastic sites, been founded in the eleventh century. Unusually, however, it was not a Benedictine foundation but was given its own rule by its founder Robert d'Arbrisel and was quite unique in that both men and women could join, living in separate wings or buildings of the property, coming together in the abbey church for Mass and other ceremonies and always presided over by an elected abbess rather than by an abbot. The Order, the Fontevraudistes, in time set up branches throughout France, Spain, Portugal and England, and continued to operate until the French Revolution, but the great abbey at Fontevraud is the one for which the Order is most famous. After the death of her husband, Henry II, and of her eldest son, Richard the Lionheart, Eleanor of Aquitaine retired to the abbey to end her days, and she, Henry, Richard, and Isabelle of Angoulême (the second wife of King John, who succeeded his brother Richard) are buried in the abbey church.[15] From its earliest days, then, this abbey had royal favour, and many aristocratic and noble ladies "took the veil" there or, like Queen Eleanor, retired and lived quietly there. One or two abbesses were princesses before entering and the daughters of Louis XV were educated there in the eighteenth century, when the abbey was probably at its *apogée*. When the Revolution came, the two hundred nuns and monks were dispersed and the buildings wrecked. Then, like the abbeys of Cîteaux and Clairvaux, the place was turned in to a prison under the Second Republic, and the great Romanesque abbey church was fitted out with multi-storeyed iron cells for the prisoners and catwalks for the warders; the nuns' gardens and vegetable plots became exercise yards. The prisons at Fontevraud and Cîteaux were closed in the 1960s; the Cistercians moved back to their motherhouse at Cîteaux and the French State set about restoring Fontevraud. The

---

[15] King John was, I think, the first king after William's conquest of England in 1066 to be both born in England (1166) and buried in England on his death (1216), in Worcester cathedral.

abbey buildings are now presented and maintained by the Ministry of Public Monuments. The restoration has been carefully done. The abbey church is once again clear and uncluttered, the limestone walls and pillars soaring upwards, the tombs of Queen Eleanor and her family lying serenely in front of the high altar, the cloisters and courtyards again immaculate... it really is a site not to be missed. There is, of course, quite a large village at the gates of the abbey by now, with a good hotel and several restaurants if you need to eat or sleep before going into Saumur, the nearest town, a really lovely place where there are two gorgeous *hôtels de charme*, the Hôtel Anne d'Anjou and the Hôtel St Pierre: you will want to stay in both!

We, however, on this day went on not to Saumur but to Loudun and Richelieu after our visit to the abbey. Loudun is a rather pretty little town built on the side of a low hill and famous not so much for its architecture as for its angels, or to be more precise, for the events which occurred there in the seventeenth century when Mother Joan of the Angels was the Prioress of the local Ursuline convent. *The Devils of Loudun* is a novelistic account of the story by Aldous Huxley and a very good read. *Mère Jeanne des Anges* and her nuns accused the parish priest, *Père* Grandier, of witchcraft and of introducing a team of devils into the convent. The church in France and the government (at that time they were more or less the same thing, as Cardinal Richelieu was Louis XII's chief minister), did not really want to hear about such medieval matters, which they probably rightly saw as hysteria rather than diabolic possession. *Mère Jeanne's* well-connected family, however, wanted their kinswoman's name to be blameless, AND the Richelieu family, the Cardinal's family, the de Plessis, as the local dukes could not forever ignore the approaches being made by their petitioners. So, Cardinal Richelieu eventually gave in, a trial was held, and poor Père Grandier was found guilty and burnt at the stake in the market square of Loudun. The demonic possession of the other nuns suddenly ended (had it ever existed?) but *Mère Jeanne* continued to be "troubled". Various learned doctors and spiritual advisers were sent to Loudun to help her and to exorcise any devils remaining. For more than thirty years she maintained the role she had perfected as a pious, devout and even saintly person bravely struggling with the Evil One. She was received by the king and queen and the great cardinal and with royal approval the convent and school for young ladies at Loudun prospered, *Mère Jeanne* continuing as Prioress (and astute businesswoman) until shortly before her death there in 1665. Anyhow, the market square in Loudun is now called *Place Grandier* and the rather handsome church where Fr Grandier was parish priest has a nice plaque honouring his memory (and not that of *Mère Jeanne des Anges!*).

After our quick look at Loudun, we drove the twenty-five kilometres or so to Richelieu, notable not just as the birthplace of the great cardinal but also as the site of perhaps the first serious exercise in town planning in Europe since the days of the Romans. The de Plessis family had a large medieval château at Richelieu and at the height of his powers as prime minister, the cardinal decided to demolish the fortress and to replace it with a beautiful Renaissance-style mansion; and to demolish the adjoining town, replacing it with a new and perfect town, clean and green and carefully planned down to the last detail. And he did, at vast expense! The mansion was destroyed at the Revolution save for the wrought iron gates and the vast park and perimeter walls, but the new town remains and is quite fascinating. It is laid out as a perfect square, the streets all on a regular grid pattern, the whole surrounded with moated walls pierced on each of the four sides by handsome gatehouses. Two large tree-lined squares, the *Place Royale and the Place Cardinale*, lie on the central axis within the walls, lined with arcaded stone buildings of more or less the same height. A handsome Baroque church stands in one square and we parked there to have a look around. Many of the buildings seemed to be of the *hôtel particulier* type, i.e., four or so storeys high, built right to the street with an arched carriage entrance two storeys high in the centre, often closed off either by a high wooden door or else by handsome wrought iron gates that gave the passer-by a glimpse of a leafy courtyard and broad steps leading to front doors flanked by elegant iron lanterns. The whole town, however, though perhaps perfectly planned for the seventeenth century, did not seem to be flourishing in the twenty-first century. The streets once wide enough for carriages to pass easily must now be one way to the larger motor vehicles. Four gates are no longer enough to allow an easy flow of traffic. And the planned formality and very visible order suggested to me that the rigidity of the cardinal's thinking may well be continued in the regulations and ordinances of the present town authorities: the place seemed frozen in time, static, still. The recent closure of the railway to Chinon and Tours seemed likely to choke the last bit of life out of the town! It was by this time dusk and so we then piled into our faithful C3 and headed home to Verneuil.

Although it is only a small town, with a population of about 7,000, Loches at some times of the day experienced that nightmare of bigger places, traffic congestion. The very centre of the old town was pedestrianised, of course, but the narrow streets leading into the centre were not, and although most were *sens unique*, or one-way, delivery vans had to park close to their delivery points, taxis had to drop their paying passengers close to their destinations and little space was left for ordinary people like us to park their cars while doing a spot of shopping. On one occasion, we had left the hired car in the big car park at the railway station and on returning found that somebody had crashed into it, damaging the rear and driver's side rear mudguard. To my surprise there was a note wedged under the windscreen-wiper saying, in French of course, "So sorry. My phone number is… and my car registration number is…". Not being at all sure what to do, I drove to the *Gendarmerie*, explained to the duty officer what had happened and said that as we were planning to leave Loches the next day and France at the end of the month, I would be grateful for advice. The young officer was so polite and so helpful. He said that on handing the car back to the hire company, we would be asked if we had reported the incident to the police and if the other driver had admitted responsibility. I showed him the note and he volunteered to phone the number there and then to verify that the other driver did accept responsibility. He did so, jotted down the details and I heard him say "and you will call in here to the *Gendarmerie* tomorrow to sign the statement."

He turned to us and said, "Don't worry. All will be well. Enjoy the rest of your stay in France". I just hoped that French tourists in Australia had similarly pleasant encounters with the Australian police… and with Australian motorists!

On the next day, we left Verneuil-sur-Indre and headed for Chantelle in the Bourbonnais, where we were to have an overnight stop at St Vincent's Abbey, run by the Benedictine nuns. Our lunch stop was to be in Bourges, ancient capital of the duchy of Berry, where we would visit the cathedral of St Etienne, one of the "big five" Gothic cathedrals of France[16]. As this and the next day were going to be the longest drives on our itinerary, we had decided to save travelling time by using the motorways where we could and so we made it to Bourges in good time. I had been to Bourges many years earlier, arriving by train and walking up to the town centre and the cathedral. This time, of course, we arrived by car and to my dismay discovered that the town is now surrounded by new suburbs and light industry and an almost defensive barrier of overpasses, underpasses, motorway exits and entrances and roundabouts garnished with the usual enigmatic signs. Our well-learnt trick of going around the roundabouts until we spied the most likely sign served us well and we selected *Centre Ville* and found a large car park near the cathedral.

We had planned to buy the ingredients for a picnic lunch before visiting the cathedral and were puzzled to find that most of the shops seemed to be closed. The tourist information office near the cathedral was, however, open and there we learnt that the shops were not closed for lunch but for the weekend! It was a Friday, and the day before had been Ascension Thursday, a public holiday (did someone say religion is dead in France?), and much of France had apparently decided to *faire le pont* or bridge the gap between Thursday and the weekend by taking a holiday on Friday too! So the plan was abandoned and we found a *boulangerie* open where we were able to buy something for our picnic lunch. The cathedral, fortunately, was not closing for lunch and so we

---

[16] The Big Five: Amiens, Bourges, Chartres, Paris and Strasbourg.

went in. It was as vast and high and impressive as I remembered it but seemed rather dusty and neglected after all the beautiful buildings we had seen in the previous week. A restoration programme had recently begun and much of the western end was wrapped in scaffolding. The weather had become rather overcast by this time and so the magnificent stained-glass windows were not glowing quite as brilliantly as I remembered them, but they remain in my memory as the great glory of Bourges, their gorgeous reds and golds rivalling in intensity the brilliant blues of Chartres. We then returned to the car through spits of rain and ate our sandwiches there before setting off again for Chantelle.

We whizzed along in the direction of Montlucon, following the valley of the Cher and pursued by a growing bank of storm clouds. Near St-Amand-Montrond we left the motorway and took the quieter departmental road in to Chantelle, a rather tired little town which, like Bourges, seemed to have decided to *faire le pont* to the weekend. Though the place was largely closed, the streets were cluttered with trucks and caravans and iron poles and lengths of canvas... being got ready, it turned out, for a giant fair and bric-a-brac sale to be held over the weekend. We managed to find a *Bar-Tabac* that was open and ordered our usual coffee and *croque monsieur* preparatory to an evening meal and night in a monastic enclosure!

Chantelle is perched on a rocky promontory surrounded on three sides by the Bauble, a small river given to wild flash floods after heavy rain. The highest part of the promontory is occupied by the abbey. Centuries ago, Chantelle was the chief fortress of the counts, later dukes, of Bourbon. By building a battlemented wall across the open end of the U-shaped promontory around which the river flowed, the Bourbon family acquired an almost impregnable few acres of high ground, and there they built a fortified château, a large priory, and a fine priory church in between. In the seventeenth century, the then duke fell out of favour with the king, his cousin, and as a result the king's chief minister, Cardinal Richelieu, had the château demolished! The family retreated to their town house in nearby Moulins, while the Benedictine monks remained in the priory until the Revolution, when they were dispersed and the buildings ruined. In 1853, a community of Benedictine nuns moved to the site and gradually restored the place. We were warmly welcomed by the guest-mistress and shown to pleasant rooms in the guest house. After Vespers, we shared a good evening meal with the few other guests and then went back to the rather chilly church for Compline. After Compline, the nuns filed out of the church past the abbess, a diminutive woman with a big smile, who blessed each nun with a good asperges of holy water from the bucket held by her assistant and then headed for the house guests, giving each of us a good dousing too! In the morning, our good resolution about an early start after breakfast was sabotaged by the various and numerous temptations in the abbey shop and space had to be found in the Citroën for the biscuits, chocolates, nougat, soaps, oils, perfumes and books that the good nuns cheerfully sold us! The last sound we heard at the abbey in

Chantelle[17] was not the church bell but the cash register! We did not, however, begrudge them a single euro, as their welcome had been so warm and genuine... and as the heating, plumbing and rain-proofing bills in that medieval pile must be horrendous.

From Chantelle, we headed for Périgord. We had planned a lunch stop in Limoges and to take in one or two of the famous porcelain factories there, but we had spent too much time (and money!) at Chantelle and so decided to omit Limoges and to take a more direct route through Aubusson. There were no motorways available for this cross-country leg and the drive took us through the lower valley of the Allier, across the Limousin plateau and, at one stage, within sight of the snow-capped Massif Central.

Aubusson turned out to be a quite fascinating stop. It is located in a valley where, centuries ago, the rushing river Creuze had been used to power the various machines used both in processing the wool and in weaving the tapestries for which the town was renowned. Aubusson had been very prosperous up until the time of the French Revolution and, after a century of decline when there were no longer multiple aristocratic buyers willing to pay dearly for Aubusson tapestries with which to furnish their châteaux and town houses, Aubusson's fortunes revived in the twentieth century when somewhat less

---

[17] Helen remained in touch by email with the nuns in Chantelle and made several online purchases of their products over the years, discovering that since 2010 their cosmetics, chocolates etc. along with the products of many similar monasteries throughout Europe, can be easily purchased on a single, co-op website, www.boutiques-theophile.com. Many of the monasteries listed also offer accommodation to travellers like those monasteries and abbeys referred to in Footnote 13.

grand tapestries again became in vogue. Artists such as Jean Lurçat and Georges Braque began designing scenes intended to be turned into tapestries and produced masterpieces such as Lurçat's *Le Chant du Monde*. We made time for a quick visit to the recently refurbished *Centre International de la Tapisserie* and then had an excellent meal at a very busy little bistro facing the medieval *Pont de la Terrade* across the Creuze. We then pressed on through Eymoutiers and St-Yrieix to our destination, the small town of Excedeuil in Périgord[18]. We arrived at about five p.m., did a little shopping, and then found our way to the cottage which we had booked on *Gîtes de France*, and which was in a little hamlet about two kilometres outside the town.

Our landlady was sitting reading in the garden of her own cottage next door. I pulled up and got out of the car to ask which cottage belonged to Madame Richmond when she spoke first saying something like, "Ah, there you are monsieur et madame! I have been sitting here all afternoon waiting for you! Did you get lost?"

I straightway realised that we had caused her inconvenience and so apologised profusely. "Why did you not phone and say you were running late?" she asked.

Happily, I was able to reply that I did not have her phone number and had only ever communicated with her by email. At this, she said that I had not been communicating with her by email but with her daughter in Paris, who should have given me the phone number. "*Hélas, Madame*, I was not given a

---

[18] Périgord is the old name for what is now called the départment of Dordogne, the term introduced at the time of the Revolution. Périgord is split into four sub-divisions: Noir, in the north around Sarlat; Blanc, in the centre around Périgueux; Vert, around Brantôme; and Pourpre, around Bergerac.

phone number," I was able to say with a suitable shrug of the shoulders and a turning down of the lip and so the blame shifted in the direction of the distant daughter.

"Ah, these young people today!" sighed Madame, and the atmosphere began to improve. "Well, you are very welcome," Madame finally said, and she led us through the garden to our cottage. It was such a pretty place! Old farm buildings built of the local honey-coloured stone, both cottages had steep *Périgourdin* tiled roofs, little dormer windows with diamond-shaped windowpanes, tall chimneys, rambling roses, hollyhocks and blue iris everywhere. Our cottage had three bedrooms, two bathrooms, kitchen and living-room, all with exposed stone walls and with enough low exposed beams, particularly upstairs, for all heads to be bumped several times a day. Madame gave us the keys, lots of instructions, answers to our various questions and the information that she would be returning to Paris the next day and that when we left we should leave the keys under a certain plant pot for her housekeeper to collect and use. Madame, who really was a nice old soul, did indeed drive off early next day and we had the whole property to ourselves.

The next day was Sunday and we decided to have midday dinner at the *Chapon Fin*, the main hotel-restaurant in the centre of town and recommended by Madame before she left. We found that Excedeuil is quite a prosperous little farming town, dominated by a partly ruined and partly inhabited twelfth-century castle. Apparently, Richard the Lionheart had besieged the castle, which successfully resisted and an exasperated Richard took his revenge by burning the town down instead. Although that all happened eight centuries ago, our local informant, the chap in the little tourist office, spoke as if it had happened in his own lifetime! There is an interesting fourteenth-century church and, just down the road is the fifteenth-century truffle market mentioned by Stephanie Alexander in her famous cookbook. A little way along the street from the market is a large stone building which was originally a *commanderie* or garrison of the Knights Templar, suppressed in the thirteenth century. I dropped Helen at the church for ten o'clock Mass and went off to the local Internet café to do some work on my laptop. We met up again after Mass and made our way to the *Chapon Fin*, Helen relating how lively the Mass had been, with a group of teenagers providing the music (mostly drums and two guitars) and leading the singing. We had a table on the terrace at the *Chapon Fin* and were again able to combine a fine meal with lots of people-watching. This became our regular practice in the Dordogne: the midday meal on a terrace in a small town as a break from our serious programme of sightseeing and the evening meal back at "home" where we could put our feet up.

From our base in Excedeuil, we did some great trips: to Hautefort and its wonderful château and formal gardens high on the hill; to the medieval fortress at Castelnaud and to the fifteenth-century château of *Les Milandes*, restored by the American singer Josephine Baker and funded by her estate as a more than usually comfortable orphanage. After Excedeuil, we set off for Belvès, in Périgord Noir, the south-east of the Dordogne Valley, allowing for a long lunch stop in Sarlat, which was as busy and fascinating as ever. The maze of narrow, medieval streets, the numerous little squares with their fountains and statues, the dozens of tall, honey-coloured stone fifteenth- and sixteenth-century houses... and even the tourists and tourist-trap little shops make it still seem very like the busy market town it was centuries ago. Of course, it helped that, as in most parts of France, the authorities had some time ago insisted that all telephone, pay-tv and electricity cables be put underground and that advertising hoardings and neon signs be banished from historic precincts, so the streets of Sarlat really do look much as they did in centuries past... but perhaps cleaner and in better repair!

From Sarlat, we went on through Beynac and La Roque Gageac, both right on the banks of the Dordogne River, to Belvès, where we had booked a few nights at the *Manoir de la Moissie,* a B&B on the edge of the town. Belvès, like so many of the towns in Aquitaine, is built defensively high on a rocky ridge. At one end of the ridge is the former castle, now the local hospital, then a street of fine old residences including the country house of the archbishops of Bordeaux: Clément V, the first of the Avignon popes, used to holiday there when he was merely Archbishop of Bordeaux. Then comes the market square (with pillory), which is the town centre, and from there a narrow street of shops (and including the best hotel in town, Le Clément V) runs west to the former Dominican church and friary (now the *Hôtel de Ville*) and a street sloping up to the former Benedictine priory (now the parish church, closed and under reconstruction). Beyond the church, the road continues to rise towards the sixteenth-century *Manoir,* where we stayed. The building had been extensively restored recently and we were very comfortable. Our hosts were rather intriguing: monsieur was working in the large garden when we arrived but came in and showed us to our rooms and chatted willingly about the house and the village. He also set out breakfast for us in the morning and explained that madame had set off for work in Bergerac before we were up. The next day, however, it was madame who did breakfast, saying she was going in to work a little later than usual. There was no sight or mention of monsieur. I had somehow got the impression, from monsieur, that she worked in interior decoration or furnishing but madame put things right by saying that she was the managing director of a large housing construction firm! From Belvès, we made day trips to the bastide towns of Beaumont, Domme and Montpazier, to the *Château de Biron* soaring up over the pretty little village at its gates, and to the former Cistercian *Abbaye de Cadouin*.

Cadouin is a pretty little village with lots of half-timbered houses and winding streets and lies deep in a beautiful forest of ancient beech and oak trees. The Cistercian abbey there had, in the twelfth century, somehow come into possession of a precious relic. Pilgrims had flocked in, and a massive building programme had to be undertaken to handle them: a big, new church, a guest house, an enlarged monastery and a very fine cloister, much of which remains today. Despoiled at the time of the French Revolution the abbey church was reopened in the 1830s as a parish church in the diocese of Périgueux, which it still is. The guest house was recently refurbished and is now a rather fine backpackers' lodge, doing very good business with ramblers, bushwalkers and nature-lovers. The abbey church and particularly the cloisters are very beautiful and make the detour through the forest very worthwhile.

The really intriguing story about Cadouin, however, relates to the relic: it was believed to be *Le Saint Suaire*, the winding sheet or part of the shroud used to wrap around the head of Christ when he was placed in the tomb. The pilgrimage to venerate the relic was hugely popular from the Middle Ages right up to 1935! I was amazed to learn that the pilgrimage had resumed after the Revolution and again after the First World War and that great crowds came by car, bus and train until 1935, when the local bishop stopped the ceremonies. He based his decision on a scientific study of the *Suaire* just then completed which said that the fabric dated in fact from the twelfth century, not from the time of Christ, that it probably came from Egypt, not from Palestine, and that the until then undeciphered markings on it were Arabic script, possibly a quotation from the Koran! In June 2006, when we were in Cadouin, there was a notice in the room in which the *Suaire* had been kept saying that the relic was not currently being exposed as it was undergoing "restoration". I understand that the sign has been in place since 1935!

We left Belvès the next day for the Abbey of Sainte-Foy in the tiny village of Conques, which we reached late in the afternoon after a winding drive through the mountains on the western side of the Massif Central. With some difficulty, we found a car park and then walked to the abbey and the guest house or, rather, pilgrim's hostel. Conques was, and still is, a major halt on the pilgrim road to Compostela and I had written some months earlier saying that Helen and I would be on the *Chemin de Compostela* in June and would like shelter for the night[19]. All quite true, as I did not say how much of the Compostela Track we would be doing. We were given a

Conques

---

[19] Again, see footnote 13 and www.leguidestchristophe.com

warm welcome by a rather brisk Dutch woman who turned out to be someone who had already walked to Compostela (from Holland!) and she and her husband, another veteran of the trail, were spending two weeks of their summer holiday working as volunteers in the hostel. I had made a mistake with the dates and had booked us in for the previous day but they forgave me and found two beds for us, the last available as there were ninety-two pilgrims there that night! I caused a few eyebrows to be raised when I asked about the best place to park the car overnight: "You have a car?" was the startled reply and the Dutch lady quickly added that there was an undercover car park at the four-star hotel just down the road. We said no more about the car but went back to the car park, packed a small bag each, leaving our wheeled suitcases out of sight in the boot, and walked back to the hostel. We had come a long way, even if we had not walked, and we had been in and out of umpteen churches and abbeys in the previous two weeks, several of them on the pilgrim trail, so we didn't really feel too much like impostors!

We were just in time for Vespers in the marvellous abbey church, and then for a visit to the *Trésor*. Conques, probably because of its remoteness and inaccessibility, is the only place in France, I think, where the Revolutionary zealots in the 1790s did not get their hands on the treasures of the church such as gold and silver candlesticks, silk vestments, paintings and sculptures. In the case of Conques, the great treasure was the reliquary containing the skull of Sainte Foy (Saint Faith, a young girl martyred by the Romans in the 3rd century), an extraordinary and strangely beautiful bust-like piece covered with gold, jewels and gemstones dating from the seventh century. It is now kept in an elegantly designed, ultra-modern and highly secure Treasure House or *Trésor*. Displayed with it are many other objects of immense historical and artistic value, including a gold and silver reliquary of the True Cross presented to the abbey by the emperor Charlemagne in the nineth century, gold and silver processional crosses and gilded and enamelled portable altars dating from the Middle Ages, and so on. Some of the more bizarre objects are the reliquaries said to contain numerous and assorted fingers, toes, shinbones, shoulder bones etc. of various saints. There is even an exquisite small(!) enamelled reliquary, inlaid with gold and silver, said to have been made to contain *Le Saint Prépuce*, the foreskin removed when Christ was circumcised! On emerging from the *Trésor*, we had a little walk around the abbey and the village, taking in gulps of fresh mountain air after that last encounter with medieval devotion, and then went in to the hostel for dinner with the other ninety pilgrims.

Proceedings were conducted by a very gracious and competent guest-master, one of the Norbertine Canons who now run the abbey in place of the Benedictines who left at the time of the French Revolution. Grace in the hostel refectory was said in Latin and then in French and English and Dutch and German and Italian and Spanish. The priest then explained, in French and Italian, that after dinner we were all invited to attend Compline in the abbey church and to sit in the stalls in the sanctuary of the church rather than in the pews in the nave, and that the Prior would give a special blessing to all the pilgrims leaving next morning for Compostela. He also asked us all to devote five minutes, before eating, to learning a little pilgrim song from the Middle Ages which he taught us, *Ultréia et Suseia* something or other, roughly meaning, as I recall, "ever onward, ever upward, faithful to the end" and to be prepared to sing it when asked to do so in the church that evening. Then we tucked into a substantial meal of baguette, eggs, fish pie and green salad, washed down with a good supply of the local wine. Helen and I had been seated at a long table with a group of thirtyish fellows from central France, all on their way to distant Compostela on foot in the morning. The unofficial leader of the group seemed to be the seventy-three-year-old father of one of them, an old chap sitting next to me. Monsieur confided that he was only walking for two weeks this time and that he was a little reluctant to leave Conques where the welcome was always so warm, "the best on the whole trail," he said.

After dinner and another little walk we went in to the church for Compline. We pilgrims (ahem!) all sat in a semicircle around the high altar and after Compline the guest-master went around the semicircle asking each pilgrim to say his or her first name and where he or she was from. "Helen from Australia" and "John from Australia" caused a ripple of interest but were far from being the only ones from beyond the borders of France. We then sang our little pilgrim's song, received a "special blessing for those leaving for Compostela in the morning on foot" (ahem!) and a sprinkling of holy water for good measure. We all then adjourned to meet in the gloaming outside the main west door of the abbey, where the guest-master appeared and gave a wonderfully witty and incisive explanation of the "Last Judgement" carved into the tympanum above the door. After that, we went back into the abbey church which was by now quite dark. Suddenly the lights came on, the organ pealed, and we had a thirty-minute concert of classical music while we roamed about the church, up the towers, along the clerestory galleries, wherever we felt like going. The ubiquitous guest-master again! Then, on the stroke of ten p.m., as promised, the music stopped, the lights went out one by one and we and the other pilgrims hurried off to bed. In the morning, Helen and I went to eight a.m. Mass followed by breakfast but saw no sign of the other pilgrims… they were apparently early risers and were by then already well on their way to Compostela! "Ever onward!"

(ii) Conques to Marseille

We set off soon after nine for our next stop, a B&B in Lautrec, a village fifty kilometres east of Toulouse. Our route took us close to Decazeville, a former coal and iron ore mining centre, around the hill on which Rodez is perched and on to Cordès-sur-Ciel, Gaillac and Lautrec. We reached Cordes in good time for lunch, parked at the bottom of the hill, and found a nice little restaurant where we had lunch on the wisteria-draped terrace at the back of the building overlooking the peaceful rural landscape. After lunch, our legs felt just a little wobbly and we baulked at the prospect of climbing the stone staircases and steep cobbled paths up to the hilltop village square. Help suddenly arrived in the form of *Le Petit Train* which appeared from around a corner and stopped to load passengers a few metres from the restaurant. For two euros apiece, we were gently transported to the top of the hill and deposited just outside one of the gates in the medieval walls. We spent an hour or so wandering around the picturesque streets and in and out of the many little shops tempting tourists with all sorts of exotica. There were quite a few studios selling the works of local artists, paintings, glassblowing, sculptures, woodcarving and so on and quite a few interesting antique shops but we limited our purchases to a few postcards and gradually worked our way down the hill on foot, resisting the temptations to right and to left. Travelling by air between Europe and Australia, boring and uncomfortable though it is, has the great advantage of strict limits on the amount of luggage permitted onboard the aircraft. That thought saved us many a time from accumulating carloads of mementoes, large and small, as we made our way through the French countryside.

Once back on board the Citroën we set off for Lautrec again and, after a bit of trouble finding our way into the village (yet another fortified hilltop one), we were parked in the small main square by five o'clock, our target arrival time. All we had to do then was find our B&B, *La Terrasse de Lautrec*, which the hosts had said in an email was in the rue de l'Eglise. We found the church easily enough, but it was in a small square rather than in a street. We walked all around the church and the square but could find no rue de l'Eglise. We then found ourselves back in the main square near the car so I approached an elderly couple sitting in the sun at their front door and asked them.

"But monsieur, there's no such street in the village," they said. "What exactly are you looking for?"

I said I was looking for a B&B in the rue de l'Eglise and they replied by pointing to a building on the western side of the square saying "Well, there's the B&B, it's in the square, and it's called *Les Glycines* (The Wisteria). I replied that I was looking for a B&B called *La Terrasse de Lautrec,* so it could not be that one, to which the couple replied that the large building on the other side of the square was also a B&B, recently opened, but they did not know its name. We thanked them and walked over to the building they had pointed out. There was no name or number on it and no sign of a plaque saying rue de l'Eglise, but we rang the bell anyway.

A woman answered quite promptly and before I could speak, she said in English "Oh, you must be the Australians!" So we had arrived! Our difficulties in finding the place were airily dismissed as we were shown to our rooms and when I asked about parking the car (in our exchange of email, madame had promised us secure and covered off-street parking in their large garage) the reply was, "But there in the square where you have put it, of course!"

Let's move on!

Our hosts were a pleasant couple, both Paris-born, in their late forties who had met while working as executives for Marks and Spencer in Paris. The company had suddenly decided to withdraw from the French market and our hosts had decided to invest their "golden handshakes" in a B&B. They had recently bought the property in Lautrec, which was close enough for monsieur to commute to Toulouse, where he had secured another good position in a large company, and they were enjoying life in the provinces. Each had children from earlier marriages but no children lived with them in Lautrec, and madame concentrated on developing the B&B, with assistance from monsieur over the weekend. The building was quite intriguing, offering a rather severe, grey, three-storey façade to the square onto which it opened without any front garden or even footpath. The high central doorway, originally a carriageway, opened inwards to a lofty entrance hall, with big glass doors opposite leading through to a terrace and formal garden surrounded on three sides by the central block of the house and two lateral wings and open on the fourth side to a stunning view out over the countryside. The fourth side of the garden was actually a low wall built on the top of the outer edge of the old town walls, the street that once ran between the walls and the house having been filled in and transformed into a beautiful garden! There was quite a dizzying drop from the garden wall to the road below where it climbed up to the village; the middle distance was taken up with farms, vineyards and olive groves, their neat but unfenced divisions making a wonderful patchwork in greens and ochre with splashes of yellow from fields of sunflowers. In the distance a wavy blur of blue hills rolled away towards the *Montagne Noire*, Black Mountain, whose slopes constitute the catchment area for the waters used in the sensed but not seen *Canal du Midi*. The owners did not really know the history of the building other than that it dated in part from the sixteenth century and had once had a street between it and the ramparts. They suspected that it had had an "ecclesiastical" purpose, perhaps as the house for the village priests, as the church was close by, or perhaps as a boarding school for the sons of the rich: there is a not dissimilar building further along the street which was once a convent and boarding school for young ladies.

Our hosts had spent a lot of time and money restoring the building and garden (a new swimming pool, surrounded by dressed stone and blue irises was almost ready for use) and furnishing the place with some quite fine antique pieces, lights and wallpapers. There were three couples already in the B&B when we arrived and after introductions and an *apéritif* in the garden admiring the wonderful view we all had dinner together that evening in the candle-lit dining room. One of the couples consisted of an Armenian American woman married to a very pleasant Frenchman, so both English and French were spoken around the table and Helen and I were made very welcome by everyone.

These other guests all left the next day, returning to Paris, and Helen and I got on with our busy schedule! We went to ten o'clock Mass in the village church and just squeezed in as it was First Communion Day in the parish and the church was full of the all-in-white First Communicants, proud parents and grandparents, fidgeting older children, flash cameras and so on. After Mass, the crowd spilled out into the square and everyone (including Helen and I) shared "Communion Cake" passed around in baskets by the fussing mothers.

Helen and I then drove in to Albi for lunch at a restaurant on the edge of the river Tarn recommended by the other house guests (*Le Pont du Tarn*) and for a look at the Toulouse-Lautrec paintings in the gallery there. After an excellent lunch on the terrace with its stunning view across the river we went first to the cathedral, Sainte Cécile, which looms up on the cliffs above the river. It is an extraordinary building, the square stepped tower so high, the bricks with which it is built looking so old, almost Roman or even Egyptian, and the flamboyant stone lacework of the main portico (strangely positioned along one side of the nave) looking more like the entrance to a fairy-tale palace than to a fortress church. When we got inside, we discovered that the cathedral was already full: it was Pentecost Sunday and, as in the cathedral at Tours, an Ordination ceremony was about to start (at the rather strange hour of three p.m.). Some people made room for us on seats in a side aisle and we were able to watch the ceremony in close-up on the closed-circuit television. There were three ordinands, two European and one African, and part of the ceremony consisted of very rhythmic African music and singing. The bishop seemed quite a charismatic man, admired and respected by the congregation, inserting little jokes into his homily and clearly popular with the eighty priests of the diocese gathered together for the Mass.

By the time that was all over, it was too late to go to the art gallery so we deferred that visit and headed home to Lautrec. The next day, we drove the short distance to Castres, left the car at the station and took the train to Toulouse for the day. We were, in fact, lucky to catch the train as we got lost in the narrow one-way streets of Castres and although we found the station easily enough, we were on the opposite side of the railway lines to the car park and couldn't see any way of getting across. A passer-by gave us directions which eventually got us to the car park, just five minutes after the train's scheduled departure time. Happily, the train was ten minutes late leaving (it was, in fact, a public holiday, Pentecost Monday, and so perhaps the timetable had varied) and so we just made it! It was a pleasant change to be gliding along in air-conditioned comfort through the countryside and with somebody else driving! When we got to Toulouse, we headed in to the centre of town, the very handsome arcaded eighteenth-century *Place du Capitole*, and the tourist information office where we picked up a map. We had three major things to see: the eleventh-century basilica of St Sernin, the largest Romanesque church in the world; the thirteenth-century church of the *Jacobins*, where the Dominicans had been founded; and the thirteenth-century cathedral, St Etienne. If you add to these destinations the *Gare Matabiau*, where we had arrived and from which our return train would leave, you have more or less a square with each side being a kilometre long, the tourist bureau being right in the middle. So whichever way we tackled the job we faced a four to five-kilometre walk. The day was warming up and likely to reach

30 degrees, so rule number one was to walk on the shady side of the street! Rule number two was to stop frequently and to take adequate refreshment! We observed these rules carefully and made it back to the station five hours later safe and sound, but a bit weary. Most of the *Toulousains* seemed to have taken the day off, although the French government had in 2006 made the holiday optional for the first time. We were lucky in that the streets were not as congested as usual and we did not have to cope with crowds of tourists at the main sites.

St Sernin certainly is impressive both for its size and for the very *Languedocien* tiered octagonal tower, which we saw copied, on a smaller scale, in churches throughout the region. The Jacobins is interesting for its strange double nave, supported by a row of columns down the middle of the church, for its largely intact cloisters and for the historical association with St Dominic and St Thomas Aquinas, the latter being buried in the church. The cathedral of St Etienne is a strange place: built in several stages, the original nave and side aisles are twelfth century and Romanesque, while the major extension of the nave was built in the fourteenth century and is in *Languedocien* Gothic. Doubling the overall size of the cathedral, it is quite bizarre, as the two naves are not aligned, the newer one being set ten or twelve metres to the east of the earlier one. All these great buildings are constructed of the slim, pinkish bricks for which Toulouse, "*La Ville Rose*", is famous and they do give an air of antiquity, almost Roman antiquity, to much of the city. Toulouse is an interesting historical mixture with these early medieval buildings, the handsome townhouses from its prosperous days of the sixteenth and seventeenth centuries and the locks and ports of the *Canal du Midi*. We walked along part of the Canal as it is right outside the main railway station and was built in the seventeenth century linking Toulouse to the Mediterranean to the east and, just south of the city centre, to the Garonne which flows west to the Atlantic. With a population of over 600,000 Toulouse is booming nowadays, is France's sixth-largest city and is the home of *Airbus Industrie*, builders of the supersonic Concorde and the giant A380, and the European rival of the USA's Boeing.

We caught our train back to Castres and had a less hectic look at the town than had been possible in the morning and then drove home to Lautrec and our B&B. The next morning, after orange juice, fresh croissants, home-made jams and coffee and tea *à volonté* in that beautiful sun-drenched garden we set off for the *Gorges du Tarn*. We made a small detour to give us another visit to Albi, where we took in the marvellous Toulouse-Lautrec collection (in the thirteenth-century *Palais de la Berbie*, originally the bishop's palace). We then made our way through St Sernin-sur-Rance, St Pierre, St Affrique, St Rome-de-Cernon and St Rome-de-Tarn to Millau, which we approached along the south bank of the river to pass underneath the great bridge over the Tarn, the *Viaduc de Millau*. We then turned south and climbed up the side of the valley to join the motorway (the *Autoroute du Soleil* which links Paris with Languedoc and the Mediterranean) and drove across the bridge heading north. The highest point of the bridge is 343 metres above the river (higher than the Eiffel Tower). The *Viaduc* looks so neat and simple and yet is, in fact, an extraordinary feat of modern engineering. Soaring above the river, the railway, the old road and the outskirts of the town itself, it was opened in 2004 and is in 2020 still the highest bridge in the world.

We left the motorway at the next exit north and turned east towards the gorges of the river Tarn which we picked up at Le Rozier and which we followed at water level for some time before commencing the steep climb up to one of the main lookouts, *le Point Sublime*. From there, we could look across the canyon to the bleak plateau or *causse* on the other, slightly lower, side as well as right down into the canyon where to left and to right the river twisted and turned. We could see canoes and boats and even campers on the sandbanks, while on rocky outcrops here and there we could see the keeps and castles of the local *seigneurs* and robber barons of days gone by. We had lunch at the little *Point Sublime* restaurant and then, turning east, drove down the narrow winding road to river level at La Malène. This is a tiny village nestling beneath the cliffs of the Tarn on one of the few patches of cultivable land along the floor of the canyon. There is a rather cute little château there, now turned in to an elegant hotel and restaurant and, guarded by the château, a low-level bridge across the river. We crossed the bridge to take the road across the *causse* to our overnight destination of Meyrueis, beginning with a hair-raising switchback climb up the canyon wall to the lip of the gorges and the start of the lonely road across the plateau to the next river and Meyrueis. I had never before been on such a frightening road and never want to again! The road surface was just wide enough for one vehicle and certainly not wide enough for a truck or bus. There was virtually no unmade edge, just the cliff-face on one side and on the other a low stone parapet about thirty centimetres high beyond which was the drop down to the river. The road climbed the cliff-face parallel to the river, zig-zagging every three hundred metres or so to gain height. It was only at the "devil's elbow" of these zigzags that the road widened a little to allow two cars to pass. I remembered that "up" traffic had priority in such situations and was relieved to see that the two cars which did start down the road while we were there did, in each case, pull over at hairpin bends, come to a stop, and wait for us to climb up and pass. We exchanged friendly waves, theirs cheerful, mine nervous! I think that there must have been half a dozen of these hairpin bends on the road and when we finally got to the top I said to Helen something like: "Thank God that's over, but it sure was a wonderful view!" Helen replied, however, that she had been too scared to look at the view, so we were both very glad to get to the top! We then had an easy run across the moors to the valley of the river Jonte, where another but less frightening descent took us down to Meyrueis for the night.

We had booked at the Hotel Le Sully, the main part of which was a sixteenth-century townhouse right in the middle of the main street and facing the gurgling mountain stream that is the river Jonte just there. The terrace of the hotel's dining-room is across the road from the main building, right on the edge of the stream, and that is where we had our evening meal. Helen seemed to have forgotten her encounter with the tripe in Caen and so we ordered a regional dish as our main course, *aligot*. It is basically a creamy puree of potatoes flavoured with lashings of garlic and served with a very spicy local sausage; we both enjoyed it but it would probably not be a good choice for people planning a romantic evening together! A bowl of good country soup and the usual wonderful bread had made a good first course, and we followed the *aligot* with a green salad and then a light dessert of *Ile Flottante*. After dinner, we strolled about town in the long twilight. At the junction of several streams and tracks across this inhospitable part of the country, Meyrueis has been since the Middle Ages an important market town. The isolation and inaccessibility of the area probably explain why it developed a reputation as a place where religious non-conformists might be safe. There had been a small Jewish community there from the thirteenth century, the ruins of the synagogue being still visible. The Huguenots arrived in the seventeenth and eighteenth centuries and there is a large Protestant church there now, built in the 1840s to an unusual octagonal design. As if to counteract these non-conformist influences the Catholic parish is in the hands of the Jesuits (we were intrigued to find the SJs beavering away in such an out-of-the-way place!). The twelfth-century castle was largely dismantled in the seventeenth century by you-know-who, Cardinal Richelieu, for the usual reason of strengthening the central and royal power and weakening local powers. Nowadays, Meyrueis seems to sell itself as a centre for eco-tourism, extreme sports such as caving, white-water-rafting and horse-riding... and it seemed to be having some success when we were there.

The next day we left for Avignon, with another winding road to Florac and then Alès, which we skirted around, and on to Uzès, where the de Crussol family, dukes of Uzès, still live in their ancient château. Uzès is a very pretty town with big, old plane trees lining the main streets, largely lined with tourist-trap restaurants and shops. Uzès has an important summer festival of classical music, is very handy to Avignon and its festival, and seems to be immensely popular with French tourists of the middle and upper classes: it is one of "the" places to go in summer for many of the "nicer" people in Paris! We had a pleasant lunch on a café terrace under the plane trees and then continued on our way. Our one stop between Uzès and Avignon was at the *Pont du Gard,* where the aqueduct built by the Romans in 60 A.D to bring water to the Roman city of Nîmes, fifty kilometres away, crosses the Gard river. The aqueduct functioned for a thousand years and even today is enormously impressive. We walked across the lower level and watched people swimming and boating in the river below: it was getting pretty hot for early June and so we retreated to our air-conditioned Citroën for the final run in to Avignon.

From 1309 and the arrival of Pope Clément V until the French Revolution, Avignon was an independent city-state, like Singapore nowadays, and it became part of France only when seized by the Revolutionary Council in 1791. Although the popes had moved back to Rome by 1418, Avignon (with the attached lands known as the *Comptat Venaissin*) was ruled by a Papal Legate and became a sort of oasis of peace, culture and tolerance in fifteenth-, sixteenth- and seventeenth-century Europe, falling into a decline only from early in the eighteenth century. The view of the city from the opposite bank of the Rhône, as we approached through Villeneuve-les-Avignon, is most impressive. The medieval walls still surround the city and although the moats have been filled in and turned into roads or car parks these signs of the twentieth century are mostly hidden by the leafy plane trees. The turrets and battlements of the papal palace and the tower of the cathedral still dominate the skyline, as they did eight centuries ago, and as we whizzed across a modern road bridge, we saw not it but the *Pont Bénézet,* of *Sur le Pont d'Avignon* fame, its broken arches knee-deep in the Rhône as the river swept by the city. We were booked into a small hotel, Le Mediéval near th*e Place Pie* (*Pie* = Pius in French), the square where the main multi-storeyed car park is located, camouflaged by vines and greenery above the air-conditioned *halles* (markets) on the ground floor. Parking in the narrow streets is almost impossible so we left the Citroën in the car park and set off with our luggage for the hotel. Although I had stayed in Le Mediéval before, it took me nearly an hour to find it this time, having left Helen minding the luggage and sitting on a shaded terrace out of the afternoon heat. I had not remembered the name of the little street and none of the first three people I spoke to had ever heard of the hotel! We eventually got there and the staff were as usual extremely helpful. The rooms were small but immaculate, each with an en-suite. Once the home of a cardinal, the building dates from the sixteenth century. It has been run as a hotel by one family for the past fifty years and had been closed for six months in 2005 for renovations and the installation of the very welcome air-conditioning! We had only two nights there and each evening had an excellent dinner at *Les Artistes*, one of several mostly outdoor restaurants in the *Place Crillon*, recommended by the people at Le Mediéval.

We put in a full day of sightseeing next day starting off with *Le Palais des Papes,* which I recalled as enormously interesting and terribly tiring: those endless stone corridors and winding staircases! June is not the best month to visit the palace as the main courtyard is by then being readied for the Avignon Festival in July. Such was the case when we were there and the banks of cameras, lighting consoles, temporary seats, portable loos and other paraphernalia were beginning to clutter a number of areas. But the place is so big there were plenty of unspoilt rooms to explore and lots of fascinating snippets of information to be gleaned from the very good audio guides issued to each tourist on paying the admission fee. I came away full of enthusiasm for the place while Helen was, I think, disconcerted by the signs of the power and luxury of the medieval papal court. After lunch, we found the energy to "do" the cathedral, *Notre Dame des Doms,* and the *Musée Calvet,* a marvellous eighteenth-century aristocratic townhouse worth the visit just to enjoy the building, although the collection of paintings and sculptures it houses is world class.

The next day, Friday, we were to leave Avignon for Aix-en-Provence, but we started off by going to the market in the *Place Pie* and studying the many stalls there. We had of course done this in various towns and villages already visited but the market in Avignon was a very large one and was housed in a modern air-conditioned and spotlessly clean building which, especially in summer, made this sort of exercise less risky there than in the depths of the country! The fruit and vegetable stalls, the flower stalls and the fish stalls were really much the same as in Australia. French butchers, however, do not seem to cut the meat the way Australian butchers do and seem much more willing to prepare the meat to suit individual householders' requirements, making it almost oven-ready: trimmed, spiced and tied up with white string in intricate patterns. Stalls that were not common in Australian markets were those selling nothing but cheese (the labels carefully explaining whether from cow's milk, goat's or sheep's, whether from pasteurised or unpasteurised milk, and the style and geographical origin of the cheese such as Camembert, Brie, Cantal, Roquefort, Epoisses, Marcellin, Port Salut etc.); those selling nothing but different kinds of olives, displayed in great wooden tubs; those selling nothing but herbs and spices, their displays bright with bunches of fresh lavender and heady with baskets of cloves, cinnamon bark and so on. There were two coffee shops in the market building but we decided to go across the road and to have our breakfast coffee and croissants at a busy little terrace café *en face*. The *patronne* seemed to run her business single-handedly and with considerable brio. When we asked for croissants with our coffee (everyone else was just dunking plain bread, I think they were, after all, market workers rather than rich tourists) she cheerfully advised us to pop next door to the *Boulangerie* and *Pâtisserie* to buy some and to bring them back to our table. We followed her advice while she "held" our coffees but, alas, we discovered that the shop next door had one of the most tempting displays of *pâtisseries* we had ever seen, so it was not possible to just have croissants! As we were still in the former papal enclave, I took the opportunity of introducing Helen to an ecclesiastical sweetmeat, and so I asked the shopkeeper whether they had any *Pets de Nonne* (a "Nun's Fart", consisting of a tiny puff of choux pastry, deep fried and rolled in caster sugar). As the shop assistant replied (quite matter-of-factly) that they did not have any Nun's Farts that day I settled for a couple of *Sacristains*, a sort of twist of puff pastry lightly baked until golden and sprinkled with coarse-grained sugar and slivered almonds. We went back to our table on the terrace and enjoyed a rather more indulgent than usual breakfast!

We then made a somewhat late start for Aix-en-Provence but as we used the motorway, without getting lost, we arrived in Aix without incident, found our hotel, the Hôtel Paul near the cathedral, checked in, and headed off for a walk and lunch. We found a pleasantly busy restaurant near the *Tour de l'Horloge*, in the *Place de l'Archevêché*, managed to get a table in the shade, and each had a salad, a glass of chilled rosé and, of course, some great French bread. Our energy replenished we went back to the St Sauveur cathedral (it had been closing for lunch when we had first got there: even churches close for lunch and a siesta in the *Midi*!) and went inside. It is a strange and interesting place, built more or less on the site of a Roman temple to Apollo which stood here on the edge of the Roman forum. "Aix" comes from the Latin *Aquae Sextiae*, the name given to the thermal springs beside which the Roman general Sextius set up a camp in 122BC which developed into an important Roman garrison town. The oldest part of the cathedral, the adjoining fourth-century baptistry, is a domed octagonal building with the dome resting on eight marble columns thought to have come from the Roman forum. The cathedral is a curious mixture of Romanesque and Gothic architecture and there are fine Romanesque cloisters alongside. Across from the cathedral and a little way down the street are numerous fine seventeenth century *hôtels particuliers*, one of which is now the town hall and several of which are now faculty buildings of the University of Aix. Further still down the hill, after passing through a delightful muddle of narrow streets, little squares, plane trees, statues and plashing fountains, you come to the end of the old town and find, in place of the former city ramparts, a broad boulevard, the *Cours Mirabeau*, lined with huge plane trees, smart cafés and chic shops, while the central median strip includes fountains and statues of the city's notables such as good King René and the poet Mirabeau. Beyond the *Cours Mirabeau*, the town suddenly takes on the orderliness of a planned city, with a grid pattern for its streets: it was laid out in the seventeenth century by Cardinal

Mazarin's brother. It was in this part of town that we found the *Musée Granet,* the gallery holding a major collection of the works of a favourite local son, Paul Cézanne, and we managed to visit the museum on the opening day of a special exhibition marking the centenary of his death. In the evening, we had a lovely meal at a table under the stars in the *Place des Cardeurs* near the *Hôtel de Ville* and then walked back up the hill to the Hôtel Paul and to bed.

We set off around ten o'clock next day for Marseille, via the motorway, and arrived in next to no time in the vicinity of the *Gare St Charles,* for which I had been aiming as a point from which I could get my bearings (being much more familiar with railway stations than with roads in France!). To give Helen a quick overview of the city we then drove out along the rue Paradis and the tree-lined Avenue du Prado to the *Place Castellane,* then turned towards the sea and at the *Plage David* turned right to follow the *Corniche Président Kennedy* back to the *Vieux Port* and the city centre. It was a sunny Saturday morning, with a cloudless blue sky, the Mediterranean looking even bluer and the crazy, chatting, gesticulating Marseillais were out in droves, shopping at the street markets, driving madly around in their convertibles (fifty years ago it was on motor-scooters!) or just strolling and socialising at the terrace bars and cafés lining the main streets. We eventually found an underground car park, near the *Préfecture,* and checked my things in at the Hôtel Estérel where I would be staying the night. Helen was to take the TGV to Paris in the afternoon for her flight back to Melbourne the next morning. We decided to phone Singapore Airlines in Paris to confirm Helen's flight but could not get past the answering machines saying that "Office hours are nine to five, Monday to Friday." The very helpful chap at the desk in the Hôtel Estérel volunteered to try but he, too, had no luck. He then rang Singapore Airlines in Melbourne and got the same result. He then looked at the SIA website, found the flight listed in the departures scheduled for the next day and suggested Helen assume all was OK, go to CDG in Paris as planned, check the flight out at the airport terminal above the underground TGV station and spend the night at the airport hotel she had booked. We agreed that that seemed the best thing to do and so set off on foot for the CBD.

We strolled along the rue St Férrol, one of the main

Notre-Dame-de-la-Garde

shopping streets, then down the *Boulevard de la Canebière* to the *Vieux Port* where we picked our way between the fishing boats selling their catches to local housewives and the North Africans selling junk to the tourists. We walked halfway along the *Quai du Port* towards the *Fort St Jean* and then boarded

Le Petit Train for a quick look at the older parts of the city and a gentle ride up the hill to *Notre Dame de la Garde*. There we were able to break the "hop-on, hop-off" journey and admire both the view and the basilica, and we took the opportunity of having a light and delightful lunch at the *L'Eau Vive Restaurant*[20] which occupies the basement of the basilica. Then we hopped back on board *Le Petit Train* and were gently trolleyed down to the *Vieux Port* by a slightly different route letting us see some of the more modern parts of Marseille. We made time for a bit of shopping in the street market near the Stock Exchange and then walked back to the car park to collect Helen's luggage from the Citroën. We took a taxi up to the *Gare St Charles* in good time for the TGV which would take Helen directly to the underground station at CDG airport, said our goodbyes on the platform, and on the dot of 17.14 the train glided off towards Paris… and our odyssey through France was over! The dial on the dashboard of the Citroën said that we had done 3,800 kilometres. I think we would both have liked to turn around and do another 3,800 through other parts of this fascinating country!

---

[20] The *Eau Vive* restaurants are run by the *Travailleuses Missionnaires*, a congregation of nuns and lay people founded in France in 1950 which runs orphanages and schools around the world, and which supports itself through these restaurants in Argentina, Belgium, Burkino Faso, Czech Republic, France, Italy, New Caledonia, the Philippines, Portugal, Peru and Vietnam.

Chapter 5
Quiche Lorraine And Savoiardi

(i) Nancy

Porte de la Craffe, Nancy

One holiday in France with a friend, like me in the autumn years of life, we arrived in Paris by train from Le Havre and so found ourselves at *Gare St Lazare*. As we were en route to Nancy, the capital of the duchy of Lorraine, we had to change from the *Gare St Lazare* to the *Gare de l'Est*. We had allowed two hours in which to do this and to have lunch and we almost came to grief in that I suggested that rather than take a taxi between the stations, we should walk and stretch our legs.

After dragging our luggage along a crowded *rue de Châteaudun*, we turned at my suggestion into a quieter side street seemingly running in the right direction but which, alas, soon turned in the wrong direction and began to go up hill. At that stage, I realised my mistake: with our years and our luggage, it was nonsensical to attempt to walk from one station to the other. So, with a *"Pardonnez-moi, monsieur,"* I stopped a passer-by with a mobile phone in his hand and asked him if he could call us a taxi. He very obligingly did so, refusing to take any payment for the call and within a few minutes a taxi arrived, we climbed aboard and very soon pulled into the forecourt of the *Gare de l'Est* with time for a quick lunch at the ever-reliable *Chez Paul*.

Then we boarded our TGV for a fast trip to Nancy and were safely checked in at our hotel soon after four. It had begun to drizzle by then and so we settled for a rest and then a sortie in search of the evening meal. This took us to the *Place Stanislas*, the really beautiful main square and centre of social life in Nancy, and in a side street we found a little "husband and wife" place where we settled for local fare: quiche Lorraine, *salade Vosgiennne* and wine from Toul. The next day we did a *Petit Train* tour starting in the *Place Stanislas* and concentrating on the pre-eighteenth century parts of the city, all fascinating. Then we gave the afternoon and the following morning to visiting museums. The two big ones in Nancy are located in the former palace of the dukes of Lorraine, begun in the fifteenth century, and in the elegant eighteenth-century building in the *Place Stanislas* which was, before the Revolution, the *Royal College* of *Medicine*. We tackled the ducal palace first as it is more given to the history of Lorraine and Nancy and, being in the Old Town, fitted in well with our

Petit Train tour and interest in the nearby church of the Cordeliers, where the ducal family members are buried. The palace does contain an extraordinary collection of ducal and regional memorabilia, all presented in a rather haphazard fashion, but it was the building itself that most interested me. Like the Cordeliers church next door, the rather plain exterior hides a fascinating interior and we spent the whole afternoon wandering through its corridors, galleries and gardens.

The next day we made an early start and managed to visit the elegant, eighteenth-century pavilion in the *Place Stanislas*, cleverly extended at the rear by a stunning glass and steel wing that doubles its size which, as the *Musée des Beaux Arts*, has a fine collection of classic and modern visual art. After that, we took a bus out to the other side of the city to visit the Museum of the *Ecole de Nancy*. This *musée* is situated in the beautiful *Villa Majorelle* dating from the 1890s and built in the Nancy style, a precursor and probable inspiration of the Art Nouveau, Art Deco and Art Modèrne styles. The *musée* has a wonderful collection of furniture, light-fittings and glassware. Then we took a bus across to the station and took a TER thirty kilometres south to Toul, which had been established as a bishopric in the fourth century and was the seat of prince-bishops in medieval times, the eleventh-century Bishop of Toul being elected pope as Leo IX. Toul, rather than Nancy, became the site of the cathedral of the Primate of Lorraine, Nancy the ducal capital not becoming a bishopric until just before the time of the Revolution. Although the newly created diocese managed to survive the French Revolution, the bishopric of Toul did not and as a result the great Gothic cathedral in the centre of Toul now has a strange, empty and unused feel: it has been eclipsed, administratively, by the eighteenth-century Baroque cathedral in Nancy. The narrow streets around the cathedral lead to the massive ramparts of the town, begun two thousand years ago by the Romans, extended in the thirteenth century by the prince-bishops, strengthened by Vauban for Louis XIV in the seventeenth century and renewed in the nineteenth century. They are, for the most part, still there and have been repelling invaders from Germany, France and Burgundy etc., for over a thousand years. We found a bright and busy little bistro near the cathedral and had a pleasant, light lunch, washed down with some of that delightful light *vin de Toul*. By then, two museums and a major cathedral began to feel like enough for one day and so we caught an afternoon train back to Nancy, our hotel and a nap before dinner.

In our walks through Nancy we had noticed the *Restaurant Excelsior*, on the ground floor of an interesting *Art Nouveau* building quite near the main railway station and, as the friendly concierge at our hotel had said that the *Excelsior* had been delighting customers for nearly a century with fine food in a beautiful *Belle Epoque* setting, we decided to have our evening meal there.

The *Excelsior* did not disappoint! It was a big room with large windows along the front and side, fitted out with *Art Nouveau* wrought iron light fittings, red velvet banquettes, lots of tables for two or four people, acres of white linen tablecloths and gleaming crystal and silver tableware. Black-clad waiters wearing long white aprons moved silently about, helping diners to their chairs, bringing food and wine, wheeling around the mouth-watering dessert-trolley and demonstrating their skills at the table-side *guéridons* where *steck flambé*, *crêpes Suzettes* and other spectacular dishes were being served. Soon after our arrival, a well-dressed elderly couple was ushered to the table next to ours, gave us a polite nod of acknowledgement and quickly settled into what looked like a very romantic dinner for two. A beribboned bunch of white roses arrived for the lady whose fingertips were gallantly held and kissed by the gentleman, while a waiter opened and poured a bottle of *Pol Roger*. We ourselves had a wonderful meal, the pleasure enhanced by the discreet but touching display of love at the adjoining table... a courting couple? A golden wedding celebration, perhaps? It certainly gave a golden glow to our last evening in Nancy. From the *Excelsior* it was then but a short walk back to the hotel and preparations for an early train the next day for our trip through Epinal to Remiremont on the southern border of Lorraine.

(ii) The fighting nuns of Lorraine.

Well, they were not really nuns by the time the fighting occurred but the feisty ladies of Remiremont put up such a spirited defence of their abbey and little town as to keep at bay the troops of the king of France. Definitely a story worth investigating! Moreover, a friend in Australia of French descent had mentioned that his grandparents had had a small farm some fifty kilometres west of Melbourne and that it had been called "Remiremont". Why not do a little investigating, I thought, while in that part of France?

Remiremont, tucked away in a bend of the river Moselle near the Vosges mountains and the border with Switzerland, turned out to be one of the most interesting and picturesque little towns in Lorraine and indeed in the whole of eastern France. For six hundred years or so, it had been the capital of a tiny, independent principality about the size of Liechtenstein but ruled not by count or duke or prince-bishop (as were Salzburg and Cologne, for example) but by a Lady Abbess, a Princess Abbess, in fact. Lorraine (Lotharingia) was the "middle kingdom", lying between Frankreich (France) and Ostreich (Austria), the three portions into which Charlemagne's great Holy Roman Empire was in the ninth century divided between his three grandsons. The "middle kingdom" was destined to fragment quite quickly into a number of counties, dukedoms, electorates, principalities and small states scattered along both banks of the Rhine. For the most part, these small states were inhabited by the descendants of the Germanic tribes that had so bothered Julius Caesar and the Roman empire a thousand years earlier. These territories were fought over for centuries by the neighbouring monarchies. Lorraine and its eastern neighbour, Alsace, have for a thousand years or more been multi-lingual and multi-cultural, maintaining that they were neither French nor German but an amalgam of the best of both cultures.

In the seventh century, a hundred or so years before the time of Charlemagne and St Benedict, two Irish monks, St Romaric and St Amé, had founded a monastic community in a wild and lonely part of the Moselle valley. It was a "double" community after the style of monasteries in Celtic Ireland, where the monks and nuns lived, worked and prayed in separate but neighbouring monasteries grouped around a central, shared church, with the whole settlement run as a single institution. This new foundation was ruled by an abbess rather than by an abbot. Given the historically subordinate role of women in Europe and indeed virtually everywhere in the world at the time, this arrangement, borrowed from the Irish ideas of monasticism and akin to the double monastery of St Brigid in Kildare, marked out Remiremont and a small number of other abbeys in France as innovative and different. The foundation at Remiremont grew steadily but after two hundred years or so the monks had withdrawn and the community of nuns had decided to join the newly-established Benedictine Order.

By 1048, shortly before Duke William of Normandy set off to conquer England, the first Duke of Lorraine accepted the role of "Protector" of the abbey of Remiremont. A few years later the abbey and the surrounding lands were excised from the duchy of Lorraine and accorded the status of an independent principality but, like the duchy itself, nominally within the Holy Roman Empire. In 1088, Pope Urban II, who was travelling in the area, decreed that the abbey would in future be answerable directly to the pope rather than to the local bishop, the Bishop of Toul, in matters spiritual, so the abbess of Remiremont came to hold both temporal and spiritual powers over the abbey, the town and the surrounding lands. A century later, the abbess and her nuns negotiated an extraordinary deal with the pope: they would give up the rule of St Benedict, the cloister, the nuns' plain black habit and the vows of poverty, chastity and obedience; they would continue to live as a pious community of women but separately, in their own houses, grouped around the abbey church; they would daily attend Mass and sing the Divine Office, especially Vespers, and would be obedient to their elected abbess, but otherwise would be free to live as aristocratic and noble ladies. They would share in the growing revenues of the abbey, be free, with the abbess's permission, to travel and to visit their families, to receive guests including gentlemen friends and could even leave and marry, if they so chose. (The French philosopher, Michel de Montaigne, who visited Remiremont in the seventeenth century recorded his admiration of the abbey and of the way it was run... and expressed his appreciation of the hospitality of the noble ladies and of the small barrel of fine wine received from them while there). No longer nuns but, rather, a "chapter of lay canonesses", they would themselves decide, by vote, which young ladies to accept as novices, (termed "nieces") and they would require, for acceptance, that <u>all</u> parents, grandparents and great-grandparents be of <u>unsullied noble birth</u>. (In the eighteenth century, King Louis XV of France visited the abbey and is said to have joked that his own family tree would not qualify him for admittance.)

In 1284, the Holy Roman Emperor Rudolph II married Isabella, daughter of the Duke of Burgundy, in the abbey church at Remiremont and a few years later he gave the title "Princess of the Holy Roman Empire" to the abbess. This independence

Remiremont, les arcades

of the principality inevitably led to conflict with powerful neighbours, the duchies of Lorraine, Burgundy and Bar and the kingdom of France in particular. The situation was rendered all the more difficult by the fact that the canonesses were nearly all daughters of the neighbouring noble families, several abbesses being royal or ducal princesses by birth. After three hundred years of this independence, the then Duke of

Lorraine invaded Remiremont in 1565. The town and abbey were stoutly defended by the townspeople, but in the end, the duke prevailed, removed the "independence flags" approved centuries earlier by the emperor and declared Remiremont to be part of the duchy of Lorraine once again, albeit a "self-governing" part. A hundred or so years later France, under Louis XIII, invaded the duchy of Lorraine and in 1638 besieged Remiremont. The townsfolk, this time led by the abbess herself and the other canonesses, defended the walls, blocked a breach and prevented the French from occupying the town until relief came from the troops of the duke (who was the brother of the abbess). But the French won out in the long run, with the whole of the duchy of Lorraine, along with Remiremont, becoming part of the kingdom of France in 1737 when the new, young duke, Francis of Lorraine, married Maria-Theresa of Hapsburg, daughter and heir to the Austrian Emperor. Francis moved to Vienna and by agreement between the French king and the Austrian emperor, Lorraine was absorbed into the kingdom of France. Francis's sister, Princess Anne-Charlotte, was then abbess of Remiremont. A remarkable woman, Anne-Charlotte divided her time between her abbey and the court of her brother and his wife, Empress Maria-Theresa, in Vienna. In Vienna, she would have spent time with her niece, her brother's youngest child, Marie Antoinette, the future ill-fated queen of France. It was abbess Anne-Charlotte who commissioned the building of the present abbess's residence in Remiremont, a handsome building now used as the Town Hall and offices. The abbesses continued to administer the principality until the French Revolution in 1789 when, despite the efforts of the local people to retain and protect their unusual local government, the "Noble Ladies of

Remiremont" were abolished by the revolutionary authorities in Paris, and the abbey and its lands were declared to be "the property of the nation". The abbey's chancellor (the equivalent of the town mayor) was voted by the populace to go to Paris as their representative and negotiator and was guillotined for royalist sympathies. The canonesses were ordered to disperse, the abbey church was closed and the town's name was changed to Libremont, "Freedom Hill" rather than St Romeric's Hill.

The ensuing years saw a decline in the prosperity of the town, no longer the centre of a principality and an international destination, and the population shrank as people formerly employed by the abbey left to find work elsewhere. The abbesses and *chanoinesses* of Remiremont are long gone but their abbey church of St Pierre, the *Palais Abbatial* and the individual houses of many of the canonesses grouped around the church in the *Place Mesdames* are still there. The buildings and the little town (population in 2020 of around 10,000) that gradually grew around them are well worth a visit. There is even a direct TGV service twice a day from Paris, via Nancy, to make smooth your way! The main street of Remiremont, where everything of interest to the visitor is within walking distance, leads from the station to the well-maintained abbey church and *Palais Abbatial*. It is lined by attractive arcaded buildings housing shops, apartments, and a centuries-old coaching inn, *Le Cheval de Bronze*, where it was a delight to stay and chat about the town with its loquacious patron. The main street is lined with many restaurants where one can savour local specialities such as a quiche Lorraine to begin with, of course, as you are actually IN Lorraine, and perhaps a Remiremont speciality such as a *nonnette de Remiremont* (a small, round, slightly domed and iced cake made with fermented local honey, eggs and spice), or a *loriquette de Remiremont*, a triangular shaped small cake sprinkled with sugar and made according to a traditional, local recipe with powdered almonds, eggs, honey and milk; and, of course, here in the valley of the Moselle, a glass of local wine! What a feast! Here's to *les nobles dames de Remiremont*!

(iii) Savoiardi

Le Chateau de l'Ile, Annecy

The name Savoie[21] derives from the Latin term used by the Romans to refer to the lands straddling the mountains running from Lake Geneva down to the Mediterranean. When Rome withdrew from the area in the fifth century, a "barbarian" tribe

---

[21]*Savoie* in French, Savoy in English and *Savoia* in Italian. The inhabitants are therefore called *Savoyards* in French, and also in English, but in Italian they are *Savoiardi*, the same term as is used for a type of biscuit first made in Savoy and now known as a ladyfinger in English and as *boudoirs* in French.

from the north took over and established the kingdom of *Burgonde*, or Burgundy, which in the ninth century was absorbed into Charlemagne's "Holy Roman Empire". After his death and the division of those territories between his three grandsons, the kingdom of Burgundy became part of France. It was soon divided up into smaller fiefdoms such as the duchy of Burgundy and several smaller states including the counties of Genève, Maurienne and Savoie, ruled by local lords. Through a mixture of war, negotiation and marriages, Savoy absorbed several of the other states and emerged in the fifteenth century as a duchy: a small, rather poor, mountainous state, but one strategically controlling the alpine passes between Italy and France. In the sixteenth century, the capital was moved from Chambéry to Turin and the House of Savoy saw its fortunes as being made on the fertile plains of northern Italy rather than in the mountains disputed with France and Switzerland. In the mid-nineteenth century, astute negotiations saw the House of Savoy invited to become the first royal family of the newly formed kingdom of a united Italy. Leaving mountainous Savoy did indeed pay off!

After having spent a few pleasant days in Lorraine, my friend and I caught a TER via Epinal to Dijon where we had lunch at the station, then a TGV to Macon and finally another TGV from Macon to our destination, Aix-les-Bains in Savoy. We arrived around eight in the evening, making it an almost twelve-hour trip and, having had lunch and snacks along the way, we were happy to just hit the hay once we had checked in to our hotel across the road from the station in Aix. While Aix-les-Bains is one of the major towns in Savoy and an important spa centre, our two projects on that visit were to make a day trip to Annecy and another one to visit the former royal abbey of Hautecombe, across Lake Bourget from Aix. The next day, therefore, we boarded the ferry of the *Compagnie de Bateaux du Lac du Bourget* for the half-hour trip across and along the lake to the abbey.

Founded in the twelfth century as a Cistercian abbey it had in the fifteenth century been chosen as the burial place of the counts of Savoy when their capital had been the nearby city of Chambéry. When the counts became dukes and moved their capital over the mountains to Turin, Hautecombe continued to be the family burial choice. Duke Victor Emmanuel of Savoy became the first King of a united Italy in the 1860s and he and his successors, up to and including the last king and queen of Italy, were all buried in Hautecombe. It is a wonderfully isolated, wild and romantic setting for a great piece of architecture, whether civil or religious, with the towers reflected in the lake and the whole seen against a background of dense forest sweeping up the steep slopes of the surrounding mountains. We were disappointed to discover that only the abbey church is open to visitors, as the Cistercians' twenty-first-century successors, the *Congrégation du Chemin Neuf*, use the historic monastic buildings as headquarters and training centre. The church was cluttered with tombs and memorials and rather garish late Baroque paintings and statuary and was a bit spooky! But we loved the lake trip there and back!

The next day we went by TER to Annecy, only fifty minutes away from Aix and also built on the edge of a lake, Lac Annecy. It seemed to us a much lovelier town, with its narrow streets and pastel buildings, a happy mix of elements from Switzerland, Venice and the Côte d'Azur. We had lunch in a sunny little square, walked by the lake, popped into the church where St François de Sales used to work (he was born and raised locally), heard the organist practising in the cathedral and caught a later-than-planned train "home" to Aix. There we splurged on an evening meal at the very posh Hôtel Bristol! Crystal chandeliers, a dining room-cum-ballroom that could seat three hundred guests, coffered ceiling three storeys high... and a cast of just sixteen diners at eight tables, with one masterly waitress: it could have been a scene from Terence Rattigan's *Separate Tables* or perhaps from a sequel to *Dinner For One*, the TV sketch featuring that multi-skilled old waiter, James, serving the lady of the house, Miss Sophie, and her imagined guests at her ninetieth birthday dinner. A lovely way to end our visit to Aix-les-Bains!

Chapter 6
Bourbon and Burgundy

L'hotel de ville, Arnay-le-Duc

(i) Arnay-le-Duc

My cousin Helen and I one year hired a car in Nevers and drove via Autun to Arnay-le-Duc. We left Nevers, slumbering on the banks of the Loire and the Nièvre where those two rivers meet, and then took the winding road up to Château-Chinon, built on a rather isolated and forest-clad plateau astride the borders of the dukedoms of Bourbon and Burgundy. After a lunch stop in Château-Chinon, where François Mitterand had been mayor before being elected President of France for two successive *septennats*, we descended through the pine forests to Autun. Originally named Augustodunum in honour of its founder, the emperor Augustus, not long after Caesar's conquest of Gaul, Autun was laid out as a model Roman city with high walls, monumental gates, forum, theatre, and temples, significant vestiges of which remain to this day. The very interesting twelfth-century Cathedral of St Lazare contains the remains of St Lazare of Aix, the fifth-century bishop of Aix-en-Provence who travelled to Palestine late in life and who died in Marseille on his return from the Holy Land in 441 AD. If, like me, you are not really into relics, the cathedral is nonetheless of immense interest. It dates from the early twelfth century and is reputedly one of the best examples of Romanesque architecture in Europe. Admittedly, there are later additions such as the Gothic spire, but the overall result is harmonious. Perhaps the most interesting embellishment is the wealth of medieval sculptures over the main doorways and atop many of the columns in the nave. That intriguing old scallywag, Talleyrand, was Bishop of Autun before throwing in his lot with the Revolution, renouncing the church and becoming the wily foreign minister and indispensable adviser in turn of the Revolutionary Council, Emperor Napoleon and the restored Bourbons Louis XVIII, Charles X and Louis-Philippe! He accumulated a vast fortune from turning his coat many times and his beautiful Château of Valençay in the Loire Valley is still lived in by the Talleyrand family and is an absolute must-see when you are visiting the famous Loire Valley and its châteaux.

Another thirty kilometres from Autun saw us arrive in Arnay-le-Duc, a large village now rather than the important town it was in the past because of its location at the crossroads of both Roman and medieval trade routes. We had booked in at a small *chambres d'hôtes* near the main street and made it our base for the next few days. The husband and wife who ran it were charming people and made us very welcome. He was a retired chef and was happy to serve us a special Burgundian dinner on our last night there. On our first morning, we explored the village which boasted one of the smaller châteaux of the Condé family, gifted to the town by a sixteenth-century duke. As a sign of their gratitude for that very considerable supply of free building materials, dressed stone, timber, lead and glass, the townspeople voted to add *le Duc* to the town's name. There is a pretty little fourteenth-century church and an imposing building now used as a museum, the *Maison Régional des Arts de la Table*, which dates from 1681 and operated as the *Hospice Saint-Pierre* for almost three hundred years, staffed by nuns from the famous hospice in Beaune. Another interesting building is the *mairie,* or town hall, housed in what was once an Ursuline convent and school for girls, a pretty turreted building looking more like a miniature Loire Valley château than a convent school.

From Arnay-le-Duc we next day drove the thirty-five kilometres to Beaune and spent the day exploring the town, lunching extravagantly and superbly on the terrace of the *Le Conty* restaurant near the *Place Carnot* and admiring the wonderful *Hospice de l'Hôtel-Dieu*, marvellously preserved and presented as a fully equipped hospital of Renaissance times. Another day trip took us to Dijon, the capital of Burgundy, for more Burgundian cuisine at lunch and to visit the ducal palace. There is so much to see in Dijon, which I had visited several times in the past, that it seemed best to concentrate on a few things rather than to drag my companion around the city from one monument to another. The ducal palace is in the most interesting part of the city, the old town, and looks across the main square, formerly the *Place Royale* and now the *Place de la Libération*. Although it has a neo-classical façade reminiscent of Versailles, the palace incorporates buildings dating from the Middle Ages through the Renaissance to the eighteenth century. The tower of Duke Phillip the Good rising up behind the central block dates from the fifteenth century and, if you can find the energy to climb the three hundred or so steps to the top, as I did in my youth, you are rewarded with a panoramic view of Dijon and the surrounding countryside. The central block of the palace, now a museum, is still furnished as a royal residence while the two side wings are now used respectively as town hall and fine arts museum. Perhaps the most interesting part of the very fine arts collection is the group of statuettes known as the *Pleurants de Dijon*. These are eighty-two figurines representing mourners (*pleurer* = to weep) attending the burials of the early dukes of Burgundy. The dukes were originally buried in the Carthusian Abbey at Champmol but after the Revolution and the dispersal of the monks, the tombs were moved first to the cathedral and then to the ducal palace, where they may now be seen in the Great Hall: truly one of the greatest achievements of fifteenth century art. On leaving the ducal palace, we refreshed ourselves with a glass of *Kir* in one of the many nearby cafés. Felix Kir was not just the source of the name of this refreshing drink, a glass of white wine with a dash of Cassis, but was its actual inventor. He was also a Catholic priest, resistance fighter during the Second World War, mayor of Dijon and local MP for twenty years… and honorary Canon of the cathedral of Dijon: a feisty and much-loved local character.

    On our last day at Arnay-le-Duc we headed off to Nuits-Saint-Georges, the very epicentre of Burgundy's greatest wine estates and itself a picturesque little town. The main street, the *Grande Rue*, has been pedestrianised and a walk along it gives one a huge choice of restaurants, *pâtisseries*, *chocolateries*, *hôtels* and *caves de vin* in which to yield to temptation. Of course, it is not a good idea to visit *les caves de vins fins* (*cave* = cellar) when one has a car to drive! So, after another gastronomic lunch that, for this driver, had to be accompanied by one rather than several glasses of Nuits-Saint-Georges, we drove the extra twelve kilometres or so to the Abbey of Cîteaux. This is where the Cistercian order had been founded in 1098 as a sort of purist breakaway from the Benedictine monks. The Cistercians aimed at a simple life based on prayer and meditation and supported by farming; they sought to build their monasteries in isolated, rural areas, *le désert*, rather than near centres of population. Cîteaux had been an immediate success and "daughter" houses had quickly sprung up all over Europe. Much of the abbey had been destroyed when it was closed down at the time of the Revolution and the few surviving buildings had remained in private hands until 1898 when they were purchased by monks returning from exile abroad. A rather futuristic new church had been completed in 1970 and the abbey is again a working monastery with about thirty monks. After nine hundred or so years of monastic labour, the forest and swamps of Cîteaux have been turned into the rich farmlands and superb vineyards stretching from Beaune through Nuits-Saint-Georges all the way to Dijon, although the abbey today is just a small farm with cheese-making as its main source of income. As I had visited a number of Cistercian houses in France, England, Ireland, Canada and Australia, a visit to the "mother house" had seemed appropriate when in Burgundy. So much history since 1098, such peace and calm, and such a warm welcome from the lay guides and friends of Cîteaux! But there is relatively little to actually see and unless you share this interest in Cistercian history and monasticism this detour is probably best omitted. The choice of Arnay-le-Duc as a base was probably another decision not to recommend. Autun would have made a much better base for exploring the area, being a larger and livelier place with many accommodation possibilities, having a very attractive and historic town centre and there is a rail service available with hire car agencies near the station. Beaune would also be a good base for visiting the area but its fame would probably mean that it would be much more crowded in the tourist season and considerably more expensive than Autun.

(ii) The Morvan

After spending a few days in Arnay-le-Duc we headed north to the Benedictine Abbey of *La-Pierre-Qui-Vire*, deep in the forests of the Morvan. Saulieu was our lunch stop. It has existed from Roman times and there are some very interesting buildings to admire: narrow, winding streets with half-timbered houses, the twelfth-century basilica of St Andoche, the *Tour Auxois*, part of the medieval walls of the old town, another lovely little hospice built on the model of the great hospice in Beaune, and even a string of gastronomic restaurants housed in beautiful old buildings, including the Michelin three-star *La Côte d'Or*. After our somewhat humbler but still excellent lunch, we set off up the winding road through the forests of the Morvan, through the village of Saint-Agnan with its beautiful lake and on to the abbey. *La Pierre-Qui-Vire* is not an ancient monastery, having been founded only in 1850. It quite quickly flourished, establishing "daughter" houses in France, Africa, Asia and the USA (in

Oklahoma). Located in an isolated part of the forest the abbey seemed an ideal place in which to pause from a rather hectic round of sightseeing. We arrived late in the afternoon, the weather having deteriorated, shall we say, with dark clouds replacing the morning's blue skies and a cool if not cold mountain breeze greeting us as we alighted from the car. The monks, however, made us very welcome, showed us to comfortable rooms in the modern and warm guest house and said that Vespers would commence in about half an hour in the abbey church and would be followed by the evening meal in the guest house. After settling into the rooms, we set off to explore a little and to make our way to the abbey church, a large Gothic-revival building completed in 1871 and now masked by a rather strange, modernistic façade added in 1992. Once inside, all thoughts of architectural incongruities fled and I felt immediately transported to a different world. It was a dim, silent world lit only by the flickering light of candles and the last gleam of sunlight escaping the storm clouds and penetrating the stained-glass windows of the church. There were already a few people sitting quietly in the nave and a few monks already in their choir stalls: it was about five minutes before the main body of monks filed in, took their places and, with a signal from the abbot, began the Gregorian chant of Vespers. The most memorable part of the experience, however, had been the sight, on entering the church, of a brazier about two metres high placed on the first step of the sanctuary and directly in front of the high altar, a column of incense rising steadily and silently and disappearing into the high vault above. One of the Psalms says something like "Let my prayer rise as incense before the Lord...". I have never before or since seen such a subtle and successful "warming up" session or prelude to a church service. Magical! Unforgettable!

We stayed at the abbey for three nights, descending from the forested heights to make two day-trips. The first was a round trip to Vézelay, through Bazoches in the morning and back through Avallon after lunch. Bazoches is a tiny but pretty village at the foot of a gentle slope on which sits the wonderful *Château de Bazoches*. The château was commenced in 1180 by the local feudal lord, Jean de Bazoches, and in 1675 it was purchased by Louis XIV's great military engineer, Vauban, who greatly altered, enlarged and embellished it. The château is still lived in by the descendants of Vauban who have, interestingly enough, intermarried with descendants of Jean de Bazoches, so that one can say that after more than eight hundred years the original family is still in residence! Part of the château is open to the public and the formal reception rooms, all exquisitely furnished in eighteenth century style, are quite stunning. The formal gardens and park are well maintained and offer a sweeping view of the surrounding countryside. From a belvedere or bastion in the grounds, there is a fine view of our destination, Vézelay, only twelve kilometres or so away.

The village of Vézelay is built on the top of a rocky hillock, probably an outcrop of the Morvan plateau. People were living here, Celts or Gauls, before the Romans came and the site of the battle in which Julius Caesar finally conquered the Gauls is on the plain below. The view from Vézelay is really outstanding, with lush fields, carefully tended vineyards and charming villages stretching out across Burgundy. The main attraction, apart from the view is, however, the great basilica of Saint Mary Magdalen, *La Madeleine*, begun in the eleventh century and one of the most important pilgrimage sites in early medieval Europe. Eclipsed by other sites in the fourteenth century, pillaged in the sixteenth-century Wars of Religion, destroyed by fire, rebuilt and then almost demolished during the Revolution, the basilica was recognised by the French government in the nineteenth century as a monument of great national significance and has been carefully restored. The medieval carving of Biblical stories above the main doors and around the nave are exceptionally interesting and the vast, lofty interior is lit by sunshine pouring in through the clerestory windows. There were very few visitors there when we went in and the beauty of the place, the silence and the light were quite uplifting. We then returned to the real world by strolling around the quaint little village, studying the menus and selecting a place for lunch. We chose the *Lion d'Or*, partly because of the interesting Burgundian menu and partly because of the beautiful building and elegant terrace restaurant. It turned out to be quite superb... rather expensive, but truly memorable.

It was time to make our way home to La Pierre-Qui-Vire and although we did adhere to our original plan of driving via Avallon we lacked the time to do much more than admire the town from across the river. It looked to be a larger version of Vézelay as well as being a prosperous little market town. The remains of the ramparts, the fortified gates, the tall clock tower and the collegial church in the main square all pointed to centuries of importance in the history of Burgundy. But we had to hurry on and just made it up to our forest hideaway in time for Vespers and a little quiet recollection in the magical setting of the abbey church.

Our second day trip was to the *Abbaye de Fontenay*, a Cistercian abbey founded by St Bernard in 1118 and just a few kilometres out of Montbard. The abbey quite quickly grew to be one of the most important in France, with over two hundred monks at its peak. It survived sacking twice by the English during the Hundred Years' War and again by the Huguenots during the Wars of Religion. It was closed down at the time of the French Revolution, the monks dispersed and the buildings sold off. In 1820 the property was purchased by the Montgolfier family (nephews of the inventor of hot air ballooning) and was redeveloped as a paper mill which operated successfully until 1875 when it was closed and the unused buildings were left to deteriorate. In 1905, a wealthy Lyonnais married a Montgolfier daughter and the couple began the restoration of the abbey, a Herculean task now completed and being maintained by the couple's descendants. Set in the middle of a forested valley, Fontenay is a perfect example of the Cistercian idea of monastic life: a community living simply and austerely, away from the bustle of town life, supporting itself through farm work and devoting a large part of the day to prayer and reflection. The structures saved from ruin include the large and luminous twelfth-century abbey church, the cloister, chapter house, scriptorium, and dormitory and the eighteenth-century house of the Commendatory abbots, now the country home of the owners. The whole lot is thoughtfully presented for visitors to enjoy the silence, beauty and peacefulness of the place... if you visit only one monastic ruin while in France, this is probably the one to choose!

From Fontenay, we returned to Montbard, itself an interesting little market and industrial town and enjoyed lunch on the terrace of the Hôtel de la Gare... perhaps a puzzling choice, but the easy car parking was an attraction and the restaurant had been recommended by travellers we had met in the morning at Fontenay. We skipped the dessert course as we were then heading off to Flavigny-sur-Ozerain, some twenty kilometres to the west and, it seemed to me, an ideal place in which to look for a dessert. Flavigny had been used as the setting for the film *Chocolat* in 1999 starring Juliette Binoche and Johnny Depp and is indeed picturesque. It is perched atop a steep little hill and consists of a tangle of cobbled streets and Medieval and Renaissance houses crowding around the village church and a former Benedictine abbey. The abbey had been famous from Medieval times for the production of herbal medicines and *douceurs*, or sweets, and these *pastilles*, *Anis de Flavigny*, are still available and are one of the main souvenirs available for purchase by tourists. They come in several flavours and are delicious! After a couple of hours exploring Flavigny, we set off for our monastic home at LPQV, with a stop halfway in the village of Epoisses, famous for its luscious, creamy (slightly smelly) cheese. A little sampling followed by a modest purchase (the monks at LPQV also made a very good cheese so we felt a little like people carrying coal to Newcastle) and we were off and up into the forest, arriving in good time for another magical, mystical Vespers and the evening meal. The next morning, it was a case of *adieu* to the good Benedictines and *en route* for further adventures.

(iii) Moulins

Two cousins and I travelled by train from Geneva to Moulins one fine spring day on what should have been a smooth trip by TGV as far as Lyon and then, after a half-hour connection, on to Moulins by the Lyon-Tours *Intercité*. Alas, our day of travel turned out to be a day of lightning and random train strikes in France and both of our booked trains were among those suddenly cancelled. The unflappable Swiss railway clerk in

Geneva's Cornavin station found us seats on a Swiss train heading for Spain through Lyon and in Lyon's Part-Dieu station a patient and helpful French-Vietnamese clerk found us a train going to Paris via Le Creusot-TGV, where he suggested we alight and find a taxi to take us the few kilometres to nearby Montchanin. We did that and there picked up a crowded little motor-train that took us on to the ducal city of Nevers. There we had a connection with a Paris-Nevers-Moulins-Vichy *Intercité* express, which arrived on time and which finally saw us reach Moulins only five hours later than originally planned. We had booked rooms at the delightful Hotel du Parc, which is opposite the station, and were just in time to check in and repair to the dining room and order dinner before the kitchen technically closed. The management and staff were wonderfully welcoming, the meal was superb and the rooms beautifully furnished and comfortable and after the most hectic of days, we tumbled into our beds and went straight to sleep. We woke to a sunny spring morning, an excellent breakfast including croissants straight from the oven and thus comforted we set off to explore Moulins.

  The Bourbon family had founded Moulins in the eleventh century as the chief town of the region and, in time, their clever use of marriage and military alliances (Béatrice de Bourbon married a younger son of the king of France, Louis IX), saw them become counts and, in time, dukes of Bourbon. Secure in their position they moved their principal place of residence from their medieval fortress-château in Chantelle to a luxurious Renaissance-style palace they built in Moulins across the square from the present cathedral. The court of the dukes of Bourbon in Moulins soon rivalled the royal court in Paris and, eventually, the ninth Duke of Bourbon was accused of treason by François I and killed in battle, and the dukedom was absorbed into the French Crown. Ironically, the duke's distant cousin, Henri Bourbon, King of Navarre, succeeded to the throne of France when François I's grandson, Henri III and the last monarch of the Valois dynasty, died without a closer male heir. Not only did the Bourbons outlast the Valois kings and in time become Kings of France[22] but, following the death of the childless Carlos II of Spain in 1700 and under the terms of his Will, the Spanish throne passed to a Bourbon prince, the nephew of Louis XIV. He succeeded to the throne as Phillip V, and his Bourbon descendants still rule in Spain, the present king being Phillip VI.

Moulins today is an interesting city, compact enough to be visited easily on foot and containing in its old centre enough medieval, half-timbered houses, Renaissance town houses, and splendid civic buildings to satisfy most tourists. Visiting the *Tour Jacquemart*, a remnant of the city walls, the strange collegial-cathedral with its twin naves, the *Pavillon de Beaujeu* (remnant of the ducal palace and now a fine arts museum) and the National Collection of Stage and Film Costumes, housed in a former military barracks on the edge of town pleasantly filled the day on either side of a delightful lunch in the *Grand Café*, a fabulous *Belle Epoque* restaurant in the *Place de l'Allier*. Moulins is a good base for trips around the area and on the second day, we took a morning TER to Paray-le-Monial, about an hour's ride east into the Charolais region. We arrived in time to stroll through the very lively

---

[22] As a token of gratitude for the support of France in its fight for independence from Britain in 1776, the United States government named part of the states of Virginia and Kentucky, Bourbon County('Bourbon' being the family name of the French kings). That part of the country became famous for its distillation of whisky (from corn rather than from rye as in Scotland) and Bourbon lives on as the king of spirits in the USA.

street market in progress in the town centre, managing to resist the temptations of the farmers' produce stalls by thinking of the reservation we had made in advance for lunch at the *Restaurant de la Basilique*, which specialised in local produce and Burgundian cuisine and where we did indeed have a wonderful meal.

Paray is probably most noted for its twelfth-century abbey church, a smaller version of the great Romanesque church at nearby Cluny which was the biggest church in the world until the construction of the present St Peter's in Rome. While Cluny was sacked, burnt and even blown up during the Revolution, the church in Paray survives intact and attracts admirers from around the world. Another place of interest in Paray-le-Monial is the convent and chapel of the Visitation, site of the seventeenth-century apparitions of the *Sacré Coeur* (Sacred Heart) which launched that devotion throughout France and the world. After visiting both the abbey and the Visitation convent we had time to detour through the historic heart of the town on our way back to the station, where we arrived in good time for our train back to Moulins. Next day we had a relaxing morning and light lunch in our wonderful hotel and then walked across the road to the station and took an afternoon train to Vichy and Clermont-Ferrand.

Chapter 7
Through the Massif Central

(i) Clermont-Ferrand

Clermont-Ferrand is the gateway to the Massif Central, a series of mountain ranges, volcanic peaks and high plateaux in south-central France with a total area about the size of the Benelux countries. The city has a population of over a quarter of a million and is close to the geographic centre of France. It is a major junction of railway lines and motorways crossing France from north to south and from east to west and has been an important centre of population since the time of the Gauls. Known as Arvenis until around 900 AD, when the name Clermont came into use, it was an important city ruled by its bishops until the fourteenth century when the counts of Auvergne took over, merging their nearby fortified stronghold of Montferrand with the episcopal city of Clermont to become Clermont-Ferrand. Although the capital of the Auvergne, it is frequently overlooked by tourists. How wrong they are! Admittedly, at first glance it looks more like the centre of the Michelin motor tyre industry, which it certainly is, than like a tourist hotspot, but a little research and a walk around its hilly streets will reveal many fascinating surprises. The city centre, the old town, is built on not just a steep hill but on the very core of a huge, extinct volcano. Most of the historic buildings, such as the cathedral, are built of the blue-black lava-based stone spewed out by the volcano.

From vantage points near the cathedral, one can see that the city is in fact surrounded by similar extinct volcanoes, as Clermont-Ferrand is on the edge of France's *Parc des Volcans* where over a hundred volcanoes, including the *Puy de Sancy*, at 1,900 metres the highest peak in central France, were once active. The *Puy de Dôme,* a volcanic peak twelve kilometres away and rising up nearly 1,500 metres, offers splendid views of the city and surrounding countryside, and is accessible now by an ultra-modern and environmentally friendly electric cog railway, *le Train Panoramique des Dômes,* a real "must" for visitors to the Auvergne and for volcano and train enthusiasts!

La cathédrale, Clermont-Ferrand

Apart from its extraordinary location, Clermont-Ferrand has a fascinating history. In 52 BC, its Gallic citizens, a tribe known by the Romans as the *Arverni (*origin of the term Auvergne), closed the gates of their stockade and successfully repelled the army led by Julius Caesar. Admittedly, Caesar returned some months later with his legions and crushed the *Arverni* and the other Gauls, capturing and executing their leader, Vercingetorix. In the city's main square, the *Place de Jaude,* there is a very fine statue of Vercingetorix, an almost legendary national hero to the French. It was here that, in 1095,

Pope Urban II launched the first of the Christian Crusades to retake the Holy Land from the Muslim forces that had occupied it after the establishment of Islam in the seventh century. To us in the twenty-first century, wearied by the politico-religious turmoil still devastating the Middle East, this may well seem to have been a big mistake and to have started off a never-ending conflict. Urban II is, however, still admired for other achievements of his reforming pontificate and his statue dominates the *Place de la Victoire* beside the cathedral. A third statue honouring a local great is that of Blaise Pascal in the nearby *Square Blaise-Pascal*. Pascal was a brilliant seventeenth-century philosopher, mathematician and scientist (think of "pascals" as a unit of measure when you next check your car's tyre pressure) and he was born and worked here.

The very handsome *Place de Jaude* is really nowadays the centre[23] of civic life in Clermont-Ferrand and a stroll to it from the cathedral can take you through the old town and along the *rue des Chaussettiers*. At number three, you will find the *Hôtel Savaron*, *"hôtel"* in its original sense of a town house, in this case the town house of the Savaron family. This fascinating place was built in 1513 by Hugues Savaron, a wealthy merchant and adviser of François I. It is now a fantastic little restaurant, called simply *Le 1513*, serving delicious and inexpensive meals, a restaurant not to be missed when you

---

[23] The *Place de la Victoire*, one of the many interesting open spaces in the city, is built on the site of a Roman forum and temple which in medieval times were replaced by the *Palais de l'Archévêque* and other religious buildings adjoining the cathedral. They in turn were demolished at the time of the Revolution and the present *Place* was created. A short way down hill is the *Place de Jaude*, a swamp and then a market in Roman times and an open public space in medieval times which became the business and civic centre of the city as distinct from the cathedral precinct which was the religious centre.

visit the city. It was pointed out to me by the conductor on the little single-carriage motor-train on which I travelled one day to Clermont from Laqueuille on the Mont Dore branch line. There being almost no other passengers on that early morning service he had spent most of the hour-long trip chatting about trains, volcanoes and his hometown of Clermont-Ferrand. Along with recommending *Le 1513*, he suggested I try a local specialty *le truffade* which I found was available on almost every menu I saw in town. The *truffade* is a sort of thick pancake, made with potato rather than flour and flavoured with garlic and sometimes also, depending on the cook, bacon. It can end up looking a bit like an ugly brown truffle... but tastes delicious! I did indeed discover that Clermont-Ferrand is far more than a junction and transport hub and deserves much more than a passing glance! The Hôtel Le Lion in the *Place de Jaude* makes a very comfortable and welcoming base from which to explore the city and further afield.

Train trips from Clermont-Ferrand [24]

(a) The Allier valley and the Cévennes

Two of the most interesting rail trips in France, both winding their way through the Massif Central, have their starting point in Clermont-Ferrand. One, the better-known, is the route along *les Gorges de l'Allier,* the valley of the Allier

---

[24] The railways in France were originally developed by private companies but all were nationalised by 1938 under the title SNCF, *Societe Nationale des Chemins de Fer Francais*. The SNCF now operates three main types of trains: the TGV, *Trains à Grande Vitesse*; the *Intercités*, standard long-distance trains using steel air-conditioned carriages; the TER, *Trains Express Régional*, short-haul trains often self-propelled single, air-conditioned carriages which can be linked together when there are many passengers.

River, to Nîmes. This is a route which I first took more than fifty years ago on board *Le Cévenol*, an *autorail* or diesel-operated motor-train built in the 1950s by Renault for the SNCF to replace steam-drawn trains on less frequented lines. Each *autorail*, brightly painted in red and cream, could carry about seventy passengers and they could be joined together to form a train of three to five units, with just one driver, in the front unit, in control of all engines. I still remember that trip, the train consisting of five units all linked together, each one so crowded with people sitting and standing that, at first, I had feared there would be no room for me. But people near the door had squashed up and I had squeezed in, luggage and all. I can still hear the diesel engines groaning with the load as the train moved off, still feel the jerking as the driver struggled to change gears and to build up speed, still smell the diesel fumes and see the whisps of exhaust curling past the open windows... interesting but far from comfortable!

Many years later I did the trip again, but in the reverse direction, this time in the comfort of a first-class carriage of an *Intercité* hauled by a massive electric locomotive. I was in Clermont-Ferrand and, at about midday one day, I went to the main station and met my brother and his wife who arrived on the morning express from Paris. In Clermont, their fourteen-carriage train was divided in two, the front half heading off down the Allier valley to Nîmes and the rear half going across the flanks of the Cantal to Béziers. I joined Peter and Pam for the trip down the Allier, bringing on board with me a large picnic basket stocked with *pâté en croute*, *cornichons*, olives, slices of ham, baguettes, three *tartes aux fruits* and two bottles of *Veuve Cliquot*. There was no food service on the train and I was determined that we would nonetheless have a celebratory lunch! The conductor arrived soon after we left Clermont, checked my ticket and welcomed us to move from our allotted seats in the otherwise empty carriage, which was by then at the very end of the train. He suggested we move to the seats at the rear of the carriage from which we would be able to look out through the open doorway that had led to the rear carriages as the train left Paris and through which we now had a fascinating view of the railway tracks and surrounding countryside, all rapidly sliding backwards as the train picked up speed. From Clermont-Ferrand the line climbs south up into the Cévennes mountains, the source of the north-flowing river Allier, crossing back and forth from one side to the other of the ever-narrowing river gorge, on eighty-two bridges and winding through forty-eight tunnels. It is really quite spectacular and, at times, goes through rugged country where there are no signs of human habitation. The high point of 1,025 metres is reached near the little junction station of La Bastide-Saint-Laurent, where we alighted. This is the watershed of the area, all rivers flowing north from here, such as the Allier, end up in the Atlantic and those flowing south end up in the Mediterranean.

We had a short wait for a connecting train on the branch line from La Bastide-Saint-Laurent which winds up through the Cévennes to the surprisingly isolated medieval city of Mende, population of about 10,000 and *préfecture* of the department of Lozère. Mende is well worth the detour and we had an excellent stay there at the Hôtel Urbain V,[25] a short walk from both the station and the cathedral. The next day we went on westward by TER to Mervejols where we parted company, Peter and Pam taking the train south to Millau where they picked up a hire car at the station to continue their trip to the south while I took the train north from Mervejols to Saint-Flour and the Cantal.

To get to Mende from La Bastide the railway line climbs up a further two hundred metres and crosses the windswept Montbel plateau before reaching Larzalier, the top of the range at 1,215 metres, and then descending through a series of snow galleries and tunnels to the headwaters of the south-flowing river Lot, which it follows into Mende and beyond. Until the introduction of the motor-trains, the line was serviced by steam and, at over 1,200 metres, was the highest line in Europe on which ordinary steam engines (not assisted by cog or ratchet or cable) were used. Soon after the opening of the line, heavy snowfalls in winter began to block trains and passengers sheltered overnight on the trains or, if they were lucky enough to be near the Larzalier station, in the station buildings while waiting for the snow-plough engine to arrive from La Bastide. To remedy the problem, several snow galleries, tunnel-like

---

[25] Urbain V was a local lad who made it to the top of the tree, from son of the local gentry to university professor of Law to papal diplomat and then to pope. After the death of Innocent VI, the cardinals could not agree on which of them should succeed but did eventually agree that the much-respected professor and diplomat should be the next pope. He was hastily summoned to attend, was made a bishop, then cardinal, and then elected as pope and is generally regarded as one of the most effective pontiffs of the fourteenth century. He died in 1370. The king of Denmark and others proposed his canonisation in 1375 and after a few centuries of bureaucratic delay he was beatified in 1870.

structures of wood or, sometimes, stone were built to protect the line in the sections where the snow tended to build up and several banks of trees were planted in strategic spots to deflect the wind and reduce the build-up of snow drifts. The line was soon dubbed *la ligne du toit de la France* (the line across the roof of France).

From La Bastide-St Laurent, the line to Nîmes begins a steady descent through Genolhac to Alès, now presenting itself as the southern gateway to the Cévennes, and then runs across the plain of the river Gard to Nîmes. Nîmes is even more worth a visit, with its wonderful Roman amphitheatre (*les Arènes*) and temple (the *Maison Carrée),* its proximity to the great *Pont du Gard* and its very good small hotels near the station, such as the *Majestic* and the *César.* The pedestrianised old centre of the city is charming and full of great places to eat and drink and watch the world go by. And, for those who really are train *aficionados,* there is always the possibility of continuing on southwards by train from Nîmes through Montpellier to the railway junction of Béziers, where one can board the train that goes back to Clermont-Ferrand through Millau, Séverac and Neussargues along the western edge of the Cévennes, across the volcanic plateau of the Aubrac and over Gustave Eiffel's famous *Viaduc de Garabit.* But who could pass through Montpellier or Béziers without stopping for at least a night or two in those historic and lively cities and who could pass through Millau without alighting for a look at that slender, spidery highest bridge in the world, the *Viaduc de Millau*? In Béziers, the city council kindly supplies a free shuttle bus to take you from the station up the steep hill on which the cathedral and city centre are built and in Montpellier, the excellent new tramway will take you from the station to the Place de la Comédie, which is really the city centre.

Millau, where the train line passes underneath the *viaduc* as it follows the river Tarn into the town centre, warrants at least a stop for lunch and an inspection. It is only a short walk from the station to the town centre where you will find the local tourist information centre ready to organise a quick visit to the viaduct and there are many good restaurants in and near the *Place Foch*, the lively centre of this interesting old town. Before the building of the great viaduct, Millau was best known in France for its gloves. The farmland around Millau has from the Middle Ages been mainly used for sheep-grazing, and while the wool went elsewhere to be spun and woven into cloth the sheepskins were tanned and value added in Millau and made in to gloves. The sheep milk was made in to the famous blue-vein cheese in nearby Roquefort. The glove-making industry declined in the mid-twentieth century with the introduction of "smart casual" clothes: Millau's industry shrank while that of Nîmes boomed (denim = cloth from or *de* Nîmes). But there are still glove-making firms in Millau and there is a very interesting section devoted to the industry in the *Musée de Millau*. There is a very good place for lunch near the historic central market, *Les Halles,* and if you are feeling a little flusher, two very fine restaurants are *Les Arcades* and, in the beautifully restored building of an old Royal Tennis court, the *Jeu de Paume*. (Remember that a double "l" followed by an "a", as in Millau, is pronounced in French in the same way as a "y" in English, so the locals will understand you when you refer to their town and the viaduct as "Me-Yo" and they may well NOT understand if you refer to the town or viaduct as "Me-Lo").

(b) The Cantal and the Aubrac.

The second great trip by train from Clermont-Ferrand is the one through Neussargues and Aurillac to Figeac, Albi and Toulouse. Longer than the route along the Allier (470 kilometres to 300 kilometres) it is no less scenic and it climbs a little higher, where it crosses the Col du Lioran at 1,150 metres. Parts of this

La Domerie, Aubrac

line were built in the 1860s and helped to establish the very first east-west railway crossing of the Massif Central linking Lyon to Bordeaux. An easier route through Roanne and Limoges was later developed, going around rather than through the mountains and taken by the international express, *Le B-G*, the Bordeaux-Geneva Express, until the introduction of TGV services in the 1980s. Train enthusiasts today can take a rather nifty TER which leaves Clermont-Ferrand along the Allier route and then, at Arvant, branches west and heads for Neussargues on the Aubrac line, where it again veers west and begins the steep climb into the mountains and extinct volcanoes of the Cantal. Twenty kilometres beyond Neussargues the train reaches Le Lioran station, located on the slopes of Mt Lioran at 1,150 metres and, if you are keen, you can alight here and take the *téléphérique* (cable-car) from just outside the station right up to the ski slopes and the Lioran ski village. In summer, the area is even more popular than in winter as there are almost endless possibilities of bushwalking, bird- and animal-watching and so forth on the high Cantal plateau and the views across the volcanic peaks, even from parts of the railway line, are breathtaking.

A little way beyond Le Lioran, the train goes through the longest of the twenty-two tunnels on the line and emerges in the valley of the river Cère, which it follows down to the station of Vic-sur-Cère, another small and picturesque mountain resort. Vic-sur-Cère has a thermal spring that was known to the Gauls and to the Romans but was largely forgotten once Rome withdrew from Gaul in the fifth century. Interest was revived in the sixteenth century and Queen Margot, wife of Henri IV, Queen Anne, wife of Louis XIII and the Grimaldi princes of Monaco visited the spring in the sixteenth and seventeenth century, while Louis XIV had bottled spring water brought to him at Versailles. The exiled Queen Ranavalona III of Madagascar visited Vic-sur-Cère to "take the waters" in the early 1900s and thought the village to be charming. The area is indeed not unlike the high plateaux of her homeland. [26] Some very interesting volcanic stone houses in the town centre date from the sixteenth and seventeenth centuries, the church of St Pierre dates in part from the thirteenth century and a very impressive Benedictine convent and school for young ladies, now the three-star hotel Le Manoir, dates from the eighteenth century. Enough to persuade you to alight from the TER and to do a little exploring and, perhaps, lunching.

The railway line continues on from Vic-sur-Cère to the "capital" and *préfecture* of the Cantal, Aurillac. Despite the prevalence of dark volcanic stone in its architecture, Aurillac

---

[26] See below under Chapter 11, (vii), Madagascar.

is a pretty place, at least in summer, with an abundance of trees and flowers in its many squares and parks along the banks of the river Jordanne. It has its château, its abbey, its very fine thirteenth-century church, Notre-Dame aux Neiges, right in the middle of town, and its *Marché aux Fromages* or cheese market for those with a nose for a nibble of Cantal, St Nectaire, Bleu d'Auvergne, etc. And it has several great little hotels right in the town centre such as the Hôtel des Carmes where I stayed and the Hôtel Le Renaissance nearby or, if you feel like splurging, the Grand Hôtel de Bordeaux. Another hour or so in the train, winding through hilly rather than mountainous country and you arrive in Figeac, with its unusual triangular station platform, and here you should alight and spend a few days!

(ii) Figeac

Figeac is a town of some 10,000 inhabitants on the banks of the river Célé, nearly six hundred kilometres south-west of Paris and on the ever-changing border between Auvergne and Aquitaine. Though an important stop on the pilgrim route to Compostela in the Middle Ages, it is not now on the "bucket list" of many international tourists and yet it is an ideal location for visitors interested in the landscape and history of this very interesting part of France. Within a fifty-kilometre radius of Figeac, you can visit Rocamadour and its extraordinary cliff-side terraces, the underground caverns and river of Padirac, Conques and its abbey, Villefranche and its Carthusian monastery, Cahors and the *Pont Valentré* and, a little bit further (sixty-six kilometres) Rodez and its great cathedral perched high on the hill, a suitable stronghold for its warrior-bishops of the Middle Ages.

Le Pont Valentré

Figeac is an ideal spot in which to experience life as it is lived in the French countryside, relatively free from the plastic and neon glitz of Hollywood and similar achievements of Western capitalism. It is a French town where most of the inhabitants are French and speak French, to the delight of Francophiles from abroad frequently disappointed by the widespread use of English in tourist centres such as Paris and the Côte d'Azur. Francophiles who are not francophone will find that a well-placed *merci, bonjour, s'il vous plaît* or even just a respectful *madame* or *monsieur* is enough to produce a smile and friendly assistance from most locals: they are flattered that the foreigner should visit their little town and usually go out of their way to help, dredging up their schooldays English, German, Italian, Spanish or whatever once the foreigner has done them the courtesy of making a little effort to speak a word or two of the local language.

Figeac is at the centre of a five-line railway junction, with buses presently providing transport to various nearby localities not served by rail. It is a quaint old market town and, unlike most French country towns of its size, it was never the centre of a diocese and has no cathedral to visit (do I hear a sigh of relief?). The Célé, which flows through the town, rises not far away in the mountains of the Cantal and is still clean and clear and gurgling merrily as it passes through Figeac. There had been a ford across the river here since Roman times and in 753 a monastery had been established on the flat and fertile northern bank of the river. The monks soon built a bridge over the stream and the tolls they extracted from travellers augmented and in time outstripped the income generated from farming. A settlement grew up around the monastery and a market and then a market town gradually developed. The monastery prospered and became an important abbey and was attached, in the eleventh century, to the great abbey of Cluny in Burgundy. The abbey church of Saint Sauveur was consecrated in 1092 and the abbot was the virtual lord and ruler of the town. The abbey, and therefore the town on the abbey lands, were independent of the two neighbouring dioceses, Cahors and Rodez, and the abbey church, still standing after nearly a thousand years of vicissitudes and modifications, is probably still the largest building in town. By the thirteenth century, tensions had grown between the abbey and the townspeople and, in 1302 the king, Philippe le Bel, intervened and decreed that henceforth the townsfolk would elect two "consuls" each year and that the consuls should assist his *Viguier* or personal representative, in governing the town. Quite exceptionally, he gave the town the right to strike coins for the realm, and the *Hôtel de la Monnaie*, or royal mint, built at his orders, still stands.

Phillipe le Bel, or Phillip the Handsome, also known as "the Iron King" for the firm and indeed harsh way in which he ruled, was not unused to clashing with the clergy. (He was the real-life king whose rule and family were the basis of the book and in the TV series *Game of Thrones*). It was he who disputed with Pope Boniface VIII the papal right to appoint bishops without consultation with the king and it was he who in 1309 persuaded Boniface's successor, Clément V, to move the papal court from Rome to Avignon. It was Philippe le Bel who persuaded Clément V to unjustly close down the Knights Templar, his wily chief minister Guy de Nogaret then seizing for the royal coffers that religious order's accumulated wealth. The king then persuaded the pope to declare the Grand Master of the Templars, Jacques de Molay, a heretic, allowing him to be handed over to the king and to be burnt at the stake in Paris in 1314. As the flames reached him the Grand Master cursed the king and his descendants and cried out that he would meet the king, his chief minister and the pope in the next world before the year was out. King Philippe le Bel, Chief Minister de Nogaret and Pope Clément V did all die within the year, but whether they all met again somewhere or other is not known!

The king's son, Philippe V, was then instrumental in seeing the bishop of Cahors elected, on Clément's death, as Pope John XXII. The abbots of Figeac who had skilfully played off both neighbouring bishoprics were no match for the king and their wealth and power rapidly declined. The consuls and townsfolk surrounded the town with strong walls in the fourteenth century but the Hundred Years' War saw it sacked by the English and change hands several times. Peace, trade and prosperity returned in the 1500s and a local nobleman, Jacques de Genouillac, distinguished himself in the wars which King François I waged against the Emperor Charles V in Italy. The king appointed him *Viguier* of Figeac and loaded him with honours and money. De Genouillac undertook diplomatic missions for the king at the court of Charles V and at that of Henry VIII in England and was charged by François I with organising the famous *"Field of Cloth of Gold"* encounter between Henry VIII and François I near Calais in 1520. De Genouillac built himself a fine Renaissance-style château at Assier, some twenty kilometres from Figeac, as well as a fine Italianate townhouse in the rue de Roquefort, still standing and used as a private residence today.

The good times under *Viguier* de Genouillac and François I were followed by the terrible times of the Wars of Religion, 1580–1605, when the adherents of the new religion, known as Huguenots in France, as Protestants in England and as Lutherans in northern Europe, fought bloody battles to control the country. With the abbots replaced by laymen as rulers of the town, unlike Cahors and Rodez, both of which were the seats of influential bishops, Figeac was an obvious and easy target for the militant arm of the Huguenot movement and fell in 1580; the large church on the hill, Notre-Dame-du-Puy, was turned in to a Huguenot fortress and held out against the Catholic royal forces until 1622. Cardinal Richelieu, chief minister of Louis XIII, then ordered the demolition of the fortress as well as of most of the town walls still standing. Perhaps the bourgeois of Figeac were never really very religious but by the 1600s the abbey had declined to the state of having only a handful of old monks living in it, men quite unable to maintain the vast buildings. The local consuls then seized the property, demolished the monastery and turned the abbey church into the local parish church. Saint Sauveur still stands in the centre of town, the large square between the church and the river being the site of the long-gone monastic buildings. This large public space, known rather ironically since the Revolution as the *Place de la Raison* (calling to mind the re-naming of Notre Dame in Paris as the *Temple de la Raison*) was where the guillotine was set up during the Terror, although only five local aristocrats met their end there.

I spent a very happy week in Figeac, renting a small but comfortable apartment in the restored sixteenth-century mansion of *Viguier* de Genouillac in the centre of town. I bought my supplies at the local market so that I could prepare an evening meal "at home" and have my main meal in the middle of the day in one of the several good restaurants in the town centre. On other days I had my main meal in the nearby places visited on rail and bus excursions. One of the most interesting sites to visit in Figeac itself is the *Place de l'Ecriture* where the *Musée Champollion* is found. Jean-François Champollion was born in Figeac in 1790 and became the most renowned orientalist in Europe. He is best known as the person who first managed to decipher the hieroglyphics of ancient Egypt. He did this by working out the meaning of the texts carved into the Rosetta Stone. The *Musée* tells this story in an ingenious way and is well worth visiting. Another little bit of culture came my way when I went to a brilliant production of Molière's hilarious *Le Malade Imaginaire* in the local auditorium put on by a visiting company from Paris. One day, I had a pleasant car trip into the countryside when I was taken by my kind landlords to see two medieval châteaux, one which had been restored at vast expense by a wealthy Parisian and one which had been purchased with the same intent by an unfortunately less wealthy Australian francophile couple some twenty years earlier and which still awaited the ever-so-costly refurbishment. Both properties were fairy-tale, dream-like places, all towers, turrets, battlements, moat and drawbridge… fascinating and beautiful but beyond the reach of ordinary mortals.

Another day trip was to Villefranche-de-Rouergue, a nearby bastide town and another absolute must for visitors to the area. Villefranche was one of the first of these fortified towns established throughout south-western France in the thirteenth century as part of the long struggle for control between the French and English crowns. It remains amazingly intact in the twenty-first century, huddled around its thirteenth-century collegial church of Notre Dame. On the outskirts (but I walked there from the railway station, so it is not very far!) is the almost intact fifteenth-century Carthusian monastery of Saint Sauveur. It was largely built with funds bequeathed by a rich merchant of the town who died while on pilgrimage to Rome. His widow carried out his wishes and, after ten years of construction, in 1642 the first monks moved in. The good merchant and his wife still lie buried in the main chapel. The monastery buildings were saved from destruction at the Revolution by the local townspeople who instead of demolishing them, as happened in many cases elsewhere, turned them into a hospice for the homeless and then into the hospital now functioning. Today, the church and cloister are open to the public as an historic monument, the monks buried in the cloister-garth over the four centuries of the monastery's existence still slumbering undisturbed beneath the green sward and rambling roses of the cloister.

Another day trip was to Padirac and then on to Rocamadour, which is a tiny medieval town clinging to the sides of the canyon through which the river Alzou flows, a fantastical jumble of stone staircases, houses, churches and chapels seemingly piled one on top of the other. In the thirteenth century, the shrine of St Amadour was one of the big pilgrimage centres in Christendom, although nowadays his existence seems, like that of St Christopher, to be more legendary than actual. Only eight kilometres away from Rocamadour is the *Gouffre de Padirac*, the biggest and most spectacular network of underground caves in France. Unfortunately, you need a car to get to both Rocamadour and Padirac, but one can be hired in Gramat, the small town on the Figeac-Brive railway line and about twenty kilometres from both. There are about forty kilometres of caves at Padirac and you access them by going down what looks like a giant sinkhole, a hundred metres across and seventy-five metres deep (you can walk down the steel staircase or take the lift). Once at the bottom, you follow your guide in the network of caverns and then come to a gurgling underground river. A fleet of twelve-person flat-bottomed boats waits at the jetty, each boatman rather jauntily dressed in white pants, striped shirt and beribboned straw boater (very like the outfits of the gondoliers in Venice). Once his passengers are aboard the boatman pushes off and guides the craft along the rushing river until it flows into a huge underground lake of crystal clear, green water. Stalactites and stalagmites and strange rock formations abound, the whole being cleverly lit in a range of pastel colours. It is an eerie, silent, wonderfully strange world. When, after warning us what he was about to do, the guide flicked a switch and ALL the lights went out, it became a slightly frightening world, as we were left in total blackness, a hundred metres below ground level... like being momentarily buried alive. When the lights came on again our group gave a slight collective sigh of relief... and it was a pleasant surprise to discover that we had travelled a circular route on foot and by boat and were now back at the bottom of the *Gouffre* and in front of the lift waiting to haul us up to ground level and sunlight. Only eighty kilometres away from Padirac are the

UNESCO-classified caves at Lascaux[27] with their amazing wall-paintings dating from 15,000 BC. The Lascaux caves[28] themselves are no longer open to the public but copies of the paintings can be seen in the excellent new museum built alongside. Padirac and Lascaux are places not to be missed while in this part of France, particularly if you are in to "potholes"!

Figeac is also a great base from which to visit Rodez, Aurillac and Albi, with its fortress-cathedral of Sainte Cécile and its wonderful collection of Toulouse-Lautrec paintings in the former palace of the bishops. All three are just a little more than an hour away by rail. Saint-Cirq-la-Popie, on the way to Cahors, is another wonderful day trip although you will really need a car. True, there is a bus (replacing the railway service to Cahors), but it stops at the bottom of a long, steep climb up the rocky ridge on which Saint-Cirq is built and unless you like marathons and mountaineering you should not attempt it. Saint-Cirq-la-Popie is a medieval village, still inhabited (although there are often more tourists than inhabitants), still vibrant, charming and beguiling, a great place for lunch and for filling your shoulder bag with craft souvenirs made locally rather than in far-away Asia!

From Figeac, the southbound train traveller has a choice between two routes to Toulouse: one via Albi; the other via

---

[27] Readers who have stayed with me as far as Padirac and Lascaux would I think enjoy the *Dordogne Mysteries*, a wonderful series of books by Martin Walker combining detective stories, regional recipes, historical references and superb descriptions of the beautiful countryside around Sarlat, Lascaux and the valley of the Dordogne and its tributaries.

[28] *une cave* in French normally means a cellar, often a wine-cellar, or an underground vault; *une grotte* is the French word for the English cave or grotto.

Rodez. Both routes are scenic and both intermediary cities are well worth visiting: a dilemma solved by visiting both!

(iii) Lyon

The Saone in Lyon

Lyon is one of my favourite cities in France and one that I know well, having lived and worked there for several years in my thirties. Competing with Marseille for the title of the second city of France, it has a similar population of well over a million but has to yield in terms of seniority, having been founded by the Romans in about 50 BC; Marseille was founded by the Greeks at least five hundred years earlier. Lyon lies at the junction of two great rivers, the dreamy Saône flowing calmly through the vine-clad hills of Burgundy and the Beaujolais and the mighty river Rhône, its chilly green waters rushing down from the Swiss Alps to the Mediterranean. The Romans built their *castrum* in a defensive position on the clifftop overlooking the meeting of the waters and a whole Roman town, known as Lugdunum, with forum, temples, baths and amphitheatre was developed there, its extensive ruins still very visible. By the tenth century, the centre of population had shifted down to the riverbanks and to the flat and narrowing strip of land between the two rivers, locally referred to as *la presqu'île* and that is where today's CBD is located. It is a tightly confined area with very narrow, winding streets in the medieval part near the cathedral and with a more planned but still restricted district between the Renaissance-era *Hôtel de Ville* and the eighteenth-century *Place Bellecour*, the only large open space within the CBD. Five funicular railways connect the flat CBD with the clifftop inner suburbs while buses, trams and an extensive metro network serve the whole Lyonnais agglomeration.

For most of my time in Lyon, I lived in the ground floor apartment, probably the servants' quarters in days gone by, of a beautiful three-storey house set in a terraced garden of about half an acre in extent. It was on the left bank of the river Saône, about five kilometres upstream from the *quai* at *Place Bellecour* (from which all distances are measured in Lyon). The owners were a charming couple with two university student daughters who lived on the first and second floors. Despite the Lyonnais reputation among the French as being very "closed", difficult for outsiders, let alone foreigners and *les Brittaniques* to get to know, the family was always kindness and politeness itself to me. One year, my seventyyear-old mother came from Australia to spend Christmas with me and my landlords treated her like an honoured family guest. They invited us "up" for an *apéritif*, and then for *goûter*, which they thought of as approximating our afternoon tea, a strange British custom which they tried to accommodate, serving Twinings English Breakfast Tea and slices of heavy fruit cake which they had located in a "British

Wares" shop in town.[29]

Next came an invitation to dinner one evening which was truly a wonderful meal and included a soufflé as the entrée, which madame laughingly explained to my mother was the standard test dish all future mothers-in-law expected their son's fiancée to have mastered. Monsieur then gallantly declared that his fiancée had passed with flying colours, her soufflé being better than the judge's own! A little later my mother and I were invited to spend the weekend with the family in their country house, driving out there in their Citroën DS, the daughters arriving later in their *Deux Chevaux*. On another occasion the parents invited us to go to the theatre with them and we saw a brilliant production of Molière's *Georges Dandin* and the following week they took us to see *Rigoletto* in the Opera House in the city centre.

While my mother had, some fifty years earlier, in a convent boarding school in Australia, taken a subject

---

[29] My landlords took some time to grasp the fact that Australians are no longer *Brittaniques*, that Australia is a sovereign nation with its own constitution and parliament and that Elizabeth II is nonetheless the Head of State and is styled "Queen of Australia". Madame had completed her secondary schooling many years earlier and believed that Melbourne was still the capital of the country (the capital was moved to Canberra in 1927). When she saw me addressing an airmail letter to my mother and that I had written "Melbourne, Vic., Australia" on the envelope ("Vic." being the official abbreviation for the State of Victoria where Melbourne is located), madame exclaimed: "Oh! *La pauvre reine*!", feeling a rush of pity for poor Queen Victoria whose former subjects were now so cruelly abbreviating her name (rather as the French subjects of King Louis XVI and Queen Marie Antoinette had abbreviated those monarchs). Perhaps my landlords were secret Royalists!

somewhat ambitiously called "Conversational French, German and Italian" she was by no means able to chat in any of those languages. Yet she spent nearly a month with me in Lyon, socialising with the family upstairs (none of whom spoke more than a few words of English), keeping house, doing the shopping at the nearby *épicerie*, *boulangerie* and *boucherie*, even picking up ideas from the butcher's wife, who had not one word of English, as how best to cook a particular cut of veal she had chosen to buy. The following Sunday, when we were walking past the *boucherie* on the way to Mass, madame the butcher's wife rushed out of the shop towards us and excitedly asked my mother how the recipe had turned out. I understood, of course, because I was in Lyon "to perfect", as the French would say, my command of the language, which I had been studying for years, but the strange thing is that my mother and the worthy shopkeeper also seemed to understand one another too! Perhaps mothers and cooks have a secret, international, language?

My mother was a keen shopper and an enthusiastic cook, and she loved trying new dishes and new ingredients, so she absolutely loved wandering through the central market in Lyon. She was particularly interested in the "Farmers Market" area, where fruit and vegetables were sold. Although it was wintertime the displays of seasonal produce, much of it from small producers and often from individual farms, orchards or vineyards, with the owner manning the stall and confidently spruiking his or her wares, intrigued and delighted her. In addition to the fruit and vegetable stalls, there were stalls selling all sorts of cheeses, wines, preserves, pâtisseries, nuts, meat, sausages and fish. And at one stall, probably unique to France, there was an old lady comfortably seated behind three large wooden tubs; one was almost full of squirming, slippery frogs, into which madame rhythmically plunged an arm and grabbed a frog. With a quick flick of her sharp knife she would chop the frog in two at waist height, throw the top half of the animal in to the middle or rubbish tub, then deftly skin the lower part in an action that looked like sliding off its green trousers (which she then threw into the rubbish tub) and then she tossed the skinned and trimmed frogs' legs, *les cuisses de grenouille*, into the third tub, where they were ready for sale to the city's gourmands! Pan-fried in butter, with a bit of garlic, a splash of white wine and a spoonful of cream they would delight many a table at dinner that evening[30].

In centuries past, Lyon was famous as the European centre for the production and weaving of silk: the fabrics that its artists and craftsmen developed and designed were used to clothe the rich and to adorn their homes... the walls of

---

[30] This visit to the markets took place in the 1970s. Since then, the French government introduced laws protecting frogs. They may still be caught in the wild, but it must be for the personal consumption by the angler and his family. The sale of "wild" *cuisses de grenouille* is now illegal. Frogs for the table are now raised in special farms, particularly in the Lyon region, but the production is small and the product very expensive. Large quantities of frozen *cuisses de grenouille* are imported from Indonesia, Turkey and Vietnam, are sold at moderate prices but are considered to be of lower quality than the home-grown article. Frogs are difficult to farm, according to one expert. It takes about a year for a frog to be big enough to "harvest" in France, while the imported ones tend to be younger and much smaller. As frogs are cannibalistic, with the bigger ones devouring the smaller ones, farmers need to move the growing frogs from one tank to another to maintain groups of uniform size. Only about 10% of hatchlings survive to adulthood (2% in the wild). They are anesthetised before being processed and despatched to market. "*Mais ces grenouilles françaises ultra-fraîches, ça n'a rien à voir, les clients les adorent,*" said a master chef in Lyon recently: "There's nothing to compare with ultra-fresh French *cuisses*, our customers adore them, and we just cannot get enough of them."

Versailles and many other châteaux are hung with silk rather than with wallpaper, and the silk was patterned and woven in Lyon. Today, Lyon silk is a fabric of choice in major fashion houses in Paris and the story of the silk industry is beautifully presented in the *Musée des Tissus et des Arts Décoratifs* located in a handsome eighteenth-century mansion near the *Place Bellecour*, while you can watch silken fabrics actually being handwoven on traditional looms in the *Maison des Canuts* by taking the funicular near the *Hôtel de Ville* up to the *Croix-Rousse*… quite enthralling.

Since further back in time, since the Middle Ages, Lyon has been the religious centre of France. The archbishops of Lyon were named "Primate of the Gauls" by the pope in the eleventh century, giving them precedence over all other bishops in France, while after the French Revolution a resurgence of religious fervour in the city saw many new religious and missionary orders established there, most with their headquarters on Fourvière Hill and Lyon was sometimes referred to as *Le Rome Français*. In recent times, the centuries-old tradition of putting a lighted candle in one's front window on the night of 8th December to honour the Virgin Mary has developed into a spectacular and magically beautiful light show, the *Fête des Lumières*, something not to be missed whether you are in Lyon in early December to honour the Virgin Mary, to buy a length of silk or for gastronomic purposes. The *Restaurant Paul Bocuse*, a little way further up the Saône than was our apartment, is just one among many of the temples of gastronomy you will find in and around Lyon: worthy successors perhaps, to the pilgrimage centres of Cadouin, Conques, Mont-Saint-Michel and Rocamadour in days gone by!

(iv) Saint-Flour

Saint-Flour, lower town

On another trip playing trains in central France, I made an overnight stop with dinner-bed-breakfast in the very pleasant and handy[31] Hôtel de la Gare in the village of Mervejols, having arrived by train from Nîmes via Mende. The next day, I took the train up the Aubrac line, which connects Béziers with Paris, and got off at Saint-Flour, where I had a few hours to wait for a connecting train to my destination, Aurillac. Saint-Flour was once the capital of Upper Auvergne, its ramparts, cathedral and town buildings dating mostly from the fifteenth century and, like those in Clermont-Ferrand, being built of dark volcanic stone. It sits high up on a rocky outcrop

---

[31] The hotel is actually part of the station building, so no taxi or porter is needed!

and was, in the fourteenth century, seen as the almost impregnable fortress barring further entrance to France from Aquitaine by the invading English. I took a taxi up the hill from the station, arranged to be collected at the same spot in a couple of hours to return and catch my onward train, and set off to explore. It was like stepping back in time, the town centre was so quiet and peaceful and devoid of traffic. The people in the tourist office seemed pleasantly surprised to have a visitor from far-away Australia and showered me with advice as to what to look at. After following their instructions, admiring the cathedral and regional museum and the views from the upper terraces, I popped into a bookshop and emerged with a book of recipes on how to cook potatoes (in thirty-nine different ways) which I still frequently use with delight. I had a glass of wine and a *croque monsieur* in a bar near the cathedral and a chat with the barman who had never before, so he said, had an Australian at his counter… and then it was time to race back to the station for my train. I had hoped to be able to visit the nearby *Pont Garabit*, built by Gustave Eiffel in 1882, but that and a closer look at Saint-Flour would have to wait for another time! Perhaps I would be able to spend a night or two in the delightful-looking *Château de Varillettes*, a few kilometres out of town, the former country house of the bishops of Saint-Flour and now an appealing small hotel and restaurant! www.chateaudevarilettes.com

Chapter 8
Heading North to Go South

(i) Amiens

After some weeks in France in the autumn of 2017, I arranged to return to Australia by ship from Dover. To join the ship I opted to travel through, and spend a little time in, northern France, an area I had long neglected. I had, I think, associated *le Nord* with the north of England where I had once worked, the "black north" of Charles Dickens. When I lived in England in the 1960s, the Midlands and North were an industrial wasteland of unemployed, dreary and disillusioned workers and I had suspected that northern France and southern Belgium were similarly rusting to death with the decline of their coal and iron industries. I had once made a brief stop in Calais to admire Rodin's great statuary group *The Burghers of Calais*, one of the burghers being Jean de Fiennes and therefore (I hoped) a distant kinsman! From Calais, I had made a short detour to the hamlet of Fiennes in the hope of finding some link with my Fiennes forebears. They had taken part in the invasion of England in the eleventh century and then in Henry II's invasion of Ireland in the fourteenth century. Their descendants settled in The Pale around Dublin, changing the spelling of the name to Fyans (to accord with Irish rules of pronunciation, where "y" has the same sound as "i"), and even providing a mayor to Dublin in the seventeenth century. Later descendants moved from Ireland to Australia as part of the Gold Rushes of the 1850s... and provided one of my great-grandparents. I was many centuries too late in visiting Fiennes to find anything more tangible than the name of the locality, but even that was in a strange way comforting and important. Though there was really nothing to see, I felt strangely at home in that gentle green countryside and my lifelong feelings of empathy with France seemed to become more understandable.

The young French president, Emmanuel Macron, elected in May 2017, had come from Amiens and a century earlier a group of nuns from Amiens had established a prestigious secondary school for girls near my childhood home in Melbourne, so I decided to take a look at the city and to make Amiens the base of this visit to the north. I booked in online at the Hotel Central-Anzac, very near the station and, after a one-hour trip from the *Gare du Nord* in Paris, I walked to the hotel and was made very welcome by the management. The hotel is a little place, unpretentious and a bit spartan, but clean, convenient and friendly. Grander but equally convenient accommodation, if you are ever looking for it in Amiens, could be found in the Hotel Carlton, directly opposite the station. The couple in charge of the Central-Anzac were used to having *les Australiens* as guests (they had probably added the word *Anzac* to the hotel's name in order to attract Australian and New Zealand customers) but were surprised and a little relieved to find that this particular Australian spoke French too. We got on very well and they were full of useful information for curious tourists.

The capital of Picardy and the *préfecture* of the *départment de la Somme*, Amiens is famous for its great cathedral, for its canals and quite unique riverside gardens, *Les Hortillonages*, and for its major role in the First World War and the Battle of the Somme, in which many thousands of soldiers from far-away lands, including Australia, died. Its situation on the banks of the river Somme had also been chosen by the Celts and the Romans as the site for a settlement and, in the Middle Ages, Amiens was an important market town and centre of tanning and weaving, prosperous enough in the thirteenth century to build its great cathedral. I had briefly visited Amiens nearly fifty years earlier when, long before the introduction of TGV services, it was on the direct railway line used by the boat trains between Paris and Boulogne, Calais and Dunkerque to connect with the ferries to England. I had broken my trip to Calais to spend a few hours looking at the cathedral where restoration work after the bombing of the Second World War was being completed. With much more time available on this trip to wander through its sublime spaces, I became convinced that *Notre Dame d'Amiens* is the most beautiful of the "Big Five" Gothic cathedrals in France, all of which I have visited and loved… but Amiens is the best! Unlike others, it was built in one burst of enthusiasm and according to the unchanged plans of the original architect. The roof of the nave is forty-two metres high, the highest in the country, the fifteenth- and sixteenth-century stained-glass windows, which almost miraculously survived two world wars, are magnificent and the whole is simple, elegant and harmonious. It stands in a large open square (perhaps one of the few upsides of the bombing of the city!) and can be admired from all sides, the best view perhaps being across the water from the Saint-Leu district.

The medieval *quartier* or district of Saint-Leu, where once the workers lived and often worked is now a trendy and picturesque area edging the river Somme and the many canals linking the city to the Somme and its estuary and is only a short walk beyond the cathedral. This is THE place for a refreshing drink after an hour or two of admiring the cathedral or the close-by *Hortillonages*.

Notre-Dame cathedral, Amiens

The *Hortillonages* (think horticulture) are an extensive network of flower and vegetable gardens on low-lying river flats used as "market gardens" since Roman times and still supplying the city with fresh fruit, vegetables and flowers which are sold at a Saturday morning market along the quays. The same quays were a good place, it seemed to me, to have lunch in between the cathedral and the "floating gardens" and so I took the advice of my hotel hosts and ate at *Le Quai* on the *quai Bélu*: a great meal on their sunny terrace and a great view across the river. After lunch, I walked along the quay and through the park to the *Maison des Hortillonages* where I bought a ticket for a boat tour of the gardens. The "boat" was a small flat-bottomed affair rather like the punts on the river at Cambridge in England but with the important difference that this boat was electrically powered and moved quite silently... apart from the noise made by chattering passengers. There was room for ten or so souls plus the guide, who both steered the little craft and gave a running description of what we were passing. We quickly moved off from the quay and were soon gliding along a narrow tree-lined canal that after a few hundred metres opened into the river. For the next forty or so minutes, we quietly made our way along a maze of waterways, sometimes passing the well-kept gardens of suburban houses, often with beautiful displays of flowers and laden fruit-trees, sometimes passing market gardens and flower-gardens with people working in them who gave a cheerful wave as we went by, and sometimes passing patches of land that seemed to be quite neglected or forgotten by their owners. Our guide was a pleasant young chap who gave a thoughtful commentary and carefully answered our questions, the tour taking on an idyll-like quality as we were gently guided from sunshine to shadow and back again to sunlight, and from the bustle of a busy city through the dreamy green world of those floating gardens. That evening, I had a wonderful meal in a little regional bistro in the rue Noyon, *Le P'tit Bistrot* and then had an early night in preparation for a busy next day.

In the morning, after coffee and croissant in the hotel's cosy breakfast room, I walked over to the station and took an early train to Villers-Bretonneux, about twenty-five kilometres away and on the way to Compiègne, my other target for the day. I had arranged to be met in Villers-Bretonneux by a taxi, as the Australian War Memorial that I planned to visit is about three kilometres from the railway station. All went well and the friendly driver met me as planned and, as we drove down the rue de Melbourne, the main street of the village, he launched into his well-honed summary of what had occurred there in 1918 and continued to draw visitors like me from

Australia. The German army had broken through the French and British lines defending Amiens and had occupied and then destroyed Villers-Bretonneux. The Australian army had stepped into the gap and had driven the Germans out and back, the turning point of the Battle of Amiens and even perhaps of the war. There were enormous losses on both sides: nearly two thousand Australians were buried in the war cemetery that I was going to visit and the names of eleven thousand more, the whereabouts of whose graves are unknown, were inscribed on the walls of the Memorial completed in 1937.

We drove straight to the Memorial and my man promised to return in an hour to take me back to town. It was a cool but sunny morning as I walked up the slope towards the building, eerily quiet despite the small groups of people about, and very reminiscent of the war cemetery at Poperinghe across the border in Belgium where I had already been. The buildings in Villers-Bretonneux are impressive and almost beautiful and the great sweep of bright green lawn, white crosses and dark green trees is stunning but so sad. As happened when I visited Poperinghe where my father's first cousin and best mate lies, I was overwhelmed with sadness and then anger at the wicked waste of the lives of these thousands of young men, most of them barely twenty years old, in "the war to end all wars". Barely a year after this Memorial had been completed, the world was at war again. And when that second World War was ended and a "United Nations" was established to maintain the peace, it took very little time for a new batch of warmongers and sabre-rattlers to start all over again. While Western Europe now seems to have learnt its lesson and to be determined to settle all differences around the council table of the European

Union, Eastern Europe, the Middle East and the USA[32] seem increasingly keen to play the world bully and to plunge the rest of us back into the chaos witnessed here in Villers-Bretonneux. When my taximan returned, I was waiting impatiently to leave that sad place and to have a hot or even a strong drink in one or all of the cheerful bars along the rue de Melbourne: the *Victoria*, the *Melbourne* and the *Sydney*. I had, however, to control this impulse and to first pay my respects to the well-kept village school, rebuilt after the First World War with money collected in Victoria and, in particular, from the school children of Melbourne, in a gesture of solidarity with the children of the devastated French village. So, after several pleasant delays and with further assistance from my friendly taximan, I made it back to the railway station in time to catch a midday train east to Compiègne. Short of time, I again splurged on a taxi and was soon across the river Oise and at the gates of the *Château de Compiègne*.

Just as Versailles is forever associated with Louis XIV, so the *Château de Compiègne* is linked with his great-grandson and successor, Louis XV. Fifteen years after succeeding to the throne (at the age of five), Louis XV commissioned the rebuilding and total make-over of the derelict royal residence which dated in parts from the fourteenth century. The re-build was not completed until the early days of Louis XVI's reign and further work was done under both Napoleon I and Napoleon III. As in Versailles, there is a monumental façade with a *cour d'honneur* facing the town while most of the state apartments are a floor above the main entrance and open at the

---

[32] I have omitted China from my little list of slow-learners as, unlike the other countries mentioned, China has not, to my knowledge, launched any military attacks beyond its own borders for at least a century.

back onto the gardens and a park which stretches away into the distance. The park and the buildings are very fine but the main glories, in my view, are the interior decoration and the furniture, almost all of it dating from Napoleonic times and most of it being absolutely exquisite. I should have arranged to spend a night or two in Compiègne as the château is so interesting and as the town itself with its surroundings also deserves a visit. It was in Compiègne that Joan of Arc was captured by the Burgundians and then sold on to the English, who promptly burnt her alive. It was at the château here that Marie Antoinette first met Louis XVI when she arrived from Vienna for their marriage and in the same château Marie-Louise met Napoleon I when, in turn, she arrived in France from Vienna for their marriage. Eight kilometres out of Compèigne at a clearing in the forest is the spot where French and German military foes have twice signed an armistice, once in 1918 and once in 1940, a one-all win-lose! A little further on is the Château de Pierrefonds, originally built in the fifteenth century and almost entirely rebuilt under Napoleon III as a "folly" and picturesque picnic spot rather than as the impregnable fortress it was originally intended to be. I had to hurry back to the station to catch a six o'clock train direct to Amiens, where I arrived an hour later and in time for another great meal at *Le P'tit Bistrot* and so to bed. The next day, I left my friendly hosts at the Hotel Central-Anzac and took the midday train to Lille.

(ii) Lille

Lille is the seventh-largest city in France (after Paris, Lyon, Marseille, Toulouse, Bordeaux and Nice). Like many of the industrial towns in northern France, Lille saw a period of severe economic decline with the closing of local coal and iron mines in the 1970s and 1980s and it reminded me in many ways of the Birmingham (in the UK) where I had lived in the 1960s. It is largely built of brick but, unlike the bricks in Toulouse, mainly slim, Roman-style pinkish bricks, the bricks in Lille are common red house bricks, as in Birmingham (and Melbourne) or brown ones (as often seen in Sydney) and, as in the Birmingham I knew, all covered in a film of industrial soot and smog. Unlike Birmingham (and other British cities), Lille does not consist of a CBD surrounded by miles of two-storeyed terraces and then, as you reach the outer, leafier suburbs, free-standing houses, the homes of the "better classes". Apart from the modern glass and concrete towers seen in all cities nowadays and from the monumental and mostly nineteenth-century stone and render government buildings such as the *Préfecture*, the arts museum, the opera and the town hall, mostly strategically placed on a tree-lined square or Paris-style boulevard, Lille is a jumble of narrow streets lined with five- or six-storeyed brick houses. While often only the width of one room plus a hallway, i.e., single-fronted, they all seem to have been built, or at least designed, by individual, idiosyncratic builders or architects... no two seem the same! They all have steep, gabled roofs such as the ones seen in northern Europe where heavy snowfalls are expected in winter, the roofline often being broken by funny little Mansard attics of all shapes and sizes, many of them having window-boxes of geraniums and other brave attempts at providing colour and greenery in the sooty surrounds. Although in many ways a grim and grimy industrial town, like Birmingham, Lille has, over the past fifteen or twenty years, picked itself up, dusted itself down, and revived a flagging economy and a dispirited population.

Much of this has been as a result of the efforts of the dynamic mayor, the very feisty Martine Aubry. Much of the CBD has been pedestrianised, a metro has been built and continues to expand, the place is being "steam-cleaned" to get rid of a century's grime and architecturally striking new cultural and sports centres have been built. A significant factor in the city's revival has apparently been the mayor's insistence that the high-speed rail lines being built by the SNCF should come right in to the city centre (to a new, chrome and glass station built alongside the nineteenth-century brick and cast-iron one) and then that the Eurostar services from London should make Lille their first stop. Lille is now a major junction for high-speed services in Europe and passengers arriving from London can now connect and just walk across an island platform, to trains heading to Amsterdam, Brussels, Cologne, Luxembourg and Marseille (where they can now walk across the platform and take a Spanish AVE to Barcelona and Madrid or a *Thello* train on to Italy). The Eurostar from London, while stopping briefly in Lille, go directly to their destination cities without any change of train. So you see that, as usual, I got almost as much fun out of hanging around the railway station and the metro as a normal tourist gets from art galleries, castles and cathedrals!

(iii) Brussels

From Lille, I went by TGV to Brussels, just for the weekend. I had booked online at the centrally located Hôtel Opéra, which seemed to suit my tastes and budget and, with a bit of help from the information desk at the *Bruxelles Midi* station, I made my way there by metro. What I discovered on arriving was that the hotel was in a pedestrianised street in Old Brussels and that each side of the street was lined with small hotels and restaurants, all of which had tables and chairs set up along the footpath. I had, again, arrived in the late afternoon and it was very clear that I would not have

The Grande Place, Brussels

to ask the hotel people where to go to get a good meal! The street led up a slight hill to the *Grande Place* and after walking there and back and studying menus along the way I opted for the little place right next door to the hotel, *Mémoires de Grétry*. The meal was so good that I decided to eat there again on the second night and again had some great food. I had racked my brains trying to think of something acclaimed in Belgian cuisine other than chocolate and waffles and did eventually remember *Carbonnade Flamande*, a sort of Belgian equivalent of *Boeuf Bourguignon* but cooked in beer rather than in Burgundy, so I ordered that. It was very good and was served with a small green salad and a large plate of chips. Then I remembered some French friends admitting that *frites* in Belgium were even better than in France… and I had to agree… and the salad turned out to be made of endives or whitlof rather than of lettuce and that reminded me of how, in Lyon, I had been introduced to endives as a salad… and as a main dish when wrapped in ham and smothered in cheese sauce. So, I did eat like a local that evening! The next evening I decided to splurge on some seafood. There was a lot of lobster being spruiked by the waiters outside the restaurants, but my weakness is for scallops, especially *à la Parisienne*, with white wine and button mushrooms and *sauce Mornay*. The menu offered scallops done with tomatoes and olives and so I perhaps cheekily said that I thought the *Parisienne* recipe much the better way of handling such delicate things as *Coquilles St Jacques* and the owner and manager invited me into the kitchen to tell the chef exactly what I wanted! The chef was closer to my age than to yours and to my relief seemed to take no offence from my rejecting the menu's suggested way of presenting scallops. "*St Jacques à la Parisienne*, you shall have, *monsieur*," he said, and so I returned to my table outside, ordered a *Kir* to sip while watching the passing parade and in next to no time was enjoying my seafood treat. It was superb!

Brussels seems to me to be a strange place, a mixture of grand nineteenth-century Parisian-style official buildings such as the royal palace, the Gothic cathedral, the "decorated Flemish" style buildings surrounding the *Grande Place*, a puzzle of backstreets that could be in Lille or even in Paris, a large batch of modern concrete, glass and chrome buildings housing the ever-expanding European Commission administration and a great circle of light industry-scapes surrounding the city. The mixture seemed somehow not to be working smoothly... rather like the peculiar mix of French, Flemish and German languages that constitute the official languages of the country. I read somewhere that the area has been bilingual since Roman times, the ruling classes in those days speaking Latin, which evolved into French, and the "peasants" or workers speaking their Germanic tribal languages, which evolved into Flemish. When I was in Bruges a few years earlier, I had been startled when people answered my French with English. I have since learnt that such is often the response of Flemish speakers, who refuse *in principle* to speak French, although unlike English, it is one of the three official languages of Belgium[33]. In Brussels, I resolutely spoke only French and resolved never to understand let alone to speak English. As it turned out, my war preparations were unnecessary and nobody in Brussels answered my French with English. A strange place, nonetheless. Perhaps this linguistic tension is one of the small prices well worth paying for being the capital of the new Europe, a community of more than 400 million people speaking a couple of dozen languages. It was, in a way, quite exhilarating to be at the heart of the great European adventure, one which was putting an end to the age-old practice of using warfare, or force, to solve differences between tribes and nations, replacing warfare with the conference table. The European Union looks like being an even greater achievement than the *Pax Romana* was two thousand years ago, as it is consensual rather than imposed by force. May the rest of the world one day follow suit!

On the Monday, I took the Eurostar to London, leaving Brussels under a cloudy sky, racing across northern France in sunshine until we approached Calais and the Channel Tunnel where the sky became overcast. Then the train plunged into the tunnel and, thirty minutes later, we emerged from under the Channel near Dover in the not unexpected drizzle, which persisted all the way to London. Back in Dover the next day, after dinner-bed-breakfast in London near the St Pancras Eurostar station, I boarded the *Norwegian Star* and headed across the Atlantic to Florida on the first leg of my journey home to Australia.

---

[33] The official languages being Flemish, French and German.

Chapter 9
In the Midi

(i) Grignan

One September, Helen and I had spent some time in central France and then decided to extend summer by visiting the Midi. We set off by train to Montélimar one morning and arrived just before midday (and midday is closing time in that land of the *méridienne*[34]). We scrambled to get to the hire car office near the station and to take possession of the car we had booked before that office closed and, having succeeded by the skin of our teeth, then drove into the town centre in search of lunch. The old town centre is now pedestrianised almost everywhere and the former ramparts encircling it have been replaced by wide, tree-lined boulevards, the *Allées Provençales*, where we were able to park the car easily and to

---

[34] In France, *la méridienne* is the equivalent of *la siesta* in Spain and having a nap after lunch, *faire la méridienne*, is a common practice in the sunny south, *le Midi*. In response to my question to friends in Lyon as to whether Lyon is part of *le Midi*, I was answered with the sort of play on words so popular in France. I was told that Lyon is *midi moins le quart*, "a quarter to twelve", i.e., not quite the *Midi*. "*Le Midi*", with a capital "M", is the geographical south of France; "midi" with a lower case "m" means midday. Lyon is not quite far enough south to be considered in "*Le Midi*" but Montélimar, 150 kilometres further south, certainly is and so is in *méridienne* country.

walk along studying menus and choosing a place for lunch, ending up in a little place called *Le Moderne*, where we had a lovely meal and were ready to hit the road soon after two. Our destination for the afternoon was Grignan and, as it was only about thirty kilometres away, we had lingered over lunch and decided to spend a little more time in Montélimar. The town had grown up around the château-fortress built in the twelfth century by the Monteil-Adhémar family, a contraction of their hyphenated name giving rise to the name of the town, Montélimar. The fortress, much altered over the centuries, still survives on the hill in the centre of town and after serving as a prison from the time of the Revolution until 1965, it was taken over by the local council and is now a community cultural centre. While one can walk up through the maze of narrow streets we took the soft option of driving up to the château, from which there is of course a fantastic view of the town and the Rhône valley. Then we made a little detour to admire the other thing for which Montélimar is famous... its nougat. The use of the name *Nougat de Montélimar* seems almost as tightly controlled as the names of regional French wines, such as champagne, chablis, cognac, etc., and we decided to visit just one of the thirteen local nougat manufacturers. The Arnaud-Soubeyran family had begun making and selling nougat in 1837 and their *fabrique* and shop had since then been moved out to the southern edge of town, was on our way to Grignan and it took only ten or fifteen minutes to get there. The Arnaud-Soubeyran premises were rather uninspiring to look at, more Disney kitsch than French elegance, but once inside, however, we were completely won over. The staff were smiling and helpful, the whole place was bright and shining and immaculately clean, and the array of different nougats and other sweet temptations was amazing.

We satisfied our shopping impulse by stocking up on enough nougat to last us for the week and then set off for Grignan, avoiding the autoroute and main roads and driving through Allan and along the D541 to Valaurie and then, through fields of recently harvested wheat and ready-to-harvest lavender, to Grignan itself, the château on its rocky eminence being seen dead ahead as one approaches, looking like the impregnable fortress it once was. We had booked at the Hôtel de Sévigné in the *Place Castellane*, found it and the free car park across the road without trouble, and were soon at the reception desk, checking in. The little hotel was really attractive. The staff were always pleasant and helpful, the public rooms were elegantly rustic, the rooms, each one individually shaped and decorated, were just perfect and there was a delightful terrace or rather walled garden for that well-earned *apéritif* or *goûter*. We quickly settled in and then set off on a quick tour of the village.

Grignan has a population of about 2,000 and grew up at the base of the rocky outcrop on the top of which the lords of the Montélimar region in the Middle Ages, the Adhémar family, had built one of their several fortresses.[35] In 1533, King François I arranged for his son, Henri, to marry the

---

[35] The family continued as barons, counts and eventually marquis of Grignan until 1732 when the line came to an end and the lands and title were purchased by the comte du Muy, younger son of an old Provençal family who became a soldier and Marshall in the army of Louis XVI, dying a few years before the Revolution. After him, the château passed into many hands, fell into almost complete ruin and then was purchased in 1912 by a wealthy Belgian widow, Madame Marie Fontaine, who spent her life and fortune restoring it. In 1979, it was purchased by the regional government and is now a national monument and cultural centre.

Italian princess *Cathérine de Medicis*. *Cathérine* travelled by galley from Rome with her cousin and guardian, Pope Clément VII, to Marseille where she was met by both her fiancé Henri and his parents, the king and queen. The pope officiated at the marriage and then returned to Rome while François I and the French court, including the newly-weds, returned to Paris in easy stages including a visit of several days to Grignan. The then Comte de Grignan was a close friend of Francois I and for the king's visit the château turned on a dazzling series of balls, banquets and masques. The suite of rooms prepared for the royal party is one of the showpieces of the château today.

In the seventeenth century, Louis XIV appointed the then Marquis de Grignan to be Governor of Provence and, under him, the château was largely rebuilt. The marquis's mother-in-law was the *Marquise de Sévigné*, a witty, well-educated woman and one of the more interesting personalities of the court at Versailles. *Madame de Sévigné* stayed at the château several times and when not there she carried on a voluminous correspondence with her daughter, both women providing fascinating social commentaries on their times. *Mme de Sévigné's Lettres* (over a thousand of them) have been printed in many languages and are still in print. It is really around the story of *Madame de Sévigné*, her daughter and son-in-law, that the tourism industry of Grignan has developed and that is what had drawn us to Grignan. In addition, I had in Australia a friend born in New Zealand of a father born in England. The surname was "Grigg", which the father said was an anglicisation of the surname *de Grignan*... and that their great-grandfather had been the last marquis, *Monsieur du Muy de Grignan*, who had fled to England at the time of the Revolution. I was intent on sending my friend a postcard from his ancestral home... and in due course I did.

We found Grignan to be as delightful as the hotel. The

village was quaint and yet very authentic, with so many ancient buildings and old houses as to make the idea of a theme park seem ridiculous: here is the real thing! There is a very interesting sixteenth-century collegial church, Saint-Sauveur, somehow clinging to the side of the cliff on the top of which the château is built. There is a thirteenth-century gate, a remnant of the town walls, with a sixteenth-century clock installed in its tower. There is the twelfth-century house of the *Bailli* or bailiff, now used as a *Musée du Livre et de la Typographie*, the townsfolk having accepted that all things to do with *Madame de Sévigné* and the publication of her letters would be good for the town and its growing reputation as a cultural hotspot in Provence. There is an even earlier twelfth-century Romanesque chapel, St Vincent, which was the parish church before the construction of Saint-Sauveur and it is now used for cultural events such as concerts and recitals. There is an annual writers' festival each summer, the *Festival de la Correspondance*, there are concerts and *soirées musicales* held in the *collégiale de Saint-Sauveur* and the château itself runs all sorts of cultural and educational events[36] throughout the year, all co-ordinated by the regional council, now the proprietor of this and two other châteaux in the *départment* of Drôme.[37]

But of course, it is the *Château de Grignan* that is the central piece in this village, a wonderful presentation of a thousand years of country living. The château is perched high

---

[36] The forecourt of the south (Renaissance) façade is used as the setting for plays and concerts forming part of *Les Nuits de Grignan* which draw audiences of 30,000 or more in July and August each year. Molière, Shakespeare, Tennessee Williams, Victor Hugo, Bizet, Haydn, Mozart and Vivaldi are among the playwrights and composers presented so far.

[37] See www.chateaux-ladrome.fr

above the village on the almost perfectly flat top of the rocky outcrop, the sides of which are almost vertical cliffs. How does one get up there? How was the fortress built in the first place? On the east side of the escarpment, there is a long, steep ramp that leads up to the fortified entrance gate. The gradient is such as can just be managed safely by horse-drawn vehicles. This is how one accesses the château today and this is how the building materials must have been hauled to the top and to the building site in centuries past. Once through the gatehouse, the roadway turns sharply to the right and visitors find themselves on a wide forecourt and looking at the south façade and main entrance to the château. The long, low building on the left is actually a terrace built on the roof of the *Collégiale du Saint-Sauveur* and the marquis and his family were able to attend Mass in the *Collégiale* without having to go all the way down the entrance ramp to village level and then walk or drive around the base of the fortress to the western side and then up the street to the front doors of Saint-Sauveur. All that the family had to do was pop through the little door in the sidewall of the terrace and they were inside the *Collégiale*, on a balcony 15 metres above the floor, out of sight of the congregation but present in the church for any ceremony they wished to attend.

The château spent most of the nineteenth century in a state of ruin but now is continually being restored and refurbished and has become a major cultural centre in Provence. Many of the rooms have been faithfully restored to their seventeenth- and eighteenth-century splendour and *Mme. de Sévigné's* elegant suite, including her study and writing desk, are there to be seen.[38] The château is endlessly interesting and our visits on two successive days were made all the more satisfying by the cheerful, friendly and knowledgeable staff who seemed so proud of their château and village.

In between visits to the château, we made two day-trips from Grignan. One was to Nyons, population about 7,000, twenty kilometres to the east on the banks of the river Eygues and almost surrounded by hills that further east merge into the foothills of the Alps. Another historic town with a medieval fortress, restored château, ancient ramparts and town gate, etc., Nyons boasts a microclimate that protects it from the Mistral[39] and makes it "as sunny as Nice". This microclimate and the well-drained soil on the hillsides have, over the centuries, helped make Nyons the centre of the French olive-growing industry, probably introduced by the Romans two thousand years ago. Our purpose in visiting was to enjoy the Thursday market for which the town has also been famous for centuries. We managed to park the car along the *Promenade de la Digue*, a quite beautiful boulevard that follows the river's west bank away from the fourteenth-century *Pont Roman*, and then walked back to the centre of town. Many of the narrow streets were pedestrianised and they and the several squares were made available for the market. When we arrived shortly after ten in the morning the whole town seemed caught up in a

---

[38] We did, perhaps cheekily, ask about bathroom arrangements in the château in the seventeenth century. Our charming guide gave a little laugh and said that they did exist and would one day be restored and be able to be viewed. She added that ideas about personal hygiene in those days differed from our own and that perhaps that was why perfumes were so popular at Versailles and ever since.

[39] The *Mistral* is a cold wind that at times blows or howls down the Rhone valley and makes life most unpleasant for man and beast.

frenzy of selling and buying... Nyons's famous black olives and olive oil, of course, fruit, vegetables, fish, meat, sausages, cheeses, honey, jams, wines, flowers, plants, pottery, clothes, handicrafts, embroidery, lengths of material, furniture, household equipment, garden tools, ice cream, sweets, hot food cooked on the spot such as pizza, paella in a giant pan, crepes, kebabs... it was extraordinarily diverse and lively and seemingly such FUN for everybody. I had never seen such good-humoured vendors, joking with passers-by, coaxing them to have a look, offering samples and titbits to tempt customers closer, nor had I seen in other markets the crowd so obviously enjoying the banter of the stall-holders, almost playfully haggling with them before concluding the deal at a price which looked as if both sides had known all along would be the agreed one.

After a couple of hours of wandering through the squares and streets, nibbling this and sipping that and slowly filling our shoulder-bags with purchases we could just not resist we finally got back to the car, plonked the purchases in the boot, and sank gratefully into chairs at a nearby brasserie, *La Restanque*, where we rested our feet, caught our breath and had a very good lunch: a tapenade of local black olives, of course, and then a shared giant *omelette paysanne* and *salade verte*. As we had ideas of an afternoon *goûter* on the way home we left it at that and after a short stroll in the park across the road we returned to the car and set off out of town.

Our destination was Vaison-la-Romaine, only twenty kilometres away through that beautiful countryside, and we easily found the *Office de Tourisme* and the large car park opposite it. Vaison was a Celtic town before the Romans arrived and replaced Celts as masters of Gaul. The Romans bridged the unruly river on whose banks the town stands, the

2,000-year-old bridge still standing and in constant use. They built monumental gateways, a six-thousand-seat amphitheatre, temples, baths, fountains, shops and houses, so much of which still stands that, in 1924, the French government renamed the town Vaison-la-Romaine. The site is comparable to that of Nyons but the riverbanks are steeper and the surrounding hills higher: Mont Ventoux, snow-capped in winter, looms not far away. We were short of time and so again decided to cheat and took *Le Petit Train* which started at the tourist bureau and rolled silently through the town, showing us a glimpse of the major sights in about forty-five minutes. While the Roman ruins are certainly impressive, I found the medieval buildings somehow more appealing: the twelfth-century cathedral and cloister in the lower town, the fifteenth-century cathedral and the medieval fortress of the Counts of Toulouse in the upper town seemed somehow closer, more familiar, more understandable. After our *Petit Train* tour, we walked over to the *Place Monfort* where we found a pretty *Salon de Thé* with a shaded terrace and there we reverted to British culture and had afternoon tea, but *à la française*, a pot of camomile tea and a delicious pâtisserie chosen from the wide selection on offer. Then it was back to the car park and the drive to Grignan, for the close of another lovely day in Provence.

  The next day was to be a day of rest. After a good sleep-in and coffee and croissants in the hotel's courtyard we set off for Saint-Paul-Trois-Châteaux, just twenty kilometres away to the south-west. Another ancient place with a Celtic and Roman background, Saint-Paul-Trois-Châteaux had become a diocese in the third century and remained the see of a bishop until the French Revolution despite its small population (about 8,000 today). It is now a busy and prosperous country town and on the advice of other guests at the Hotel de Sévigné, we had decided to drive over there for lunch before going on to our main target for the day, the Abbey of Aiguebelle. Saint-Paul did not disappoint, and we found a great little restaurant in its *Place du Marché*, where we did indeed have an excellent meal interrupted only by too many opportunities for people-watching. After lunch, we drove the twenty or so kilometres north to the abbey where we stayed until Vespers in the late afternoon.

The abbey at Aiguebelle had been founded in 1137, not long after the beginnings of the Cistercian Order at Cîteaux. It had been closed for about thirty years after the Revolution but had reopened in 1815 and the monks had set about repairing the severely damaged buildings: the church had been used as a stable, the cloister as a rubbish tip, and so on. The reopened monastery had flourished and in due course had opened branches or "daughter houses" in France and abroad, notably in Morocco and Algeria. The monastery in Algeria, *Notre-Dame de l'Atlas* at Tibhirine, had been attacked by anti-Christian Muslims in 1996, seven monks were assassinated, and the surviving monks withdrew to the order's monastery in Morocco.

I had been to Aiguebelle years earlier and was sure that Helen would appreciate a chance to visit it. The buildings huddle together in a shallow, wooded valley and though they are extensive (in days gone by over two hundred monks lived there) they are very simple and low. The exception is a large guest house a few hundred metres up a slight hill beyond the church, a nineteenth century building that has recently been modernised with such things as electricity, hot water and even a lift and that is where I had stayed for three or four days. Day visitors are limited to strolling in the park-like grounds and to visiting the monastery shop, the memorial to the monks of Tibhirine and, of course, the abbey church. The church is close to nine hundred years old, very plain in the Cistercian tradition, very beautiful. We timed our visit to be able to attend Vespers, which was sung by the monks in a sort of modernised Gregorian chant, and in French rather than in Latin... it was very calming, quite uplifting: a detour to be made if ever you are in the vicinity and need to take stock of things. And then we hurried home to the comforts of the Hôtel de Sévigné and to the delights of the *bonne table* of the nearby restaurant!

The next day was our last in this corner of Provence and it was quite hard to leave the friendly people of Grignan, their fabulous château and their fields of lavender and sunflowers but we had to and so set off in the late morning for Orange, the railway station and the depot where we would hand back the hire car. With a population of about 30,000 and its magnificent nine-thousand-seat Roman theatre and other historic and architectural attractions, Orange is not a place to merely pass through or to drop off a hire car but, pressed for time, we had no alternative other than to resolve to come back one day, soon, hopefully, to stay and to enjoy an opera or other spectacle in its wonderful theatre during its summer annual music festival. *A bientôt, Orange!*

(ii) Béziers

Béziers is a city of about 80,000 in the south of France, perched on the top of a rocky (and easily defensible) promontory overlooking the river Orb not far from where the river flows into the Mediterranean. It is an ancient place, where traces of Bronze Age and Iron Age settlements have been found and where the Celts, the Greeks and the Romans had all established bases before the Christian era. The river gives it access to the sea and the wide valley of the Orb inland offers easily accessed cultivable land, much of which from Roman times has been used for vineyards and wine production.

Le pont vieux, Béziers

Béziers is on the main road and rail route between the south of France and Barcelona and on the road and rail routes between the Mediterranean French coast and Bordeaux on the Atlantic coast. Like many others, I had been through Béziers several times before I thought to stop and visit. On a beautiful late summer day, a friend and I arrived by train from Barcelona, checked in to the very comfortable Hotel Impérator, picked up a hire car and began a very enjoyable week-long stay in the area. It was still warm enough for most people to choose to dine outdoors and for the restaurant terraces under the trees of the streets and squares to be pleasantly busy. Tired after a longish day of travel, we opted to stroll along the *Allées Paul Riquet* outside the hotel looking at menus and to choose a place close by. That we did and had a pleasant, light meal at the *La Rotonde* and then turned in for an early night.

The next day we spent walking around the city. The first stop was, of course, for a coffee and croissant along the *Allées* and then, after picking up a map and guide from the tourist information office, we headed for the medieval part of town and the cathedral of St Nazaire which has dominated the Béziers skyline since its construction seven centuries earlier. It is not an architectural wonder being a bit of a mixture of Romanesque and Gothic styles and its foreshortened nave makes it seem a bit squat and box-like. However, its situation high on the hill, surrounded by a jumble of crooked, narrow streets crammed full of medieval buildings, makes it particularly interesting. Alongside it is the former bishop's palace, another medieval building, and on a sort of large ledge or terrace part way down the cliff on the riverside is the beautiful formal garden of the bishop's palace, now a public park. In 1209, royal troops laid siege to Béziers where the bishop had offered sanctuary to hundreds of "Cathars", or "Albigensian" heretics, being hunted down across southern France. The walls were breached and the troops poured in, burning down most of the town and killing virtually the entire population, Catholics and heretics indiscriminately.[40] At least

---

[40] There has long been a story, increasingly doubted by modern historians, that the commander of the troops asked the chaplain to the army how to distinguish between the Cathars who were to be killed and the Catholics who were to be spared. The reply supposedly was: "Kill them all. God will recognise his own. "*Tuez-les tous. Dieu reconnaîtra les siens.*" True or false, the siege of Beziers was one of the worst massacres in medieval European history.

10,000 civilians were believed to have been killed and reconstruction of the town and cathedral took more than a century.

Having spent the morning in the Middle Ages, so to speak, we had a leisurely lunch at the *Brasserie du Palais* on the way back to the hotel for a short siesta before heading out again to explore the rest of the city. First of all, we had to tackle another ancient church, the *Madeleine*. The *Basilique de la Madeleine* was begun in the tenth century and, like the cathedral, it was burnt down in the 1209 siege; it was heavily damaged during the eighteenth century and is again being extensively restored. Though battered and bruised it is nonetheless an interesting and even beautiful building and its position in a wide square means that it can be admired from a distance and from several different positions, including from the shady terrace *of Les Caves de la Madeleine*, a nearby café-bar offering cooling drinks on a hot afternoon and, we discovered later, excellent meals. From the *Place de la Madeleine*, we walked in to the seventeenth and eighteenth centuries in the rue du Capus and the *Place de la Révolution*, where the city's two fine arts museums are located, the main collection in the *Hôtel Fabrégat* and the more recent acquisitions in the *Hôtel Fayet*. Both collections are well worth the visit and both buildings themselves, former private mansions, are very beautiful and of great historic interest.

The next day we spent out of town, with a drive up to St Chinian for lunch among the vineyards at the very pleasant *Café de la Paix*, followed by a leisurely drive through the vine-clad countryside. Charles Trenet had grown up in St Chinian and simply by looking around one could readily see the inspiration for his ever-popular song "*Douce France*". From there, we drove through Puisseguier to Capestang and Colombiers, on the *Canal du Midi*, and then on to the tiny hilltop village of Montady where we had a wonderful evening meal at the *Restaurant de la Tour*. I had visited Montady some years earlier and wanted to see again that incredibly beautiful view from the terrace of the restaurant, out over the fields to the neighbouring hill village of Ensérune, built on the site of a Roman *oppidum*. In between the two hills, there had been a large swamp which in the thirteenth century had been skilfully drained, the water drawn to the centre and then, through an underground channel more than a kilometre long, discharged into a small stream and thence into the river[41]. The reclaimed land, roughly circular in shape, was divided into long wedge-shaped fields, their points meeting in the centre, creating a fascinating pattern of shades of green, yellow and beige, depending on the crops planted in each, when seen from the comfort of our restaurant terrace.

The big attraction on the following day was to attend the *corrida*, timed to start in the late afternoon. It seemed as if everyone in Béziers had decided to go to the bullfight that day and we had simply to follow the crowd to find the *Arènes* and take our seats. My earlier experience of bullfighting in Spain had convinced me that the warming up, the preliminaries, constituted the best part of the programme and that turned out to be the case in Béziers. The city suddenly seemed to have morphed into a Spanish rather than a French city. The brass

---

[41] Alongside this feat of medieval engineering were the seventeenth-century marvels of the *Canal du Midi*, and the *Tunnel de Malpas*, running under the Roman *oppidum* as does the railway tunnel of the nineteenth century now used by twenty-first century TGVs!

band loudly played that strange, slightly Arab-sounding music always heard at bullfights, the women, many dressed in long, flouncy gowns and wearing combs and mantillas in their hair, strolled along and shrugged their way to their seats, the men gallantly offering arms and handing the ladies to their places: the young (and not-so-young) bucks worked hard for a little bit of female attention before being almost totally eclipsed by the *muy macho* scene and events evolving in the central arena.

Along with Nîmes and Arles, Béziers is one of the southern French cities where *la tauromachie*, bullfighting, is passionately supported and we had timed our visit to coincide with the annual *Féria*. In Nîmes and Arles, the *corridas* are held in the 2,000-year-old Roman arenas but in Béziers the city fathers had in 1897 financed the construction of a purpose-built amphitheatre modelled on the *plazas de toros* of Spain, just a hundred kilometres to the south. The *Arènes* in Béziers do indeed look very like the *plazas de toros* I had seen south of the border, although with a capacity of around 14,000 the Béziers arena was more comparable to the one in Malaga than in Madrid.

Just a little behind schedule, the trumpet blasts announced the start of proceedings and the procession or *paseo* of *matadors*, *toréadors* and their assistants, all clad in colourful eighteenth-century outfits, walked solemnly into the arena to the applause of the crowd and the show quickly got under way. A big, black, angry-looking bull suddenly emerged in the arena and, after trotting to and fro seemingly to look at various parts of the crowd in a strangely menacing way, settled for standing still in the middle and watching, waiting... for what? The atmosphere was quite electric, the crowd fell strangely silent as if respectful of the bull which did not know, as the crowd did, that death would soon enter the arena. More blasts of the trumpets announced the arrival of the *picadors* on the (frightened) horses who quickly used their lances to make mighty gashes above each of the bull's shoulders, and then of the *banderilleros* who danced up to the now bleeding bull and threw their sharp darts into his flanks to further irritate him. More trumpet blasts announced part three of the fight, the arrival of the *matador* in his tight-fitting bespangled "suit of lights" and black bicorne hat, sword and red cape in hand. The first two stages of the *corrida* had been to test the bull to see whether he had an aggressive or a docile temperament and then to slash the bull's neck muscles so that he was obliged to lower his head and allow the *matador* to aim the sword thrust over the head and straight to the heart. Now everyone else had left the arena and the *matador* walked slowly towards the bull which stood still, watching him. The *matador* stopped a metre or two in front of the bull and stood very still, speaking to it (whether in French or Spanish we did not know: the bull had been raised in Spain), challenging it, taunting it, I believe to be the custom. The bull remained motionless until the matador moved, sweeping his cape in front of the bull which responded by moving forward a little and trying to catch the cape on his horns. This sort of cat and mouse game went on for a few minutes, each of the *matador*'s movements following strict procedural rules drawn up in past centuries and whenever the crowd thought a movement to have been particularly well executed a great cry of *Olé!* would erupt, breaking the otherwise spellbound silence. Death was very close: would it be that of the bull or that of the *matador*? In this case, as in most but not all cases, it was indeed the bull and it happened quickly and cleanly and the crowd roared approval of the courage and skill of the matador… and the bravery of the bull. There were six bulls to be fought that afternoon and we watched the first three and then left. It is exciting and even exhilarating to see a young athlete face down a five hundred kilogram fighting bull, but it is not part of Australian culture and does raise uncomfortable issues of animal welfare and even of morality. We decided to stick with Bizet's *Carmen* whenever in the future we felt like the company of *toréadors*. Before condemning bullfighting as an uncivilised Spanish and French way of obtaining steaks, however, it is well to remember how we in Australia (and many other "civilised" countries) behave. Our steaks, of course, come in vacuum packs from the supermarkets but we send boatloads of live cattle and sheep abroad, to the Middle East and to Asia, to be slaughtered, and often to be butchered while still alive and conscious, in ways often far more barbaric than those seen at the *corrida*.

We had much less exciting plans for the next day. The leafy boulevard on which our hotel was located was named in honour of Pierre-Paul Riquet, the mastermind of the *Canal du Midi* which links the Mediterranean to the Atlantic and was opened in 1681, one year after Riquet's death and fifteen years after construction had begun. A canal enabling barges and galleys to bypass the Iberian peninsula had been considered by the Roman emperors Augustus and Nero, by Charlemagne and by François I, but it was Louis XIV who finally took the plunge and commissioned the project, the biggest engineering project in Europe in the seventeenth century. The two hundred-and fifty-kilometre-long Canal links Béziers with Toulouse, where boats can pass through locks and join the Garonne river and then travel down that river to Bordeaux and on to the

Atlantic, a total distance of 500 kilometres as against 2,500 or so by sea through the Straits of Gibraltar. We had booked a day trip on the Canal and so after our morning coffee, we drove down to the port at Fonséranes and boarded a large old barge that had been converted into a very comfortable pleasure boat able to accommodate about forty passengers and at 9.30 a.m. off we went. Within a few minutes we were at one of the big attractions of the day, the staircase of eight locks, one immediately after the other, that our barge entered and was then lifted up from river level to the level of the Canal a hundred or so metres higher, and then away we sailed across the countryside towards the distant Atlantic.

We two were the only non-French-speakers on board and, as I volunteered to act as interpreter for my companion, the captain relaxed and gave his safety instructions and running commentary in French alone. He had quite a bit to say about both the Canal and the countryside we passed through and kept us all awake and attentive by slipping jokes into his patter at frequent but irregular intervals. It was a glorious sunny day and the barge glided along without any noise or fumes. We quite quickly left the built-up area around Béziers and, for most of the day, glided through land given either to vineyards, cereal cropping or groves of olive and almond trees. The Canal was lined for most of the way with centenarian plane trees, their dappled light and shade and reflections in the waters of the Canal being quite beautiful. From time to time, we met other craft travelling in the opposite direction and one or the other would pull into the bank to make passing easier and safer. We passed under several pretty hump-backed stone bridges and went through several small villages where the Canal seemed to form one side of the main street, the Canal bank taking the form of a stone-paved quay, often with a *café-bar*, *boulangerie* or *négociant de vins* to tempt passers-by.

After a couple of hours, we tied up at the large village of Colombiers, where we were encouraged to "go ashore" and stretch our legs (and open our wallets). Once back on board we set off again and after a further few kilometres arrived at, and passed through, the one-hundred-and-seventy-metre-long *Tunnel de Malpas*, completed in 1680, the first canal tunnel ever built in the world, or so our captain claimed. Not far past the tunnel we pulled in to a shady, wider part of the Canal and were served a very pleasant three-course lunch. The main course was announced by the captain as *lapin chasseur* and as my companion had, I knew, an aversion to rabbit, I hastily translated this as chicken chasseur, and the *sauce chasseur* being so good, and the red wines served with the meal being so plentiful, the rabbit was judged to be delicious by all diners, including both foreigners. Coffee was served after lunch, accompanied by a glass or two of *Cataroise*, a rather powerful local liqueur. Despite the name, which I thought unlikely to have been favoured by those austere and puritannical Cathars, it seemed to relax both inhibitions and throat muscles and soon had us all joining in the boating songs the captain and his merry crew quickly had us singing. By the time we got back to Béziers around four o'clock, we were certainly ready for another afternoon of Spanish culture, but in the form of a *siesta* rather than that of the *corrida* of the day before.

Our next burst of activity was to have a relaxing day at the beach. There are many great possibilities close to Béziers, such as Valras-Plage, Marseillan, Cap d'Agde (the biggest naturist beach resort in Europe) and Sète. We decided to make a round trip of it, passing through Frontignan to get to Sète, where we would lunch and swim and then head back along the narrow strip of land linking Sète to Cap d'Agde and then on to Béziers. We got away mid-morning and with only light traffic were in Sète around eleven, parked the car and set off to explore (and to find a good spot for lunch).

While Sète has about twelve kilometres of beach along the isthmus connecting it to Cap d'Agde, the town itself is more a port, commercial, fishing and ferry[42], than a beach resort, and as it has a history dating back nearly four centuries it was well worth exploring before we ate and relaxed. The town centre is built on an artificially created island, one with a low hill in the middle, the Mont Saint-Clair, from which there are great 360-degree views of the sea and of the lagoon which separates the island from the mainland. The port was established in the reign of Louis XIV as the Mediterranean terminus of the *Canal du Midi*, which flows into the lagoon. In 1680, the *Canal Royal* was cut through the narrow isthmus separating the lagoon from the sea and a long and massive seawall was built to create an artificial harbour. A tall lighthouse at the end of the seawall was constructed, along with two fortresses, one at the base and one near the top of Mont Saint-Clair. The *Canal Royal* enabled barges from the *Canal du Midi* to access the new harbour where goods could be transhipped to ocean-going vessels that would then sail out to other Mediterranean ports. The lower fortress, the Fort St Pierre, is now a fantastic open-air theatre. In 1983, a second canal linking lagoon and sea, the *Canal des Quilles*, was built a few hundred metres west of the first canal, completing the "insularity" of the town centre. While the *Royal* name has gone, the seventeenth century canal remains

---

[42] There are seasonal ferry services to Algeria, Morocco, and Palma de Mallorca in the Balearic Islands.

and is still the real "main street" of Sète, being lined on both sides with handsome buildings and really looking quite like a little bit of Venice. We strolled along the quays on the southern side and had difficulty choosing one among the many enticing places to eat, finally settling on a seafood restaurant called *La Calanque* which offered "local specialities" and where we shared what was indeed a good mixed seafood platter. We attempted to walk off some proportion of that excellent lunch by another foray into the town, this time up through the *Quartier Haut*, the old town of narrow streets and shady squares around the church of St Louis and below the walls of the *Fort Richelieu* atop the Mont Saint-Clair. We then found our way back to the car and set off for the beach. There were two rather pretty little beaches on the south side of the island and then a long stretch of beach seemingly running all the way to Cap d'Agde. And there were people and cars everywhere! It was at the end of August, peak holiday time, and we had foolishly forgotten that the beaches of the Mediterranean coast attract crowds of holidaymakers from inland France but also, even perhaps more so, from the chilly countries of northern Europe and that at the beach in August one is likely to hear more Dutch, English, German, Swedish and so forth than French. We slowly drove the full twelve kilometres along the isthmus without seeing anything other than crowded beaches and full car parks and soon found ourselves at the outskirts of Agde where we decided to drive into the centre of town, have a cool drink and decide what to do. We found a car park near the cathedral and the *Office de Tourisme*, collected an information brochure, found a pleasant-looking *brasserie* overlooking the river, and sat down to rearrange the afternoon. Interest in the beach had faded when the good folk in the tourist office assured us that Cap d'Agde was much more popular than the beaches we had driven past on the way from Sète. We gave up the idea of a swim!

Agde is rather like Sète in that it is on flat even marshy terrain and sits at the base of a low hill, in its case the Mont Saint-Loup. Instead of being wedged between lagoon and sea, it is on the banks of a river, the wildly unpredictable Hérault, a few kilometres from its mouth. Agde is a very old settlement dating back to Roman and Greek times. It became a bishopric in the sixth century and parts of the present cathedral date from the ninth century. We decided to have a quick look around the town centre and found the riverside drive with its historic buildings, *brasseries* and *térrasses* rather pleasant but the dark volcanic stone used in the cathedral and most of the historic buildings gave the town a rather sombre look. By four o'clock, we were ready for home and so hit the road, still a bit hot and bothered but probably a bit wiser. We should have just gone to the beach, and gone early in the day, should not have tried to combine swimming and sightseeing and should not have expected the Mediterranean beaches in mid-summer to be as crowd-free as beaches in Australia usually are! As the French say, *"Les voyages forment la jeunesse et déforment les valises!"* [43]

(iii) Narbonne

One day, Helen and I caught a TGV which whisked us south to Narbonne on its way to Spain. There we were met by the

---

[43] Roughly translates, a touch more prosaic in English, as: "you live and learn"!

owner of the apartment[44] we had rented for the week and she drove us the short distance from the station to the cathedral, opposite to which stood the eighteenth-century building in which the apartment was located. The owner was so nice and the apartment so wonderful that our whole impression of Narbonne took on a very *rosé* aspect from the outset. In Narbonne, we just relaxed, almost pretending we were locals. Off to the baker before breakfast for fresh bread or croissants, down to the market at lunchtime for fresh mushrooms and slices of ham to make an omelette, up the street to the general store for a bottle of chablis, across the Canal to the wickedly tempting *pâtisserie fine*, *La Note Sucrée*, for a choice of dessert… great fun and very restful!

We had two projects for Narbonne, apart from relaxing: the first was to make a trip to Carcassonne and the second was to visit the Abbey of Fontfroide. We made the trip to Carcassonne one day, travelling by a morning train and then by the shuttle bus from the station in the "New Town", begun in the thirteenth century, across the river to the "Old Town", begun in the eleventh! The old town had been extensively restored in the late nineteenth century and is now said to be the best example of a medieval fortified town in Europe. We wandered around the narrow streets, which are very like those at Mont-Saint-Michel and almost as jam-packed with tourists. The whole place, including the château and the cathedral is, however, built of caramel-coloured brick and stone, more cheerful than the rather gloomy basalt used at Mont-Saint-Michel. We had a good lunch on the vine-covered terrace of a little restaurant in the old town… and caught a late afternoon TGV back to Narbonne and our wonderful apartment.

---

[44] "La Suite de la Cathédrale", Narbonne

Narbonne itself tempted us to defer the trip to Fontfroide and to spend a day quietly exploring the town proper. It had been established by the Romans in the first century AD as their main port for the invasion and conquest of the Iberian peninsula and there are many Roman ruins there, including a bit of the paved road, the *Via Domitia*, built to link Iberia via Provence to Rome. The unfinished cathedral of St Just is fascinating architecturally and for the strange stories associated with its construction and failure to be completed. *The Canal de la Robine*, which flows through the centre of the city linking Narbonne to the *Canal du Midi* is lined with wide stone quays along which there are handsome townhouses, terrace cafés, the ubiquitous plane trees and many flowerbeds and flowerboxes. It acts as a sort of linear park and set of lungs

The Pont des Marchands

for the whole city. On either side of it are the narrow streets of the medieval town. These include a street of shops and houses built atop a bridge spanning the *Pont des Marchands*… just like the larger and more famous *Ponte Vecchio* in Florence.

The archdiocese of Narbonne was abolished at the French

Revolution but had been one of the most prestigious in France, occupants of the seat having included two bishops who were subsequently canonised, two who became pope and others who were cardinals from the Medici, Este, Bourbon and Guise family (the latter being the uncle of Mary Queen of Scots). The last archbishop of Narbonne was Arthur de Dillon, born in Paris to Irish parents who had fled Ireland after the Battle of the Boyne, Arthur Dillon Senior rising to the rank of general in the French royal army. Archbishop de Dillon had an extraordinary life, died in London in 1806 and was buried where the French TGVs now arrive in St Pancras station: his remains were transferred to Narbonne cathedral in 2007. The archbishop's palace, now a fine arts museum as well as the town hall, is an intriguing building with parts of it being over a thousand years old and the eighteenth-century wing still largely furnished as it was for the last archbishop.

Unfortunately, we both felt too tired to tackle the trip to Fontfroide the next day and so we decided to abandon that project and to have another day of rest before setting off on the next leg of our tour of *le Midi*. Fontfroide, we told ourselves, would be much the same as the abbey of Fontenay in Burgundy, which we had already visited. We were wrong. Both are Cistercian abbeys in remote forest settings and both have been restored and preserved by great philanthropic families but Fontfroide, I subsequently learnt, is more complete, even more beautiful, and is a vibrant artistic centre of architecture, painting, music and many other art forms. We made a mistake there and Fontfroide should be on the "must visit" list of anyone who gets as far as Narbonne. The abbey is some fifteen kilometres out of town and there is no public transport so a car is needed, but from what I have since heard and read the effort of getting there is always well rewarded.[45]

So after our day of rest we took the morning TER to Marseille, arriving in plenty of time for a leisurely lunch before our connecting train to Nice. We opted to eat in an unusual restaurant in the *Gare St Charles* that I had discovered the previous year, the *Bistrot Bocaux*. It had a menu that ran to six or eight pages, an extraordinary list of choices and each choice was a pre-cooked meal ready and waiting in an airtight jar. The jars, (*un bocal* = a jar) hundreds of them, were all displayed on the shelves that lined the large glass-walled room on the station concourse and, with the autumn sunlight behind, them, they made an arresting sight! I had *Duck à l'Orange* while Helen had *Coq au Vin*, and both meals, you may be surprised to learn, were very good. Certainly, a step up from many a railway refreshment room or in-flight meal served on an international flight!

(iv) Nice

After that surprisingly good lunch at the *Gare St Charles*, we pressed on to Nice, enjoying the fabulous scenery of the *Côte d'Azur* as our TGV glided along, the Alpes Maritimes on our left and the sparkling blue Mediterranean on our right. Storied railway stations succeeded one another: Toulon, Fréjus, St Raphaël (alight here for St Tropez), Cannes, Antibes and then Nice, "Queen of the Riviera". Helen had wanted to make her last stay on this trip in a monastic setting and the place chosen, the abbey of *Notre-Dame de Laghet*, entailed a fifteen kilometre drive up into the hills behind Nice. We decided

---

[45] See www.fontfroide.com

common sense was better than valour and so we went by taxi rather than by the tram and bus link available. Our destination turned out to be a strange place, a quaint mixture of the old and the new. We had quite good en-suite rooms, there was a lift, and the meals were very good for an institution that catered for from twelve to a hundred people at one sitting... crowds at conferences or on big religious feast days. The nuns were very welcoming and the setting in the hills was quite beautiful. The bus down to Nice, however, ran only three times a day and one did feel marooned there and, to some extent, caught in a sort of time warp, with the nuns in full traditional habits, bells ringing throughout the day, and lots of candles and incense and even a bishop or two in purple pontificals at some ceremonies. We did catch the bus down to Nice one day and had a rather splendid lunch at a restaurant called *Safari* on the *Cours Saleya*, surrounded by the baskets and buckets full of gorgeous flowers for which the *Marché aux Fleurs* in that square is famous, but our final few days were mostly spent winding down in the peaceful gardens of the Benedictine nuns. Then we indulged in another taxi back to town: first to the airport, where Helen boarded her flight home to Australia and then, for me, to a modest hotel, the Hôtel Central, which I had discovered on an earlier visit to Nice and where I was to be based for a further week to indulge my passion of "playing trains".

Firstly, I was keen to try out the recently reopened railway up to Grasse and so next morning I set off. The Hôtel Central is, as the name suggests, within walking distance of the station, the shopping centre and the main tram route along the rue Jean Médecin which in ten minutes will take you down to the seafront and the *Promenade des Anglais*. I walked up to the station, had my morning *café crème et croissant* and boarded a smart new TER for Cannes and Grasse. The run around the *Baie des Anges* to Antibes and Cannes is always beautiful and that morning was no exception. I had to change trains in Cannes and fell into conversation with a charming middle-aged couple waiting on the same platform. After a few minutes of chat, the husband, obviously detecting from my accent that I was not French, hazarded the guess that perhaps I was "*un Anglais*"? I hastened to correct him and said that I was Australian, born in Melbourne. "*Ah, Monsieur, et moi j'habite la rue de Melbourne à Villers-Bretonneux et ai été élève dans l'école reconstruite après la Grande Guerre par les écoliers généreux de Melbourne,*" etc. And his wife had gone to the same school too! Both husband and wife insisted that, as an Australian, I should include Villers-Bretonneux in my tour of France, that they would be delighted to show me around and that I would see that the village had kept its word and had never forgotten, and would never forget, that those brave young Australians had literally given their lives to save the villagers from the Germans all those years ago. Before I could explain that I had already visited Villers-Bretonneux, my TER arrived and was soon climbing up into the hills behind Cannes.

The trip took only thirty minutes and offered splendid views over Cannes and the coast as we climbed up and then along the escarpment, as Grasse sits nearly five hundred metres above sea level. From the station to the town centre, there is a further steep climb now done, if like me you need help, in a shuttle bus replacing an earlier funicular railway. Grasse turned out to be quite hard work, all steps and stairs (*les montées*) and steep little lanes (*les traverses*) and shady little squares (*les placettes*) filled with antique shops and wine bars and *chocolateries* and *pâtisseries* and bistros and other cruel temptations: far harder to resist than the glitzy sophistications of the *Croisette* in Cannes or the *Promenade des Anglais* in Nice! Grasse had, until the Revolution, been the seat of a bishop and the former bishop's palace, largely dating from the Middle Ages and now used as the town hall, sits alongside the former cathedral at the very top of the hill. When you have had enough medieval magic, you might follow my example and explore a little of Grasse's other claim to fame, its perfume industry. Since the seventeenth century, Grasse has been the centre of the industry in France and the growing, harvesting and processing of flowers and the marketing of perfumes now employ several thousand locals. A visit to a perfume factory is, I can assure you, a very pleasant experience. I toured the Fragonard plant but all the great perfume houses there welcome visitors. Then it was time to head back to the station and the TER down to sea level, Cannes and Nice for dinner, bed and breakfast and preparations for the next day's excursion.

My second train trip out of Nice was to be an <u>international</u> one, but one of just a mere sixteen kilometres, to the Principality of Monaco. The railway line hugs the coast and passes a succession of fabulous views of the Mediterranean, the rocky shores, the sandy coves, the palm trees, the pine trees, the eucalyptus, the frangipani, the hibiscus and so on, gliding through Villefranche-sur-Mer with its terraced villas on your left and its enchanting bay on your right, Beaulieu-sur-Mer and its beaches, and it then winds around the foot of the picturesque medieval village of Eze. Then the train plunges into a short tunnel and comes to a stop in the partly underground station of Monti Carlo. You have crossed the international border and have arrived in the capital of Monaco!

The tiny principality is oh-so-crowded with visitors in summer but, in spring and autumn, it is the most picture-postcard-perfect rendition of a sophisticated, elegant seaside playground for the world's rich. Ordinary mortals may watch, for no charge, and the passing parade is endlessly worth watching, but be careful if you think of buying anything... food, drink, ice cream, sunglasses, a hat, a towel! Far cheaper to jump on the train and make the twenty-minute trip back to Nice and its Monoprix and markets.

If you leave Nice soon after your coffee and croissant, you can be in Monaco by ten a.m. and have time to "do" the town, admire the Prince's Palace, visit the Oceanography Centre and the cathedral (where Princess Gratia née Grace Kelly is buried), and be back in Nice for a late, light lunch. That is what I did, anyway. And then I had an afternoon to spare and so took a bus up to Saint-Paul-de-Vence for another quick look. Saint-Paul is, in many ways, a scaled-down version of Grasse, a largely intact medieval hilltop village, set in the hills a little way inland from the *Côte d'Azur*. Saint-Paul is of course much smaller than Grasse and its main industry now is tourism. On days when a cruise liner with thousands of passengers on board drops anchor off Cannes or Nice or Villefranche and sends busloads of them up to Saint-Paul on a half-day trip the place would be unpleasantly crowded. But on quiet days, such as the late autumn day when I was there, it is calm and peaceful, snoozing in the afternoon sun. Red and yellow roses filled urns and tubs at front doors, branches of purple bougainvillaea tumbled over garden walls into the narrow streets, elaborately curled wrought iron gateways revealed glimpses of shady courtyards and cats napping in sunny corners. Saint-Paul has been very popular with artists over the past century, Chagall, Matisse, Modigliani and Picasso among many others chose to live and work there at various times and there are many small art galleries in the village selling their and other artists' works. There are also plenty of antique shops well-stocked with beautiful pieces and I was especially attracted by the wonderful uses of wrought iron... lanterns, lamps, picture and mirror frames, small tables and so on. I resisted all temptation until, alas, I came to a charming little tea shop, the *Timothée Café*, and there I succumbed to the delights of both a *tarte aux fruits* and a delicious, creamy *mille feuilles*. That was the end of sightseeing for the day and so a slow and careful walk back to the bus stop saw me safely on my way back down to Antibes and Nice.

My fourth sortie from Nice took me by tram and bus up to Cimiez, once a hillside village on the outskirts of Nice and now a very fashionable residential suburb. People have been living around Cimiez since well before the arrival of the Romans and there are extensive ruins of Roman temples and villas throughout the area. It was still a small rural community in the sixteenth century when Franciscan friars established a monastery on one of the hilltops, a monastery that now, with a beautiful church, cloister and garden, is a major tourist attraction with its peaceful atmosphere and glorious views down over Nice and the sea. It was, however, the arrival of *les Anglais* on the *Cote d'Azur* in the early nineteenth century that transformed Cimiez from a rural village to a society hotspot. It was the English aristocracy and Victorian millionaires, seeking to escape the damp and cold of the English winter, who were the first to appreciate the mild winter climate of the area and to start building holiday homes followed by increasingly luxurious villas, hotels, baths and casinos. Queen

Victoria, her uncle Leopold I of Belgium, Napoleon III, czar Nicholas II, "everybody who was anybody" went there in the last quarter of the century. The Russian aristocracy took to spending the three months between Christmas and Easter in Nice and a Russian Orthodox church and then a cathedral were built in Nice with their support. And in the twenty-first century, Nice and the *Cote d'Azur* are again awash with Russian voices as the post-Soviet oligarchs and millionaires discover the delights of *la Côte*. In 2010, a direct train, the Riviera Express, Moscow-Nice and return, was introduced by the Russian and French railways, travelling via Warsaw, Vienna, Milan and Monti Carlo. It consists of three VIP luxury sleeping cars, six first-class sleeping cars, one second-class sleeping car (presumably for the ladies' maids and the gentlemen's valets), two restaurant cars and a service car. The trip takes about fifty hours, with a change of bogies near the Polish frontier where the wider, Russian gauge meets the standard European gauge. The train runs once a week in each direction with extra departures arranged to meet surges in demand. A one-way ticket in VIP class costs around €1500, €650 in first class and €400 in the solitary second-class carriage. This would not seem to be a train for the workers!

Queen Victoria in her old age spent nine winters on the Riviera, staying in Menton, Hyères, Cannes and Grasse and then, for the next five visits, in Nice where she booked out the whole of the Grand Hotel de Cimiez on her first two stays and for her third, fourth and fifth visits, taking over the western half of the brand new and quite magnificent two hundred-room Régina Hotel, which had been built with her patronage in mind. The hotel, the Régina, is still there dominating the scene although it is now sub-divided into a number of luxurious private residences. After her death, a rather handsome statue of the queen was installed in the grounds of the hotel by the municipality of Nice, grateful to her for her patronage and for having consolidated the reputation of the *Côte d'Azur* as THE playground of Europe's rich and royal.

There is not much for ordinary mortals to do in this enclave of the super-rich once the beautiful villas, the Franciscan monastery, the Matisse and Chagall museums and villas, the gardens and the views have been visited and so I summoned a taxi and set off further into the hills, asking the driver to take me to the village of Castagniers. It took nearly half an hour to cover the fifteen kilometres of winding uphill road as the views were so distracting and the driver so keen to talk about the area, where he had been born and of which he was so proud, but eventually he put me down at the gates of the Cistercian abbey, *Notre Dame de la Paix*, my destination. After admiring the church, the buildings and the gardens I adjourned to the abbey shop as I had heard that the chocolate made and sold there by the nuns was something special. Having made my purchases, I then asked the nun in charge how best to walk in to the village, whereupon the customer waiting to be served after me, a young chap who turned out to be the local vet, offered me a lift. As a result, I ended up in a neighbouring and slightly larger village (Asprémont rather than Castagniers, as that was where the vet was going) sooner than expected and in time for a late lunch. My friendly vet had recommended the *Hostellerie d'Asprémont* in the main square and that is where I had an excellent meal, a *salade Niçoise* and a carafe of rosé followed by coffee and my BYO dessert of Cistercian chocolate. A number 76 bus then made its appearance and carried me safely down to Nice where I boarded a tram that took me back to the station and to my hotel.

La Promenade des Anglais

I can never pass the Nice-Ville station without thinking of Queen Victoria. She was in her seventies when she "discovered" the *Côte d'Azur* and started wintering there, travelling incognito as "Lady Balmoral" to avoid endless official receptions in France, although, of course, everyone knew who Lady Balmoral really was. She made the long trip from Windsor Castle, crossing the Channel in the royal yacht *Victoria and Albert* and then covering the twelve hundred kilometres from Calais to the Mediterranean in her specially built Royal Train, all eight carriages of it, with enough room for the eighty to one hundred people in her entourage. She was accompanied by a princess or two (her daughters or grand-daughters), ladies-in-waiting, a couple of generals as gentlemen-at-arms, half a dozen footmen, her maids, her French chef, her much-favoured Indian servants in their splendid Indian costumes (she apparently relished the title of

"Empress of India" which she had assumed in 1876), a couple of Scottish pipers in their kilts and, on her first trip, even John Brown, her *gillie*. Brown found he could not tolerate so much sunshine and stayed at home in Balmoral when the queen ("Mrs Brown"?) again holidayed in France. Once the royal train had crossed the Channel and was running on the French railway network, all station masters and signalmen along the queen's route were always instructed from Paris to give the train top priority. As the queen's habit was to rise and be dressed by her ladies each morning between nine and nine thirty, the royal train came to a standstill at that hour wherever it happened to be and ALL trains in the area were required to stop too, lest one should by mischance inadvertently pass the windows of the stationary royal train. In the queen's wake, the visitor population had boomed,[46] palatial hotels such as the legendary Hotel Negresco, had been opened to accommodate the wealthy visitors, an opera house was built and attracted the greatest singers and dancers of the day and the many small fishing ports along the *Côte* were soon crowded with the luxurious ocean-going yachts of Europe's upper classes. By the early twentieth century, the numbers of aristocratic visitors began to decline but they were soon replaced by millionaires from the New World and after the Second World War by those of the Middle East. Nice continues to reign over the *Baie des*

---

[46] Interestingly, the high season on the *Côte d'Azur* nowadays is the summer, when the rich and the beautiful flock to sunbake on the beaches and to party in the clubs at night. In Queen Victoria's day the high season was the winter, when one went to the *Côte d'Azur* to escape the dark, damp, cold of winter in industrial revolution England and northern Europe. And, of course, in Victorian and Edwardian times one avoided the summer sun, "sunbaking" was quite unthinkable and summer was the time for tennis parties and cricket matches on immaculate green sward in England.

Anges and Queen Victoria's statue continues to preside from the hilltop in Cimiez, a reminder of those halcyon days when her subjects could boast that "the Rivera is ours".

(v) Corsica

The fifth of my little adventures by public transport around Nice involved first a quick trip across the seas to Corsica, followed by train travel covering the entire length of the Corsican rail network. Corsica Ferries offer a fast daylight service and a slower overnight service between mainland France and the *Ile de la Beauté*, as Corsica is sometimes called. I took the noon sailing from Nice to Bastia: it was a fine autumn day, the sea was calm, the sky was blue, the ferry was large and new and fast, and after watching the very picturesque port of Old Nice slowly disappear, I headed for the restaurant and had a very fine lunch and a great chat with tablemates also visiting Corsica for the first time. My purpose was a little more specialised than theirs, in that I was going to Corsica to play trains, intending to return the following year for a more in-depth stay. It was dusk and after six when we arrived in Bastia. I made a beeline for the Hôtel Bonaparte which I had been told was within walking distance of the ferry berth, not expensive and quite good. I had not booked in advance and was lucky to get one of the last rooms but was soon installed and ready to have a light evening meal and then to head for bed. The hotel staff suggested a small place nearby, *Le Baptiste*, and so I walked the couple of hundred metres over there. It was a simple, very "local" place, seemed very popular and gave me a great seafood meal which with a bottle of lager had me soon ready for bed and a good sleep.

In the morning, I had a short walk to the railway station

for the 9.00 train. I had decided to take the Ajaccio train as far as Corte and to change there to the branch line that goes down to the west coast, to make overnight stops in Corte and Calvi, and then to retrace my route to Corte and to continue on from Corte to Ajaccio. Corsica is a very mountainous island and building the railway was a difficult undertaking back in the 1880s. A narrow (one metre) gauge was used because of the many tight curves that would be needed and it took ten years to complete the 160 kilometres from Bastia to Ajaccio, requiring thirty-two tunnels and fifty-one bridges. The trip promised to be spectacular! I was surprised to find the train almost full as we rattled out of Bastia and across the narrow coastal plain to Casamozza, where we started the steep climb up in to the mountains. It took just two hours to get as far as Corte, the mountain fortress and onetime capital of Corsica, and there I alighted and hailed a taxi to take me to the Hôtel de la Paix. Corte is very hilly and not a place in which to drag around one's luggage while trying to find one's hotel! The staff at the Hôtel de la Paix were very welcoming and full of advice as to where to eat and drink and sightsee.

Being no longer young and fit and never having been keen on mountaineering, I decided to avail myself of *Le Petit Train* to "do" Corte without working up a sweat or straining any muscles. I have always been inclined to snigger a bit at these strange contraptions, trolleys rather than trains and now seen almost everywhere that foot-weary tourists are found gamely "sightseeing", but never again will I laugh. Taking the *Petit Train* tour in Corte was one of my best decisions and I strongly recommend it as the painless way of seeing the citadel and the *Belvédère (lookout)*, both pretty difficult to access on foot, and all the other fascinating nooks and crannies of this interesting old town.

The next day, after a leisurely breakfast I caught the 10.30 train back as far as Ponte Leccia and had a virtually immediate connection with a train on the branch line down to Calvi. Once down to near sea level, the line traverses flat scrubby land before arriving at Ile Rousse with its strange reddish hills and then runs along the very edge of a series of bays and beaches to Calvi, where we arrived in time for lunch. I stayed at the Hôtel Belvédère, a short walk from the station and with a great view of the citadel high on its promontory and the main tourist attraction of Calvi other than its really superb beaches. The citadel is a massive piece of medieval military construction and dates from the thirteenth century when the city-state of Genoa, rival of Pisa and Venice as dominant maritime powers in the western Mediterranean, seized Corsica and ruled the island until the middle of the eighteenth century when, after a brief period of independence, it became part of France. Christopher Columbus, who is usually referred to as being "Genoese", was actually born in Calvi when it was ruled by the Genoese Republic, so Corsicans regard him as being Corsican rather than Genoese, just as they regard Napoleon I as being Corsican rather than French! I spent my afternoon walking around the narrow streets of the citadel, admiring the cathedral and the jumble of quaint old houses and the glorious view over Calvi and its bay from the ramparts.

The next morning, I was again at the station for an early departure, this time the 8.30 train back to Ponte Leccia where I changed trains and was back on the main line up though Corte to Ajaccio. This is the most spectacular part of the Corsican railway system, the train spending more than two hours climbing into the snow-capped mountains, following rushing mountain streams, passing waterfalls, plunging into tunnels, some of them spiral ones, and rattling across numerous stone and iron bridges, one of them almost as high as the Eiffel Tower and designed by the Eiffel company. At the highest point of the line, where it crosses the Vizzanova Pass, the train was 1100 metres above sea level and it then began a fairly steep and winding descent down to Ajaccio, the end of the line. It took nearly three hours to climb up and rattle down through the mountains from Ponte Leccia to Ajaccio and the scenery was quite wild and wonderful. Of course, the mountain lines through Switzerland go much higher, the engineering involved is more dazzling, the scenery even more spectacular and everything is so immaculately maintained, but I was more than satisfied with my Corsican train adventure and with the friendly people I met while "playing trains".

I shared a taxi from the Ajaccio station to my hotel, the Hôtel Kalliste, with a friendly English couple I had met on the train and spent the remains of the afternoon exploring Ajaccio. The city has a population of about 100,000 and apparently likes to be referred to as "*la ville impériale*", reminders of the Bonaparte family being found all around the place. The main street is the wide, straight and very impressive *Cours Napoléon*, the next best street is the rue Cardinal Fesch (the cardinal was the emperor's uncle), the nicest square is the *Place Foch* with a statue of Napoleon I in pride of place, and the waterfront promenade leading to the Genoese citadel is the Quai Napoléon. The city was far more interesting and attractive than I had expected. The constant reminders of Napoleon and of Pasquale Paoli (the hero of Corsica's eighteenth-century revolt against the Genoese) only added to its appeal and I decided that I should one day return to Corsica and explore much more than its railway network.

After a very pleasant dinner-bed-breakfast at the Kalliste, I boarded the midday ferry to mainland France and as the ferry pulled away, I realised that the most stunningly beautiful view of Ajaccio could only be enjoyed from the sea. The city is built along the shores of a large bay and, as one sails away and looks back the foreshore, lined with palm trees and pastel-tinted buildings, with a backdrop of low hills and behind them a great range of jagged, snow-capped mountains makes one understand why Corsica is called the "*Ile de la Beauté*".

Chapter 10
A Tale of Four Rivers: Loire, Maine, Aure And Seine

(i) Beaugency

Beaugency is about twenty-five kilometres south-west of Orléans. It is built on the banks of the river Loire and might be regarded as the gateway, or one of the gateways, to the Loire Valley and its fabulous châteaux. It is on the railway line along the Loire Valley linking Orléans through Tours to the Atlantic coast and to Bordeaux, but the purpose-built TGV line from Paris to Bordeaux nowadays by-passes Orléans, Beaugency, Blois and Amboise. TER trains still link these towns to one another as well as to Paris and the Atlantic coast with connections in Tours and so Beaugency is still easily reached by rail, but a car would be needed if you wanted to use it as a base for visiting the châteaux further west along the valley.

 I had been through Beaugency many times on my many trips between Paris and Bordeaux but it was not until 2015 that I actually stopped and spent several days there. Many years earlier, I had been in New Caledonia and had become friendly with a young couple from France who with their two children had decided to move away from Europe. Some years later, they had decided to return to France, uneasy about the political situation in New Caledonia and concerned about their children's future. They travelled back to Europe on the Lloyd Triestino liner *Galileo*, which called into Melbourne *en route* via the Suez Canal; I spent the day showing them the sights, brought them home where my mother gave them one of her, as usual, wonderful dinners and then took them back to the ship just before it sailed that night. The family ended up settling down near Beaugency and invited me to visit whenever I was in the area. My cousin and boon travelling companion, Helen, was an alumna of the Ursuline nuns in Australia and as one of that Order's earliest convents in France had been established in Beaugency in 1629 and was still operating she was keen to visit the town too.

One Monday morning in September, we travelled by train from Paris to Chartres, where we hired a car for the cross-country trip to Beaugency and beyond. We spent two nights at the very pleasant Hôtel des Poèmes in Chartres close by the railway station and spent the full day in between admiring the cathedral, one of the "big five" in France. Personally, I find the two western towers of the Chartres cathedral unfortunately jarring in their very different styles, but I will admit that the interior of the cathedral is superb, harmonious and very beautiful, while the stained-glass windows, the greatest glory of Chartres, are absolutely stunning. How all that twelfth- and thirteenth-century glass survived the bombing of the Second World War and the preceding eight hundred years of fighting in Europe seems almost miraculous. Chartres is an interesting old market town, huddled along the banks of the river Eure which winds past the steep hill crowned by the cathedral. If you are interested in medieval stained glass, Chartres cathedral is said to have the finest collection in the world.

But we were on our way to Beaugency and, on the

Wednesday morning, we set off, choosing to take a somewhat leisurely route through Bonneval, Châteaudun and Meung-sur-Loire. We decided to skip breakfast in Chartres, no great sacrifice after having splurged on a fantastic meal the previous night at the *Boeuf Couronné*, a short walk from our hotel, and we made good time to Bonneval, where we decided to stop for a *café crème* and a quick look before pushing on to Châteaudun for lunch.

Châteaudun is a very ancient town and is located at the intersection of two Roman roads. The town is dominated by the fortress and château dating from Roman times and which has been enlarged and rebuilt many times over the centuries. We parked near the château and then walked down to the very grand main square, the *Place du 18-Octobre*, where we found a table on the terrace of a pleasant little brasserie, *Le Commerce*, and had a light lunch, that old favourite of mine in such circumstances, an omelette. Omelettes always seem to be so perfect in the land where they were invented, and accompanied by some crusty bread, a glass of wine and then a coffee, our choices made for the ideal lunch. Back on the road by two we set off for, but not stopping in, Meung-sur-Loire, despite its historic château: there are so many interesting châteaux in the Loire Valley that it would be impossible to visit them all, and we arrived in Beaugency in mid-afternoon.

Beaugency is an historic place with a population now of about 7,000. People have lived there on the banks of the Loire for many thousands of years, the slight hill on the north bank affording a good defensive position which attracted both the Gauls and the Romans and the emerging lordly families in the early Middle Ages. The river has been used as a means of defence and transport since time immemorial, flowing westward to the Atlantic and, in the east, flowing past Nevers and Orléans on its way to the sea from its headwaters in the Auvergne. The small island in the wide river had, for centuries, made this locality a good spot to attempt a crossing but no bridge had been able to be built until early in the eleventh century. A bridge was then built but only with the help, so goes the legend, of the Devil himself.[47] The Loire was, and remains, a moody sort of river, usually flowing languidly along but after heavy rain in its upper reaches it can rise dramatically, become very turbulent and sweep away mills, bridges and riverside buildings. The bridge built in the eleventh century has been rebuilt and repaired in every century since and the river can be said to be both a life-giving and a destructive force in Beaugency.

We found our hotel, the Hôtel de la Licorne, in the tiny *Place du Martroi* and checked in. Helen had written to the Ursuline convent asking whether she could visit and whether they could recommend a modest and convenient place to stay. The nuns had suggested the Licorne, had assured her that a visit would be welcomed and had suggested the following afternoon as being suitable. We, therefore, had organised with my friends Bernard and Monique from Nouméa to spend our first day with the Ursulines, our second day on a drive in the countryside and the third day, Saturday, with their family in Beaugency. One of the most prominent buildings in

---

[47] In return for his help, the Devil required the soul of the first of the town's inhabitants to cross the bridge. The wily townsfolk drove a large black cat across the bridge before any other inhabitants crossed and thwarted the Evil One. To this day, the nickname for people from Beaugency is *les chats de Beaugency*.

Beaugency is the eleventh-century former abbey, very near our hotel. Part of the building is now a very fine hotel, the Grand Hôtel de l'Abbaye, part is used by the local secondary school and the abbey church is now used as the parish church. We decided to stretch our legs and walk around the buildings before dinner and perhaps even to have dinner in the hotel. After spending time admiring the building, we found that an evening Mass was about to start so we decided to sit quietly and enjoy the architecture, the atmosphere and the peace and calm. There were only a couple of dozen people attending and, after Mass, the priest walked down the aisle to the door and greeted everyone as they left, including the two strangers. An elderly couple ahead of us waited quietly until we were done and the priest had turned back into the church and the husband then spoke to us in halting English saying: "Is this your first visit to Beaugency?"

I answered in French, telling him that it was indeed our first visit and then, in answer to his next question which was in French, I added that no, we were not English but were from Australia. We all introduced ourselves in a mixture of French and English: they turned out to be from Versailles (no, not the palace, but the town which grew up near the palace!), he was a retired engineer and they had a holiday house by the river in Beaugency. Though his wife spoke no English and Helen had very little French the two of them seemed to get on like a house on fire, while monsieur and I spoke in French about touring in the vicinity. On learning that we would be in the town for a few days, the couple invited us to visit their holiday home and *prendre l'apéritif* with them the next evening and after presenting us with their address card (cards are such a useful, if old-fashioned, custom) they went on their way and we headed back to La Licorne. The Grand Hôtel de l'Abbaye certainly looked fabulous but even to dine there, let alone to stay there, looked to be beyond our budget and so we settled for an evening meal in La Licorne. The nuns' advice proved to be sound, as the little hotel was clean, comfortable, conveniently situated, had quite a lot of character in its decor and was run by very pleasant and efficient North African people. And the meals were similarly very good. So, our arrival and first evening in Beaugency had been very satisfactory!

The next day, Thursday, we had a late start and a leisurely breakfast in the hotel's little patio and then went for a stroll around the town. There was quite a lot to see apart from the abbey and the bridge and the quite numerous seventeenth- and eighteenth-century houses: the medieval *Tour de l'Horloge* which was originally part of the town ramparts and acquired the town clock in the sixteenth century; an eleventh-century church, St Etienne and the *donjon*, the *Tour de César*; the fifteenth-century *Château Dunois*; the sixteenth-century *Hôtel de Ville*, a dear little jewel of Renaissance-style architecture housing some quite fine seventeenth-century tapestry wall hangings; and of course the seventeenth-century Convent of the Ursulines which we were to visit in the afternoon. We did as much as we could and then returned to our hotel for a snack and a snooze before setting off for the convent. When we eventually arrived, we were very kindly welcomed by the nuns, particularly by one who spoke very good English and, after what I judged to be a respectful amount of time, I excused myself, pleading fatigue, and left Helen to enjoy the time with her former educators. I went back to the hotel and "took it easy" for the rest of the afternoon. Helen returned from the

Ursulines just in time to freshen up before setting out once again, this time to *prendre l'apéritif* with the couple from Versailles. Their holiday home was only a ten-minute walk up a slight hill from La Licorne and turned out to be an ultra-modern ground-floor apartment in a recently restored seventeenth-century warehouse. The living room had a wall of glass opening to a paved courtyard and looked over a tumble of chimneys, attics and slate roofs towards the tree-lined river. The room was furnished with comfortable, minimalist-style furniture and the wife, noticing our surprise at the contrast between inside and outside, smilingly explained that as their family home in Versailles was furnished in a very French traditional way, with the sort of clutter a family gathers over the years, she had decided that their holiday home would be very different: comfortable, but as simple as possible, with a minimum of housework, minimum garden maintenance and a maximum of *farniente*! Her husband chided her that she never even slowed down, let alone *far niente*, and pointed to the plates of *amuses-bouches* (savoury snacks) she had prepared for the evening and to the piece of embroidery she had picked up as soon as she had seen that we were seated: "She never stops," he said affectionately. We spent a very pleasant hour with them chatting about Beaugency and Versailles and Australia and about their families and ours and then we said our goodbyes and walked back to the brasserie near La Licorne for the evening meal. Helen and the wife exchanged Christmas cards for years afterwards, a living reminder of a lovely experience and of how warmly strangers can be welcomed in France.

    The next day, as planned, we set off by car on a round trip to Gien and Saint-Benoît-sur-Loire. We choose the road through La-Ferté-Saint-Aubin, where there is a fine château, built of stone and orange-coloured bricks (often seen there in the marshy Sologne region) and facing a "mirror", a water feature in which the building is reflected. The *Château de* La-Ferté-Saint-Aubin is still a family home, furnished with period furniture and open to the public, but we contented ourselves with an admiring look from the park and drove on through Cerdon to Gien.

Gien, like Beaugency, is built on the high side of a stretch of the river Loire at a spot where, in the late Middle Ages, it proved possible to build a bridge that could withstand the vagaries of the river. And again, as in Beaugency, a château important in French history crowns the hill overlooking the town and the bridge. Important women in French history have lived in this château: Joan of Arc, the regents Anne de Beaujeu, Louise de Savoie, Catherine de Medici, and Anne of Austria, as well as a long list of important men including Louis XIII and Louis XIV. The town, about double the size of Beaugency, was heavily bombed during the Second World War and was virtually destroyed, being later rebuilt in a more or less traditional style with the use of local timbers and polychrome bricks and the result is really quite attractive. We had, however, come to Gien not so much to admire the buildings but to purchase some of its most famous products. For the past two hundred years or so, Gien has been noted for its production of high-quality, hand-decorated porcelain, produced mostly for domestic use such as dinner services, and offered at prices slightly lower than those of its older and more famous competitors in Sèvres and Limoges. We were told, however, by the helpful people at the *Bureau de Tourisme* on the river quay, that by arriving just before midday we were arriving just as the *Faïencerie de Gien*, its shop and museum would be closing for lunch. The best course of action, therefore, seemed to be to have lunch too and to be ready and waiting when the place reopened. There was a pleasant-looking bistro almost next door to the information office and so we settled down there and had lunch. To my delight, the special that day was *Quenelles de brochet*, a sort of light and fluffy dumpling made with pike (the only way I could imagine enjoying that frightening fish!) and I easily persuaded Helen to trust me and allow me to order for us both. The Loire is noted for its freshwater fish such as pike and the meal did turn out to be delicious, accompanied by a glass of the local Sancerre and *un petit café*... and then it was time to hit the *Faïencerie*.

I had visited porcelain works in Limoges many years earlier, had bought a beautiful and elegant coffee service there and so was already "hooked" on the product and needed no sales pitch from the friendly staff in Gien. The factory, museum and shop are in an old and surprisingly dilapidated building but the product is superb. The range of designs and pieces is extraordinary and the artistry and beauty of the decoration is mind-blowing. We had allowed ourselves a couple of hours to visit the works and the shop and had agreed that it was to be mainly a case of "just looking", with a single purchase of a mug or small plate as a souvenir. Be warned: it is almost impossible to see all those beautiful pieces being made and decorated by hand without wanting to buy some of everything! Helen's credit card was taking a terrible pounding and I had to twist her arm to get us out of there before she had bought "a little souvenir" for every member of her extended family, as well as for herself, and I would have had trouble packing the pile of purchases into the car. But it was a wonderful experience and my own pieces of Gien looks down at my desk as I write, a constant and delightful reminder of that trip through the Loire Valley. We got away from Gien a little after four, setting off down the river road to Sully-sur-Loire. The people at the *Bureau de Tourisme* in Gien had advised us to cross the river in Gien and to take the road along the southern bank of the river as that would bring us to Sully-sur-Loire on the same side of the river as the château and would give us a great view of it sitting there on its island, mirrored in the waters of the Loire. We did as we were advised and stopped for a good look: Sully-sur-Loire is yet another of those fairy-tale-style castles built of white limestone, roofed in blue-grey slate and topped with a confection of candle snuffer turrets, towers and chimneys: too pretty to be real, but they ARE real, and this one remained in the family of the first *Duc de Sully* until 1962, when it was acquired by the local municipality and opened to the public.

We drove on, across the river and through the town and reached Saint-Benoît-sur-Loire in good time for a visit and for Vespers. First established in 650 A.D to house the remains of St Benedict who had died in Monte Casino, this is one of the oldest monasteries in Europe, although the buildings have been damaged, destroyed and rebuilt many times. The Romanesque abbey church that dates largely from the eleventh century, is simple, vast and very beautiful and seems to stand serenely on its rising ground watching the river and time and the foolishness of man flow by.

We decided after all not to wait for Vespers, which we discovered would be held at ten past six rather than at five as I had thought, as we were still nearly an hour's drive from "home" in Beaugency. We drove first of all to Châteauneuf-sur-Loire and then, instead of continuing along the river through Orléans and the temptations and traffic of that historic city, we turned across the river at Jargeau and went on through the woods and vineyards to La-Ferté-Saint-Aubin and returned to Beaugency the way we had left it in the morning. After an *apéritif* in the quaint bar of La Licorne we walked along the *Place du Martroi* to the big brasserie there, had a light meal, and strolled home to bed and a good night's sleep after a wonderful day.

The next day was Saturday, our last day in Beaugency and the one we were to spend with Bernard and his family. The family had changed in the intervening years: the two teenagers were now married and both working in Paris and Monique's aged mother was living in Beaugency with them. We had been invited to the midday meal and had arranged that we would be collected at the hotel at about eleven o'clock and would be walked through the market: Saturday was the big, all-day market in the main square in Beaugency, while there was a half-day market on two or three other days of the week. Markets were almost as high on our list of things to see as were monasteries! It was Bernard who called for us, armed with a short shopping list drawn up by his wife and mother-in-law: apparently, the old lady still liked to take a hand in the planning if not the actual preparation of the meals and like most families in the town the family thought it normal to go shopping two or three times a week. There was a supermarket available but it was on the outskirts of the town, by vote of the citizenry, and most shoppers preferred fresh [48] to frozen food... and the mother-in-law certainly did. So, we three worked our way around the square inspecting the fruit and vegetables in season, lingering at the cheese stall while Bernard sampled and

---

[48] The cheese, delicatessen, meat, poultry and fish "stalls" were actually very smart refrigerated vans with drop-down sides and lots of glass, chrome and fluorescent lighting.

selected his purchases, introducing us to the husband-and-wife proprietors as *"mes amis Australiens"* and causing a ripple of interest among people within earshot. At one of the fruit stalls Bernard bought what looked like half a kilo of strawberries, specifying that he wanted the *fraises des bois*, the tiny ones "no bigger than the tip of a lady's little finger", wild not cultivated berries and far more flavoursome than ones grown on berry farms.

After adding some fresh bread to his purchases, Bernard announced that the job was done and that, if we had seen enough, we would head off home. We agreed and piled into his Renault and, within ten minutes, had arrived. On the way, Bernard explained that he had recently sold his business in Orléans and had retired to the outskirts of Beaugency where Monique had grown up and where her mother still lived in the family home. It was a large and lovely old, two-storey place with a terraced garden extending down to the river's edge but it took only a quick glance to realise that the upkeep of such a property would be very demanding... Bernard said, with a wry smile as we got out of the car and walked towards the door: *"Oui, cela me dépasse un peu!"* (Yes, it is all a bit too much to manage!) It was great to see Monique again after so many years and to hear news of the two teenagers I had last seen playing on the beach in Nouméa and it was an honour and a pleasure to meet her mother, *maman* to Monique, *mère* to Bernard and *madame* to us.

Madame welcomed us to her home and waved us across the wide entrance hall to a beautiful *salon*, parquetry floor gleaming under a scattering of Persian rugs, antique chairs and tables looking as if they were to be admired rather than actually used, a tall vase of flowers on a table between the two glass doors opening on to the garden terrace... it was a bit breathtaking, like stepping on to the TV set when a Molière play or even a Jane Austen adaptation was being filmed. But *madame* sat down on one of the exquisite chairs and gestured towards a gilded settee for us while Monique disappeared (towards the kitchen?) and Bernard moved to a drinks tray on a table near *madame* and busied himself with opening the bottle of Mumm I saw peeping out of the ice-bucket. *Madame*, meanwhile, enquired politely about our travels and about Australia and then, once Monique had re-joined us and we had raised our champagne flutes to toast *santé*, good health, *madame* slipped away and Monique explained that lunch was ready and that we should move to the dining room next door and be seated. Apparently, we had delayed Bernard a little at the market and the first course of lunch was a *soufflé aux pommes de terre*, and soufflés do not wait for stragglers! So Helen and I sat at the beautifully laid table, Bernard attended to the glasses and Monique and *madame* emerged with the soufflé, or rather soufflés, as individual small soufflé dishes or ramekins had been used in this case. The soufflé was sensational, as light as a feather and yet downright earthy and potatoey in flavour and I managed to tell *madame*, who turned out to have been the chef, that my Irish forebears whose genes made me a true devotee of *la pomme de terre*, would, I was sure, want to join me in praise of the dish. A few flowery words, a glass or two of champagne and the luncheon party was off to a good start with *madame* presiding and beaming from the head of the table. The soufflé was followed by a cold *terrine de lapin en croûte* and several salads and then by a dessert of the strawberries from the market and a bowl of whipped cream. We moved out to the terraced garden for coffee and after a short while *madame* excused herself and turned to go into the house but urged us to stay on chatting with Monique and Bernard and wishing us *bonne continuation* of our visit to France. As neither Monique nor her mother had more than a few words of English and Helen had only a little more French, communication had been a bit strained as everybody tried to be polite to both *madame* and her English-speaking guest but with the old lady's departure indoors the atmosphere eased a little. Monique said that her mother was not as well as she believed herself to be and that the latest discussions between the family and the doctors had resulted in the decision she and Bernard had taken to move in and to ensure that her mother was never left alone in the house. It was not an easy situation as her mother did not want to accept that she needed care or even company! Helen and I had both been through somewhat similar family situations and discussing them, even briefly and in "franglais" seemed of interest to both Monique and Bernard. Eventually, however, we said it was time to leave and Monique came out to the Renault to say goodbye, promising to relay our repeated thanks to her mother for the wonderful day. Bernard dropped us off back at the Licorne, bringing to a close a great day and a wonderful glimpse of French family life... which turned out to be not unlike life in Australia, with the same sorts of ups and downs, pleasures and problems... but with the advantage of *madame*'s wonderful potato soufflés!

(ii) Angers

Le Château d'Angers

I had been fascinated by the names Angers, Anjou and Angevin ever since my school days, when I had heard about Henry of Anjou and his feisty wife, Eleanor of Aquitaine, their swashbuckling (and probably gay) son Richard the Lionheart, or *Coeur de Lion* as the French called him, and their seemingly rather unpleasant other son, John, of *Magna Carta* fame. It was, however, not until my old age that in 2014 I managed to visit Angers, the capital of Anjou and of the almost mythical Angevin Empire. Angers nowadays has a population of around 150,000 and so it is, as it has been since medieval times, a big and important city in France. Its glory days started when Henry, count of Anjou, married Eleanor, duchess of Aquitaine, seized the neighbouring dukedom of Normandy in 1144 and then, on the death of his cousin, King Stephen, became king Henry II of England. In 1154, he ruled, as a result, a composite empire stretching from England's borders with Scotland right across England, Normandy, Anjou, Maine, Poitou and

Aquitaine as far south as the Pyrenees. Later, parts of Provence, Sicily, Naples and southern Italy were at times ruled by Anjou. Henry II regarded Angers as his capital, sometimes moving his court upriver to nearby Chinon and spending little time in his other major cities of Rouen and London. He was succeeded by his son Richard the Lionheart, who spent only six months of his ten-year reign in England and was killed while defending his borders in Aquitaine. Henry, Eleanor and Richard were buried in the royal abbey of Fontevraud, fifty kilometres southeast of Angers, along with King John's second wife, Isabelle of Angoulême, while King John was buried in England.

Angers is located on slightly hilly ground at the junction of the river Maine with the wide river Loire. In Plantagenet times, the city was heavily fortified and it is still dominated by its immense seventeen-towered fortress, the *Château d'Angers*. I arrived there by train one chilly autumn day and quickly took a taxi from the station to the *Hostellerie du Bon Pasteur*, a short distance across the river Maine. A strange choice, you may think, but let me explain.

The *hostellerie* takes up part of an historic group of buildings, the mother house of an order of nuns, *les Soeurs du Bon Pasteur*, the Good Shepherd Sisters, founded in Angers soon after the Revolution to provide shelter to homeless and helpless women and children. A small group of *Bon Pasteur* nuns had come to Australia in 1863 and had opened a refuge for women and children in difficulty in Melbourne, many of them abandoned in the town by menfolk who had set off for the bush and the gold rushes. The need was great, local women joined the nuns to help, some lucky gold miners helped financially and by the end of the century, the Sisters numbered several hundred and had large convents, shelters and primary or elementary schools right across Australia and New Zealand (and much of the world). My father was a doctor in a Melbourne suburb where there was a second large Good Shepherd convent and rehabilitation centre and he acted as visiting medical officer there for more than twenty years until his early death. There was a very good and mutually respectful relationship between him and the various women who, in turn, completed six-year periods as Prioress. On the birth of his second child, my mother's suggestion that the baby's list of names should include Stanislaus, the name of the then Prioress, was welcomed by all. So it was that the child (the present author) grew up and occasionally visited the convent with his father. The good nuns would, while his father attended to the sick, occupy young John Stanislaus with walks in the garden or games with the convent dogs or cats, of which there were always several, or even with a glass of lemonade in summer or a biscuit or two in winter. Feeling that I was almost an alumnus of the Good Shepherd Sisters, I jumped at the opportunity of staying in the hostel that now occupies part of the buildings where the order had started. While there are, I believe, about four thousand Sisters of the Good Shepherd around the world today, they now work in small groups in the community. Huge convents like the Mother House in Angers, which was built in stages between 1857 and 1957 on a former industrial site across the river from the town centre, are no longer needed. The hostel is mainly used now, I gathered, by university students, with tourists like me and people visiting Angers on business taking up the slack during university recess. The rather plain and utilitarian nineteenth-century buildings have been completely renovated, modern central heating systems, lifts and Wi-Fi have been installed and each room in the hostel has en-suite facilities and I found it very comfortable and economical. There was a sparkling new self-service dining-room that turned on really good meals, there were beautiful gardens to stroll in and the whole lot was only a few minutes' walk from a bus stop and ten minutes' walk to the *Château d'Angers*.

The château had mostly been built in the thirteenth century by which time, with the death of King John in England, the Angevin Empire had begun to collapse. Anjou became part of France and served as the fortified frontier between France and the still-independent dukedom of Brittany. The present great fortress incorporates parts of the earlier château of the counts of Anjou and of structures dating back to Roman and even Celtic times. It still dominates the city and a visit is a real must if you are ever in the area. The views over the river and city from the top of the battlements are superb and the royal residence and chapel, the various gardens in the courtyards, in the moat and even on the battlements are quite fascinating. The wonderful medieval tapestries, *The Apocalypse*, displayed in a purpose-built gallery inside the main courtyard are of world significance and are said to have inspired the similarly wonderful tapestries in the *Musée Lurçat*, another must visit while you are in Angers.

There is a lot more to Angers than medieval architecture and world-class tapestries of course, but the historic town centre with its timbered houses, inviting squares such as the *Place Sainte Croix*, the *Cathédrale St Maurice* and the *Hôtel Pincé* do need to be seen. Back across the river and near the Good Shepherd Centre is the *Musée Jean Lurçat*, a collection of Lurçat's greatest modern tapestries beautifully presented in the handsomely restored old *Hôpital St Jean*. I spent three very pleasant days wandering around the city on foot, by tram and by bus, even making it out to the former Franciscan monastery of *Les Baumettes* in its idyllic garden setting on the banks of the Maine. I had some really good meals in the *Bon Pasteur* hostel and each one was an opportunity to meet and chat with the other guests who invariably proved friendly and did indeed mostly turn out to be university students. The few nuns I met (as they no longer wear the white habit and black veil I associated with the Good Shepherds in my childhood it was not always clear which of the staff were nuns and which were not!) were equally welcoming and seemed quite chuffed to have a guest from far away *Australie* who spoke with affection and respect of their Antipodean convents.

(iii) Bayeux

One year, I travelled with a cousin and his wife through Normandy and the Loire Valley. Our train from Tours and Le Mans arrived in Bayeux under drizzly grey skies and, as the station seemed to be in an isolated spot on the edge of town, we felt we were lucky to commandeer the solitary taxi in the parking lot. I gave

The Aure in Bayeux

our destination as the *Couvent des Moniales Bénédictines* and, fortunately, the taxi driver said he knew the place well. He added that if we had had a map we really could have walked from the railway station as it was only about a kilometre away, but we were convinced that the rain and the luggage certainly ruled that out! The *Monastère Sainte Trinité*, as it is now called, had been founded in the seventeenth century as a branch of the abbey in Caen established by Queen Matilda a few years after her husband, William, had conquered England. It occupied a range of historic and handsome buildings in the rue Saint Loup near the centre of town. The taxi dropped us at the door of the guest house wing, which was right on the street and our ringing of the doorbell was quickly answered by a cheerful young nun. She confirmed that we were expected and said that they had reserved two en-suite rooms on the fourth floor for us. She told us that it would be *plus calme* for us up there and that we would have a fine view of the gardens and other buildings. I shuddered at the thought of having to drag luggage up four flights of stairs in an eighteenth-century building with four-metre ceilings on each floor and was mightily relieved to learn that *un ascenseur* (a lift) had been installed as part of the recent refurbishment of the guest house. So, by the end of the day we were comfortably settled in our very nice rooms and ready to attend Vespers, enjoy the evening meal in the guest house refectory with a number of other guests and then attend Compline in the chapel before having an early night. There were only about a dozen nuns in the house and the two or three who dealt with the guest house were very welcoming. There were in fact many more guests than nuns, some being university students (who liked to try out their English on the exotic Australian guests), others being foreign travellers like us and some being French people who were visiting relatives in the convent. One charming French husband and wife were visiting their daughter, the nice young nun who had opened the door to us and who, after a trial period of several years, was preparing to take her final vows as a Benedictine nun.

Unlike most of Normandy, Bayeux was not bombed to bits during the Second World War and, although damaged and rebuilt, the old town centre, with its quays along the river Aure and its half-timbered houses, is very picturesque. The cathedral, begun in the eleventh century by Bishop Odo, half-brother of William the Conqueror, is very fine early Gothic (although it has a strangely incongruous little copper dome on the top of its central tower, more like a Venetian palazzo than a church). We went to Mass there on Sunday, expecting to see a smallish, elderly and largely female congregation and were surprised to find the cathedral absolutely packed out when we arrived just before the start of proceedings. We could not find seats together and just managed to squeeze into two spots a few rows apart. It turned out to be the day on which a large group of children was to be Confirmed by the bishop, so it was a Pontifical High Mass with wonderful music, flowers, candles and clouds of incense. Then there was the long line of white-clad schoolchildren moving up the aisles towards the bishop to receive the blessing, with excited parents popping up all over the place with mobile phones and flash cameras to photograph their little darlings. The bishop's attendants kept asking the congregation NOT to take photos during the ceremony, but the mums and dads took absolutely no notice. A good time was had by all (except those unhappy attendants) and when we left the cathedral at the end we were offered cakes and wine by the ladies of the parish who had turned on a celebratory snack for the whole congregation, foreigners included. We continued the celebration by having a superb midday meal in a beautiful restaurant nearby, *Le Pommier* in the aptly named rue des Cuisiniers. And that is how we prepared ourselves for the afternoon's activity and the main purpose of our visit to Bayeux, i.e., to see the Bayeux Tapestry.

The Bayeux Tapestry is now housed in a purpose-built display gallery in yet another grey, grim old building (a former seminary) giving no hint of the splendours inside. The tapestry which is a sort of comic strip depiction of the conquest of England by William, Duke of Normandy, is thought to have been embroidered by William's wife, Matilda, and her ladies a year or two after the Battle of Hastings. (It is really a very large piece of embroidery rather than a woven tapestry). The queen and her ladies used multi-coloured woollen thread, stitching on to a plain linen background, the seventy different scenes captioned in simple Latin: *Hic Edward Rex, Hic Dux Willelm*, and so on. The tapestry is seventy metres long and fifty centimetres wide and is displayed in a long, glass case lit from within, in a very long, darkened room. Visitors enter a roped-off walkway at the beginning of the display and are encouraged to slowly walk the length of the tapestry, examining each of the scenes depicted. It is all so simple, so explicit… it is absolutely enthralling and should be high on one's list of things to do when visiting Normandy.

The next day, after another great "3 C" breakfast of coffee, croissants and chat, we said goodbye to the welcoming nuns and their other guests, taxied back to the station and took a morning train to Caen, the second city of Normandy. Here, we picked up a hire car to enable us to go off the beaten track between Caen and Rouen. From Caen, we went through Vimoutiers to the village of Camembert, the birthplace of that delicious, creamy cheese now appreciated (and copied) all over the world. It was a pretty little place, surrounded by green pastures and black and white Normandy cows and replete with temptations to stop and savour the local speciality, but we resisted and pressed on to Bernay, a large and lovely old town chock-a-block with history and half-timbered houses where, after a wonderful lunch in the historic *Lion d'Or hotel-restaurant*, we left the main road and made our way through the woods to the once-great abbey of *Notre-Dame-du-Bec* about thirty kilometres outside Rouen.

Notre-Dame-du-Bec is another Benedictine house and one founded on the banks of the river Bec in 1034, i.e., thirty-two years before Duke William set off to conquer England. This abbey came to be greatly favoured by the Norman and Plantagenet kings of England, many of its monks being appointed to important ecclesiastical and governmental positions. Three of its abbots became archbishop of Canterbury, one became abbot of Westminster Abbey, five became cardinals and others became bishops or archbishops of important dioceses in France and England. The fourteenth-century *Tour St Nicholas* is the oldest building on the site nowadays, all the other medieval buildings having been destroyed over the years and replaced in the seventeenth and eighteenth centuries by the neo-classical buildings there now. There was more destruction at the time of the Revolution and the whole site was used as a riding academy by the French army from then until the end of the Second World War, when the monks were permitted to return.

I had visited the abbey some years earlier and had actually stayed for two or three nights, not in the recently built and very comfortable guest house, which had been full to overflowing, but in the monastery itself where there were plenty of unoccupied monastic "cells". That particular building dated from the eighteenth century and one of the cyclical boom times in the abbey's history. It had been built on a grand scale, with accommodation for a hundred monks in individual "cells" or rooms each of twenty square metres opening off a central corridor on the second and third floors of three wings forming a U-shaped courtyard. I had taken my meals with the monks in their refectory rather than in the guest house and, by some quirk of good fortune, had even been invited to join a small group of visiting dignitaries including an Anglican bishop and his wife from England, being given a guided tour of the monastery by the abbot himself. I had been so impressed by the history of the place and by the beauty of the setting in the forest that it was inevitable that I should insist on including *Notre-Dame-du-Bec* on this trip with my cousins! So we did a guided tour, this time led by one of the monks, and attended Vespers in the present church (installed in the vast eighteenth-century monks' refectory, as the great fourteenth-century abbey church which it replaces had been closed at the time of the Revolution and the stone and timber used in its construction had been sold off as building materials). We then set off for Rouen.

(iv) Rouen

We arrived in Rouen in the early evening and, after checking in at the Hotel Astrid opposite the station, were soon seated in the restaurant next door and enjoying a relaxing glass of *Kir* and a good dinner. After a long day of travelling across Normandy, we needed no lullabies that night! The next day we left the hotel around nine a.m. and, after a quick coffee and croissant, headed off towards the cathedral and town centre, walking down the rue Jeanne d'Arc, really the main street and almost the only straight and wide one, another example of Haussmann's influence on nineteenth-century town planning. Rouen was built on the northern bank of the Seine in one of the many lazy loops made by the river on its way from Paris to the sea, but the city has spread to the southern bank too and

Rouen, Le Gros Horloge

the agglomeration now occupies most of the land within the three sides of the giant U-bend. The river there is tidal and deep and ocean liners can come upriver from Le Havre if they manage to pass under the intervening suspension bridges. Although Rouen had been heavily bombed during the Second World War, with the cathedral and the sixteenth century *Parlement* building taking direct hits, billions of francs and euros have been spent on rebuilding and renovating and the *Ville Vieille*, or medieval town centre, now looks intact and flourishing. Much of it has been pedestrianised and so one can walk around the maze of narrow, twisting, cobbled streets gaping at the hundreds of fourteenth-, fifteenth- and sixteenth-century houses and buildings, causing no more disruption to pedestrian traffic than do people walking while talking on their mobile phones.

One can't visit Rouen without thinking about the Hundred Years' War between France and England and poor Joan of Arc.

The English made Rouen their capital while they occupied much of western France and we visited the *donjon* in which they had imprisoned Joan after her capture. On the outside, it is a rather attractive round tower, built of local white stone and capped with a slate "candle snuffer" roof, all that remains of the medieval citadel. Joan had been raped there by the English soldiery the day before her execution and next morning had been taken to the nearby *Place du Vieux Marché*, chained to a stake, and slowly burnt alive, the Regent of England, His Grace the Duke of Bedford and His Eminence the Cardinal-Bishop of Winchester presiding. There is a very tall cross on the spot now and an unusual, modernistic church built in the 1960s has replaced the medieval one destroyed during the Second World War. The tall cross, the strange church and the numerous cafés and restaurants around the square make the area one of the major tourist attractions of the city. The cathedral is most famous for the height of its spire which had made it the tallest building in the world until it was pipped by a few metres by the Eiffel Tower. A lot of work is still being done on its restoration (probably a never-ending job) but the main western façade is finished and is a wonder of stone lace, in the high flamboyant style. It had been the venue, a month before our visit, for the requiem Mass of *Père Hamel*, the priest who was assassinated in 2016 while saying Mass in the thirteenth-century parish church at St Etienne du Rouvray and we went out to the suburb to pay our respects. The church was still closed, due to be reopened the Sunday after our visit, and there were still flowers and candles around the closed front doors. We were spoken to by an elderly woman placing flowers there. She wore a headscarf and looked to me to be Algerian, speaking fluent French, crossing herself and explaining that she was a parishioner who came to the church every Sunday and often during the week, a reminder of the consequences of France's two-hundred-year colonial presence in North Africa.

On a lighter note, lunchtime came around while we were in St Etienne du Rouvray and so I asked a chap (another elderly gentleman) in the almost deserted street (the church clock struck twelve while we were there, and in rural and suburban France nearly everything closes for a two-hour lunch break) for advice as to where we might eat. He directed us to a little bistro "around the corner", a clean and tidy place which was already almost full of diners inside but where there were plenty of places available out on the terrace. And there we had a delightful meal, my cousin's wife even chatting up the owner-waiter and wife-cook and securing a handwritten version of their "secret" recipe for *Tarte Normande*! After lunch, we made our way back to town and managed to fit in a visit to the art gallery before it closed its special exhibition of early impressionism. The locals claim that impressionism was a Norman invention and they had brought together a wonderful collection of works by Norman and other artists, many of them family portraits and privately owned. In the evening, we had another great meal in a restaurant called *Can Can* in the *Place du Vieux Marché* (no, I did say "restaurant" and not "nightclub" and I can't explain the name)! We were reluctant to leave Rouen but the road beckoned, we were tourists and tourists must tour!

The last leg of this tour through Normandy took us by car down the valley of the Seine to the now-ruined *abbey of Jumièges*, greatly favoured in times past by royal patrons. Like *du Bec*, it was closed at the time of the Revolution and it was put up for sale as a source of building materials. After forty years of dismantling and neglect the ruins were bought by a wealthy family who stabilised them but did not attempt rebuilding. Unlike *du Bec*, *Jumièges* never saw a return of the monks but it has become one of the most admired and most visited monastic ruins in the country. Its site overlooks a giant bend of the Seine, which enhances the beauty of the simple, soaring architecture and we could not but wonder how on earth the revolutionaries could have brought themselves to destroy something so beautiful. I suppose the answer is that injustice, poverty and hopelessness over the years drove them to desperate acts... just as is still happening two hundred years later in many parts of the world!

From *Jumièges*, we set off down the Seine valley with a plan to see the three great bridges now spanning the river, all built after the Second World War to replace a network of cross-river ferries that had plied the river for centuries. We headed off first of all to the pretty town of Caudebec-en-Caux from which there is a great view of the *Pont de Brotonne*, the first one on our route, and then on via Lillebonne to cross the *Pont de Tancarville* to the south bank of the river which we followed down to the *Pont de Normandie*, the newest (1995) and longest (two kilometres) and on to Honfleur.

Honfleur is perhaps the prettiest little port on the French Atlantic coast with its jumble of old houses and narrow streets climbing up the hill from the quayside at the mouth of the Seine. It is an historic place too, having for centuries figured in the comings and goings of the English and French monarchs as they crossed the "Narrow Seas", often changing from ship to barge and going by river up to Rouen or Paris. It was the port from which the French explorers of North America,

Champlain and La Salle, sailed in the early 1600s but it soon afterwards became so silted up that it was accessible only to fishing boats and very small craft. For us, it was an ideal place to have a seafood lunch at one of the many little restaurants looking over the Old Harbour and across the river estuary towards our destination, Le Havre. Then we drove across the *Pont de Normandie*, through the picturesque town of Harfleur, another silted-up medieval port and into Le Havre itself.

The silting up of the various harbours in the Seine estuary in the 1500s saw the king order the construction of a new, deep-water port, to be called *Havre de Grace*, the Harbour or Haven of Grace, now just Le Havre, and it quickly became the main port on the French Atlantic coast, seconded by Bordeaux, far to the south. The city was almost obliterated by Allied bombing during the Second World War as the occupying Germans bitterly defended it and then, before retreating in 1944, dynamited what was left of it. The rebuilt city today is, we thought, rather bland, being mainly pale grey pre-stressed concrete. The town hall and St Joseph church towers do break the skyline agreeably but the main building of interest is the futuristic art gallery, the *Musée Malraux*. The gallery seems to be built of a myriad of multi-shaped glass panels held together by slim steel struts and is sited dramatically on a breakwater jutting out into the ocean a few hundred metres from the piers where today's giant cruise liners berth. Being a ship enthusiast from my schooldays, I had been to Le Havre before to visit its maritime museum. Le Havre had been the home port of the *Ile de France*, the *Normandie* and the *France*; it had witnessed the departure of the French Line's *Washington* in 1864 on the first transatlantic crossing (to New York) by a French steamship and the return in 1971 of the *Tahitien*, a ship on which I had travelled, and which was the last French passenger liner to complete a transatlantic crossing (from Australia via Panama). Another attraction of Le Havre is the range of restaurants along the *Quai de Southampton* offering great food and great views of the harbour. The seafood there seems particularly good, and I have amazed myself (and onlookers, I think) on several occasions by getting through veritable mountains of *moules marinières, crevettes, bulots* and other fabulous *fruits de mer*. The attraction of Le Havre this time was that we would be able to hand in our hire car at the station, look across the harbour to admire any cruise liners in port that afternoon and then board our ferry for the overnight trip back to the UK, settling into our comfortable cabins to pleasantly end our visit to the Loire Valley and Normandy.

Chapter 11
Outremer

(i) Indochina

My introduction to the term *"Indochine"*, the French overall reference to their protectorates and colonies of Cochinchina, Annam, Tonkin, Cambodia and Laos, would have been when, soon after the end of the Second World War, I was a teenager interested in philately. I managed to obtain a few stamps issued by the French colonial administration that had returned after the defeat of the Japanese army of occupation and was again issuing stamps marked with the single country name *"Indochine"*. The atlas among my schoolbooks showed it, coloured green (while British colonies were coloured red) and marked as "French Indochina". One stamp showed the temples of Angkor and another showed an image of Paul Doumer, the first governor-general of Indochina and another had an image of Alexandre Yersin, the founder of the Pasteur Institute in Indochina. At university in Melbourne in the 1950s, by which time I had swapped my interest in stamps for one in passenger ships, I was friendly with a student from Singapore and, in December of 1952, when he was flying home for the Christmas holidays, I asked him to inspect and photograph for me, if he could, the newest and largest liner of the Messageries Maritimes fleet, the *La Marseillaise*. The *La Marseillaise* had been built for the Marseille-Indochine run and would be calling in Singapore while my friend was there "at home" with his parents, English expatriates. He did as asked and brought back both photos and an enthusiastic account of his visit to the ship, plus a story that his parents' friends in Singapore reported that the new ship had quickly established itself as the best choice for travel to Europe, eclipsing the offerings of the English P&O, the Royal Dutch Mail and other competitors. My first personal (but indirect) involvement with Indochine occurred in the early 1960s on my first visit to New Caledonia, when I discovered that the banks there were branches of the *Banque de l'Indochine* and that even the currency, the *franc Pacifique*, was actually issued by the *Banque de l'Indochine*.[49] In the 1990s, I was delighted by the Oscar-winning film *Indochine* starring Catherine Deneuve and Vincent Perez and I was enthralled by the cinematography with its many shots of the lush green countryside and of colonial life in the 1930s. Finally, in 2011, I managed to visit Indochine, although what I found there was not at all the Indochine of my dreams but the new nation, Vietnam, utterly captivating but in a totally unexpected way.

My ship, the *Princess Daphne*, had slowly made its way across the estuary of the Saigon River, passing the early morning bustle on the wharves of *Cap St Jacques* (now Vung

---

[49] The *Banque de l'Indochine* had been established in Paris in 1875 and had been given similar banking and currency rights in all of France's Indian Ocean, Asian and Pacific Ocean territories. The bank withdrew from Indochina in 1974, merged with the *Crédit Agricole*, the *Crédit Lyonnais* and the *Banque de Suez* to become the *Banque Indosuez*, and now operates throughout France and around the world.

Tau) where passengers jostled to board the big white hydrofoil ferries waiting to take them up the river to the city. Saigon is about ninety kilometres upstream from the sea and the river is serpentine and deep but very tidal, complicating navigation for large ships: while the ferries did the trip in two hours, large ships like ours took at least three and could only travel on flood tides. We slowly steamed up the winding river, sometimes wide, sometimes narrow, flat mangrove-covered plains stretching away on either side towards distant dark green hills. After nearly two hours, signs of habitation and then of large buildings began to appear ahead through a mixture of smoke haze and shimmering heat waves. Was it a mirage or was it indeed Saigon? It was in fact a giant new suspension bridge across the river at Phu Muy, carrying the new motorway from Vung Tau to Ho Chi Minh City, gleaming white concrete pylons towering up on each bank and a long, steel span of roadway suspended from a spidery network of steel cables. The ship glided under the bridge and yet another bend in the river saw us steaming towards the wharves lining the left bank behind which rose a jumble of glass and concrete towers culminating in the seventy-two-storey blue-glass covered Bitexco Tower. This was indeed the new world of Vietnam and

Ho Chi Minh City, not that of *Indochine* and Saigon[50].

The ship tied up at the former Messageries Maritimes quay, alongside the distinctive Dragon House, the shipping line's former head office in Indochina now recycled as the Ho Chi Minh Museum. From the deck, we could look across to the massive *Banque de l'Indochine* building and, a little further along the riverside, to the Hotel Majestic at the corner of the former rue Catinat, the "main street" of old Saigon. As the ship would be in port until noon on the next day and I would be returning to spend a full week in Saigon later in the month, I was in no hurry to rush ashore and to do Saigon in a few hours. So, after a leisurely lunch on board, I teamed up

---

[50] The Vietnamese people originated along the valley of the Red River, an area known as Tonkin and dominated by the Chinese empire until 1010 when Hanoi became the capital of a separate but vassal kingdom ruled by a succession of local dynasties. In 1802, the last dynasty, the Nguyen family, moved the capital to Hué and declared themselves "emperor of Annam" as well as of the north, i.e., of Tonkin. Saigon was then a small fishing village in the far south of Annam with a small citadel guarding the ill-defined and often disputed border with Cambodia. In 1858, a French force occupied the Saigon area and in 1862 constrained the emperor in Hué to cede the southern region, Cochinchina, as a colony to France. By 1888, France had established protectorates over central Annam and Tonkin in the north and had centralised its colonial administration in Hanoi, leaving Hué to be the seat of the figurehead but powerless emperors while Saigon developed rapidly as the commercial centre of the country and as a showpiece of French colonial planning. When France withdrew in 1954, the country was divided in to two (rather than three) parts, North Vietnam and South Vietnam, and in 1975 the North invaded the South, captured Saigon and united the two parts to form the single Republic of Vietnam. While the ever-growing urban agglomeration around Saigon was named Ho Chi Minh City, HCMC, the central or "old" part is still almost universally referred to as "Saigon". For example, the central railway station is signed Ga Sai Gon (*ga* being Vietnamese for the French *gare*, station), and one of the largest universities in the country, founded under the new regime in 2007, is the University of Saigon.

with a group of other passengers to do a little sightseeing in the city centre. While the CBD really was within walking distance it was very hot and humid and so we set off by taxi, asking that we be dropped off at the Central Post Office: my research had shown it was more or less at the centre of the CBD and of what we might hope to see on a short visit. The Central Post Office is one of the more important colonial buildings in the city and was completed in 1890, its unusual glass and metal barrel-vaulted ceiling said to be designed by Gustave Eiffel, he of the famous tower in Paris. The Post Office looks across a handsome tree-lined square to the cathedral of *Notre Dame*, completed ten years earlier and built of materials entirely imported from France, bricks from Toulouse, roof-tiles from Marseilles, stained-glass windows from Chartres, the six bronze bells cast in Le Mans and the large clock in the main façade, still keeping perfect time, built in Besançon.

The tree-lined street leading back to the river from the cathedral square, formerly the rue Catinat and now Dong Khoi street, beckoned to us as we emerged from the cool of the cathedral and so we sauntered along past the chic tourist-oriented shops as far as the Le Loi boulevard intersection where, thankfully, we found the famous Hotel Continental with its shady terrace and attentive waiters ready to serve long, cool drinks such as a *Pastis* or even a Heineken. We lingered on the terrace there, admiring the *Belle Epoque* opera house across the road and the never-ending swirling hordes of motor-scooters, bicycles, barrows, cars and pedestrians. As long as one did not have to cross the stream, the flow of traffic was fascinating and almost mesmerising. How did it work? Why were there no accidents, no outbursts of road rage, no ambulance sirens every few minutes…?

Once refreshed we continued walking towards the river, keeping to the shady side of the street, popping into a few of the elegant shops at the behest of the ladies in the group who fortunately did resist all temptations and were "just looking". Then, where Dong Khoi met the riverside boulevard, we stopped for a long, cool pick-me-up in the wonderfully colonial, and almost chilly air-conditioned comfort of the *très chic* Hotel Majestic. After a little rest in those superb surroundings, we set off on foot for the ship, less than a kilometre away and felt, on climbing up the gangway, that the little tour had been a great introduction to Vietnam.

Some of us set off quite early next morning and took a taxi to the famous Ben Thanh Market, where prices were noticeably lower than in the shops along Dong Khoi! Virtually everything seemed available there, including a breakfast *à la française* of coffee and croissants or *à la vietnamienne* of a bowl of *pho* or a myriad of other snacks and street food offered by the many cafés and food stalls in that part of the market. My companions were particularly interested in ready-made clothing and the market certainly lived up to its reputation for liveliness, range of goods and opportunities for endless haggling and real bargains when one was patient, persistent and lucky. I had decided not to do any shopping until a day or so before the end of the holiday so that I would not be adding purchases to my luggage until I was packing to return to Australia. I just looked on and enjoyed the scene! It took two taxis to transport us and all the shopping back to the ship, but we were safely on board, showered and changed before sailing time at midday and so were able to again watch, from the comfort of the air-conditioned observation lounge, the ship's slow transit of the river. By mid-afternoon, we were again abreast of *Cap St Jacques*, the river pilot was dropped off to the waiting pilot launch, and the *Princess Daphne* headed northwards, leaving the statue of Christ atop the hill at the *Cap* behind as we sailed along the coast, past Cam Ranh Bay and towards Nha Trang, which we reached the following evening.

Nha Trang is set on a beautiful bay, a scattering of tropical islands strung across the wide entrance protecting the long stretch of beach and the city itself from the open ocean. A range of mountains provides a blue-green backdrop and the towers and cables of a *téléphérique* linking the city to one of the islands add a touch of modern technology to the scene. Nha Trang is one of the country's most popular beach resorts and the wide sweep of the crescent-shaped beach boasts a tree-lined promenade, not unlike the *Promenade des Anglais* in Nice and is already lined with a fair sprinkling of hotels, restaurants and other modern buildings. When we went ashore next morning, we opted, however, to look for "old" Nha Trang, its French colonial buildings and those of the Champa kingdom once centred there. The main attraction is known as the Champa Towers, the quite substantial remains of a temple complex (a smaller version of Angkor Wat in Cambodia, but Hindu rather than Buddhist) on a hilly peninsula jutting into the bay. This central part of Vietnam, like the Danang area a little further north had, a couple of thousand years ago, been settled by Malay people from Borneo and Sumatra rather than by the Han people from China, and the Champa kingdom had remained an independent entity until its conquest in the thirteenth century by the Hanoi-based Han descendants as they moved south.

The ship had organised a shuttle bus to transfer passengers to the city from where it was a short walk to the beautiful park and gardens of the Champa buildings. By the time we got there, however, it was nearly noon, hot and humid and I quailed at the sight of the hundred or more stairs leading up to the hilltop complex. There were lots of people around, both tourists and locals, and I managed to find a seat on a bench under a flowering poinciana tree and announced to my shipmates that I would stay there until they had climbed the stairs, visited the temple and came back down to ground level. There was one other person sitting on the bench, a silver-haired Vietnamese chap who was of about my own age, to whom I gave a polite nod and a *bonjour* [51] as I sat down. And we fell into conversation. It turned out that he had been born near Hanoi in colonial times when all schooling was in French, had trained as an air traffic controller initially in Hanoi and later on in metropolitan France and was now retired. He said that when the French had left Indochina he had been invited to go with them and to live and work in France but, although sorely tempted, he had not wanted to leave his homeland. He had continued working under the new national government but had then opted to move to the south when the country was divided in two and the north became quite intolerant of ethnic,

---

[51] Although France relinquished control of *Indochine* in late 1954, French remained the language of business and administration even though it was replaced by Vietnamese as the language of instruction as soon as enough Vietnamese-speaking teachers became available. The arrival of the Americans in the 1960s, in support of South Vietnam's combat with North Vietnam, saw English introduced as an optional subject in school in the South and by the time the Americans left in 1975 English had replaced French as the first foreign language spoken. The chap sitting next to me had spent his school years and his working life in the French world, had only a smattering of English and seemed happy to speak with me in French, which he spoke fluently.

religious and language differences. With a wry smile, he said that he was of mixed race, (Cham and Han), mixed culture (French and Vietnamese), and mixed religion (Christian and Cham-Hindu), adding that he had come to the temple that morning to meditate... and that he would call in to the Catholic cathedral on his way home to light a candle and say an *Ave* for his deceased wife. I responded with something of my own life, a little longer and not quite as tumultuous as his had been but full of ups and downs, as most lives are, and I was reluctant to leave him when my friends came tottering down the stairs after their tour of the temple and towers. This had been my first opportunity to talk at some length with a local and he had proven to be such a nice, cultured, calm and happy fellow.

The ship left Nah Trang that evening and by morning we were in Danang, fourth biggest city of Vietnam and, like Nha Trang, located on a wide bay lined with gleaming white sand beaches and backed by a high mountain range. The city is at the mouth of the Han River which is spanned by a number of rather extraordinary bridges, one of them, a suspension bridge nearly a kilometre long, being spectacularly illuminated that night as we sailed away. The port is at the southern end of the great curve of the bay, tucked into the lee of a rocky promontory, and it involved a thirty-minute shuttle bus ride for passengers to cross that bridge and to get to the CBD. The centre of the city seemed to be in the throes of a frenetic building boom and my hopes of finding a wealth of French colonial buildings were dashed. Nearly everything that was not being demolished or renovated was of concrete, glass and steel! We did find the cathedral, built in 1923 in a sort of low-flying Gothic style and painted an incongruous but surprisingly attractive pale pink! Perhaps it was the pleasant garden setting, with shade trees and benches for weary pedestrians, that made it seem so appealing! From that welcome oasis, it was a short walk to the Museum of Cham Sculpture, dating from a few years earlier than the cathedral and housed in an exquisite purpose-built building designed by French architects and incorporating the best of art deco, colonial and Cham styles. I found the building far more interesting than the contents! We then took a taxi back to the centre of town where we joined the ship's bus tour to Hoi An for lunch and a bit of shopping. Hoi An was the main port of the Cham kingdom centuries ago and, although the river silted up and the port faded into insignificance, the pretty little town grew into a popular watering place in colonial times and is a favourite stop on current tourist itineraries. Hoi An is, moreover, one of the best places in Vietnam to shop for clothing, its tailors reputedly among the best in the country. Some of our group set off shopping as soon as they alighted from the bus but the more sensible ones, myself included, headed for the riverside walk, which was dotted with eating places large and small, grand and modest, with cuisines ranging through Vietnamese, French, Chinese, Japanese, Indian and fusion. There were even hamburgers and fries on offer, a legacy no doubt of the American troops at nearby China Beach! After a couple of hours in Hoi An, we were hustled back to the tour bus for the drive back to the ship. We made a short stop in the nearby Marble Mountains, a low range of limestone and marble mountains separating Hoi An and Danang, in which there are many caves, tunnels, quarries and shrines... and a phalanx of determined stall-keepers at the car park offering a vast range of marble nick-nacks to unwary tourists (marble weighs heavily on airport excess luggage scales)! And so we made it safely back to the *Princess Daphne* in time for a shower and dinner before sailing away after dark and leaving the lights of Danang and that glittering bridge behind us.

Our next port of call was Halong Bay, the almost mythical *Baie d'Along* of colonial Indochina. The bay is in the northwest part of the Gulf of Tonkin, close to Haiphong, and extends over an area of 1,500-square kilometres, (the size of Greater London) and contains nearly two thousand islands, islets and rocky outcrops mostly covered in dense green jungle. The waters of the bay, once you are away from the built-up areas, are of a beautiful turquoise colour on a sunny day and the bay and the islands are often wreathed in coils of sea mist and fog on others. We arrived at around midday on a calm, very still day, with the mist slowly rising and dissolving and revealing the rocky, green islands as we steamed past, seemingly only a stone's throw away from some of them. By mid-afternoon, we had anchored off the resort town of Halong itself and passengers had until noon the following day to explore the bay independently or in organised boat tours. I felt that cruising to and from Halong on the *Princess Daphne* was enough of the watery wonderland and contented myself with pottering around the fishing port and town and indulging in a decadent afternoon tea in the Hôtel d'Halong. The hotel had been built in Art Deco style in about 1930 and was the most prominent sign of the colonial era and, we were assured, the choice of all visiting celebrities (such as Catherine Deneuve when in Halong for the filming of *Indochine*). Indeed, that film includes many shots taken in the bay that underline its almost ethereal beauty... as well as the capacity of humans to be incredibly cruel to one another and at other times to be noble and selfless. Vietnam and Indochina were pushing me towards introspection and philosophy!

We weighed anchor around midday next day and set off northwards towards Hong Kong, our final port of call. It is a pity that most travellers arrive in Hong Kong by air, as the arrival by ship and to slowly steam across that beautiful harbour is a wonderful experience. The *Princess Daphne* berthed at the Ocean Terminal in Kowloon and I was among the first to disembark, grab a taxi and head for the airport for my flight to Hanoi. As the taxi driver was unloading my suitcase at the airport, I realised that it was NOT mine! I had bought a new case for the trip, a rather unusual black and brown one with two tan leather security straps. I had thought it pretty unique but the one in the taxi boot looked identical while having a different name and address on the luggage tag! I had taken someone else's case... and had left mine on the wharf for someone else to discover and despair over! The taxi driver and I quickly decided that the only thing to do was to return to the wharf: the taxi broke all speed records for the trip back and when we arrived there were still passengers disembarking from the ship and wandering through the luggage hall looking for their cases... and there was my case, alone and loitering and waiting for me. We quickly exchanged cases, put my case in the taxi boot without eliciting comment or protest from any onlookers and sped back to the airport. Phew! I was just in time for my late afternoon flight, and I sank gratefully into the comfortable seat on Air Vietnam's Airbus A320 and in a couple of hours landed in Hanoi.

I was, I think, a little apprehensive about arriving in the capital of a communist country and one with which Australia had not long ago been at war. The airport was large and modern, the immigration, security and ground staff mostly seemed to wear military dress and peaked caps and to be rather unsmiling and severe, but the place was not very busy and with formalities completed fairly quickly we were all soon free of officialdom and out in the arrivals area. I had corresponded online with a small but attractive hotel in the old part of the city which had promised to have a car and driver at the airport to meet me but although there were many such drivers there holding up placards with the names of expected passengers writ large upon them, nobody had a placard showing my name. Happily, there was a tourism information desk and a helpful English-speaking staff member phoned the hotel and enquired about the car. The hotel replied that the driver had returned from the airport unable to locate his passenger and that I should now take a taxi from the airport taxi rank rather than wait for him to drive out to the airport again. So I quickly piled into one of the taxis at the rank, showed the driver the name and address of the hotel which the tourism people had thoughtfully written out in Vietnamese and English, and set off. The driver spoke no French and almost no English but seemed an obliging chap and had nodded reassuringly when I pointed to the address. It was by then after eight p.m. and very dark and the road into the city was unlit and seemed to go through open countryside. Eventually, we reached the built-up area and then began an extraordinary adventure which saw the driver stopping every few minutes and apparently asking passers-by where the hotel was. The streets were unlit apart from the light occasionally flooding out from the lighted windows of shops and houses we passed or from the multi-coloured neon signs that now and then appeared. It took over an hour to find the hotel! Fortunately, the tourism desk at the airport had arranged a fixed price for the trip and the driver very decently made me understand that he did not ask for more. I gave him more, in the form of a handsome tip, and went into the hotel. To my amazement, the people at the reception desk, one of whom did speak reasonable English, said that I had no booking. (Why they would have sent a car to the airport for me if I had not made a booking seemed rather curious but I let that pass and asked whether I could in fact be accommodated). They were not full, and I was offered a very pleasant room with marble floors, private bathroom and air-conditioning but on the third floor and with no lift! It was late, I was tired and I accepted with alacrity; a kind soul carried the old chap's case up the stairs and I fell into bed.

In the morning light everything did seem better. The hotel was a new building in the Old Quarter, one of hundreds of four- or five-storey buildings on one of those narrow but deep blocks so common in Asian cities. The street was narrow and crooked but tree-lined and already thronged with buyers, sellers and shopkeepers by the time I got downstairs for breakfast. The Old Quarter sits next to the Citadel and between the Hoan Kiem Lake and the much larger West Lake and my little hotel proved to be a good base from which to explore Hanoi. I set off on foot in search of coffee and croissants and found that they were available at several stalls and shops a few doors away from the hotel. One of the undeniably good things about the French colonial era was that it left the various peoples of Indochine, whether in Cambodia, Laos or Vietnam, able to produce croissants, pâtisseries and baguettes almost as good as those of France itself! I selected a café on the edge of Hoan Kiem Lake and found it so good that I returned there for breakfast each day. I ended up walking right around the lake, in easy stages of course, and paused for refreshment and then lunch diagonally across the lake in the French Quarter, where the Opera House and the Hotel Metropole were on my "must see" list, as was the President's Palace, the former residence of the French governors-general of Indochina. After a much-needed siesta back at the hotel, I took a taxi to the large West Lake for dinner at a very beautiful lakeside restaurant. The next day saw me take a tour of the Old Quarter and its dozens of streets, each one specialising in a specific craft. The tour was done in a little, open-sided electric minibus, just one or two passengers and the ever so friendly and informative driver and it was absolutely fascinating. One street was full of shops selling only silk and paper flowers, their wares filling the shop windows and flowing out on the street in coloured buckets. Another street sold just those very Vietnamese conical straw hats, another one sold brightly decorated paper masks, another one sold pots and pans, the shopkeepers often sitting cross-legged in the street hammering away and actually making various beaten metal items; another street sold lacquered boxes and trays, another specialised in fans and feathers for decorating ladies' evening wear, another sold paper money and *papier mâché* funerary objects, and so on. It was extraordinary! After that, I adjourned to my lakeside restaurant for lunch and then set off for the cathedral, St Joseph's, a scaled-down version of Notre Dame in Paris with a dash of Vietnamese decoration, and then a quick visit to the central railway station to check on tickets for the overnight train to Hué. The handsome station, opened in 1902, looked to me to have been based on the "Second Empire" plans used for the *Gare St Jean* in Bordeaux, which was completed in 1896. In Hanoi, however, the station had been heavily bombed by the

Americans in 1972 and the totally destroyed central block had been rebuilt in 1976 in a quite different and modernist style... functional rather than faithful to the original design.

All was in order with the train tickets, booked online some months earlier and, in due course, I settled into the air-conditioned four-berth soft-seat class sleeping compartment ready for the seven-thirty p.m. departure. The train left right on time and, for the first few kilometres, seemed to squeeze along a single-tracked street through the suburbs, shops, houses, back gardens, etc. all within arm-reach on either side of the train. After half an hour or so the train picked up speed and the rhythmic rocking and rolling of a night train began to lull passengers towards sleep. I had been told, however, that the three vacant berths in the compartment would be claimed by passengers boarding at Ninh Binh, two hours south, and so I decided to stay up until then so as to welcome my travelling companions to "our" compartment. At about nine-thirty, the train pulled into the station and two forty-ish Vietnamese chaps and a little boy were soon ushered into the compartment by the conductor. They had little French or English and I had no Vietnamese but everyone meant well and smiles all round, particularly in the direction of the six-year-old boy, seemed to put everyone at ease and after a bit of chat in improvised sign language and the gift of a three-inch high koala to the little boy (fortunately I had a small stock in my luggage) we all settled down for the night. We were due to arrive in Hué at about seven-thirty a.m. and, as the sun rose at about six, we all woke at about the same time and had an impromptu breakfast together when the snack trolley passed along the corridor offering tea, coffee, *pho* and bread rolls. I had a coffee and a bread roll but the Vietnamese family (father, son and uncle) waved the trolley attendant away. They had brought their own snacks and as they were travelling all the way to Saigon, another twenty-four hours on the train, they would probably have a more substantial meal later in the day. They somehow told me that they were farmers from near Ninh Binh and were going to visit family in Saigon. Among their few items of luggage was what in Australia would be called a "sugar bag" sized bag of farm-grown rice. As it was, the little boy seemed happy with a few handfuls of cold cooked rice wrapped up in a banana leaf and he was over the moon when I added a couple of muesli bars and Kit Kats to the fare on the table. I was in fact sorry to be getting off in Hué and leaving that delightful family group, feeling that I was on the way to acceptance as a friend despite the sad language barrier.

But alight in Hué I, of course, did and when I reached the security checkpoint at the station exit I was asked to show my photo ID. I put my hand in my breast pocket to retrieve my wallet and passport: the passport was there but the wallet was not! Had it fallen out during the night on the train? Was it on the floor or under the sleeping berth mattress? I raced back to the train and to our compartment and searched around, finding nothing. Father, uncle and little boy watched me in alarm: was I accusing them of having stolen my wallet? Sign language was so limiting! The conductor hustled me off the train which was about to move on. Whistles blew, bells rang, flags were waved... and then I felt something unusual in my left side trouser back pocket (which I rarely used), put my hand in and pulled out... my wallet! It had been there all the time. I turned towards the train thinking to tell the conductor and the family in the compartment about my mistake and foolishness but the train had begun to move off. The doors were closed but I saw the conductor through the glass door-top looking at me and then I saw the window of our compartment with the two men and the little boy, anxious faces pressed to the window glass. I held the wallet up as high as I could in my left hand and pointed to it and myself with my right hand and then with my right hand tried to say, in sign language, "So sorry! Silly old me! Goodbye, Thank you!" And by then the train was gathering speed and they were gone.

It was not a happy ending to my contact with North Vietnam and, in my mind's eye, I still see the father and uncle frantically searching under the seats and items of luggage for that elderly Australian's wallet; fortunately, I can also remember the flash of delight on their faces at the window as the carriage rolled past me and they saw the wallet in my raised hand.

In a rather subdued frame of mind, I took a taxi from the station to my hotel, the historic and wonderful Hotel Saigon-Morin, and to my surprise was able to check in early (it was not long after eight a.m.) to a beautiful room. After showering away the cares of the overnight train, I had an excellent buffet breakfast in the splendid dining room overlooking the river and was soon ready to tackle sightseeing duties. Hué is the third-largest city in Vietnam and in 1802 replaced Hanoi as the capital of the country. The chief sight to see is the Citadel, more accurately referred to as the Forbidden City as it is, in fact, a walled compound containing a fort and a royal palace in the form of a series of ornate pavilions, pleasure gardens and administrative buildings. Built in the early 1800s it was, like the much older Citadel in Hanoi, modelled on the Forbidden City in Beijing. The Citadel in Hué was badly damaged by the French army in the 1880s and by North

Vietnam and the Americans in the war of the 1970s, but restoration is afoot and a visit is already well worthwhile. The Perfume River divides the Citadel from the CBD and is itself one of Hué's attractions. I did an afternoon cruise to visit two of the seven royal tombs along the river which has a languid, dream-like quality and brought to mind the evocative opening scene of the film *Indochine* which shows a royal funeral procession slowly progressing along the river towards the tombs. In the evening, I had a wonderful meal in the beautiful hotel and then another early night in preparation for a long train trip the next day.

The railway line from Hanoi to Saigon was begun in 1897 and was completed in 1936 as part of the *Transindochinois* envisaged by governor-general Paul Doumer to link My Tho on the Mekong Delta in the south, via Saigon, Hué and Hanoi, with the Chinese border and even on to Kunming in western China, a total distance of over 2,500 kilometres. South of Hué, the line has to cross the Annamite Mountain range which is over 2,500 metres high and plunges straight into the sea. The modern highway now goes through a six-kilometre-long road tunnel but the train still struggles up and over the Hoi Van (Flying Cloud) Pass at 500 metres, all the time clinging to the ocean side of the mountains, and providing passengers with superb views. It took a little more than two hours to negotiate the pass and to arrive in Danang but as my destination was the hill station of Dalat[52] (which can be reached by direct air

---

[52] The name of the new hill station, DALAT, was coined by the colonial administration and is made from the first letters of a Latin phrase, *Dat aliis laetitiam aliis temperiem*, meaning "it gives happiness to some and health to others".

services from Danang or by bus from Nha Trang) I opted to stay on the train and reached Nha Trang at around nine p.m. I spent the night in a pleasant little hotel near the station and in the morning set off to Dalat.

In 1932, a mountain railway had been opened to Dalat, leaving the Hanoi-Saigon line at a junction near Nha Trang, but alas it had become another victim of the North-South war and had been closed in 1974 and so I had to take the replacement bus. The distance was a little over a hundred kilometres and the road, at times, followed the old railway line, giving glimpses of disused tunnels, rusting signals and some very steep ramps. About a third of the old line had been equipped with a cog system and the Swiss-built steam engines used ratcheted cogs fitting into a third, central, cog rail to climb the steeper grades. The final six or seven kilometres of the line have been restored and a little tourist train does the return trip from the quaint station in Dalat. One can only hope that the government's plan to restore the whole line comes to fruition soon as the trip up by train would attract many more visitors than the rather uncomfortable bus trips do at present. At all events, we arrived in Dalat around midday and I took a taxi from the bus terminal to my hotel, the Hotel du Parc.

Dalat is entirely a creation of French colonialism. In the 1890s, the colonial government had commissioned doctor and scientist Alexandre Yersin, protégé of Louis Pasteur, to explore the highlands of Indochina and to recommend suitable locations for the construction of hill stations where Europeans, troubled by the tropical climates of Saigon, Hué and Hanoi, might spend some weeks on sick leave, so to speak, and recover their good health. It would be cheaper than returning to a sanatorium in the French or Swiss Alps! Yersin recommended a site 1,500 metres above sea level on the Langbian Plateau inland from Nha Trang in the Annamite Mountains and an entirely new town was built there and named Dalat.[53] A sanatorium, villas, hotels, churches, a convent, schools, a central market, golf links, an artificial lake in the centre of town and the cog railway to give ease of access, were all built from scratch, much of the materials being imported from France. A summer home for the governor-general in Hanoi and a summer palace for the emperor in Hué soon appeared both, like many of the other major buildings, in Art Deco style, often with modifications such as steep roofs to reflect local Montagnard culture and style. There are camellia gardens, banks of hydrangeas and rhododendrons, pine plantations, rose gardens, fields of daffodils and tulips, apple and stone-fruit orchards and large market gardens growing asparagus, cauliflower, strawberries and other cold-climate fruit and vegetables. Dalat was a great success from the outset and is not at all what you would expect to see in the tropics. The Palace Hotel, built in 1922, was the grandest of these colonial buildings and is still there, now part of the Sofitel chain and well beyond my budget. The Hotel du Parc, across the road with a slightly less sweeping view, built ten years later and only a little less grand was, however, both affordable and wonderful, especially if one was on a nostalgic trip in search of Indochine, as I was.

Diagonally across the road from the Hotel du Parc was the former Bureau de Poste, now the Café de la Poste, another slightly Art Deco building and offering good meals at a more

---

[53] Similar if less elaborate hill stations were built in the Ba Na Hills, for Danang and at Sapa, for Hanoi.

modest cost than those of the two grand hotels nearby. I spent a couple of days relaxing in this cool climate and colonial luxury, walking the tree-lined streets near the hotel, admiring the many villas built along the lines of those in Provence, the Basque country and the Loire Valley, with a fair sprinkling also of Swiss chalets and even English country bungalows. I walked down the hill to the central market, housed in yet another Art Deco colonial building. I then decided to splurge on a taxi up the hill to the hotel and on finding that the driver of the taxi spoke excellent English and French I splurged even more and asked him to take me on a drive around the main sights of the city. He was such an amiable chap and had gone to Australia as a child in 1978, one of the thousands of "Boat People" who left South Vietnam for Australia when North Vietnam took over the South in 1975. He had grown up in Australia and his schooling had been in English but fortunately his parents had insisted that he maintain his Vietnamese and his French. In middle age, he had decided to visit the land of his birth and had so much liked the way things were turning out that he had decided to invest his savings in a small business, a taxi service, there in Dalat. He said it was going very well, with Dalat growing rapidly as a cool "green" holiday centre for the Vietnamese in the crowded cities on the coast and as a popular stop for international tourists interested in its unique colonial history and architecture. He took me to see the former Lycée Yersin, now a Teacher Training College, the *Domaine de Marie*, a convent and school with a curiously attractive mixture of Vietnamese and French architecture and the University of Dalat, established in the 1950s and set on a huge campus containing both ultra-modern and beautiful old colonial buildings. And of course, he took me to the railway station, modelled on that of Deauville in Normandy, smoothly blending in with the surrounding mountains and the steep roofs of local tribal architecture. Dalat was a very pleasant, calming and cooling interlude in a two-week tour of Vietnam and is a detour I would urge be built into all similar itineraries.

Saigon Opera House

From Dalat, I flew with Air Vietnam directly to Saigon where I took a taxi from Tan Son Nhat airport to the Hotel Continental in the city centre. Arriving at Tan Son Nhat was somehow much more relaxing than arriving in Hanoi had been. The airport was more crowded and much busier and the traffic on the road into the city was immediately and constantly chaotic and yet the mood was lighter, brighter, far more welcoming. By the time one arrives in the central part of the city, "District 1" as it is officially titled, the influence of a century of French presence is very apparent. Colonial Saigon was laid out on a standard grid plan, with the cathedral and the main post office facing a large central square from which streets run south towards the river, north to the Tan Dinh area and the city's oldest church, *Sacré Coeur*, built in 1877, east to the Botanical and Zoological Gardens and west towards the Governor's Palace (now the Reunification Palace) and the Tao Dan Park. The former rue Catinat, now Dong Khoi Street, runs from the cathedral to the river and was in colonial times the most fashionable street. Along it still are the Hotel Continental, built in 1880, the Opera House (1900), the Grand Hotel (1930) and, at the bottom and facing the river, the top-of-the-range Hotel Majestic (1925). Across the Opera House square (now Lam Son square) is the Hotel Caravelle (1959), famous as the "home" of many news correspondents during the war of the 1970s and just a block away on the wide and pedestrianised Nguyen Hue boulevard (formerly the rue du Marché de Fleurs) is the Rex Hotel, built in 1927 as a motor car showroom and service station and transformed into a luxury hotel in 1960, just in time to be more or less taken over by the American forces for the duration of the war! Three blocks past the Hotel Rex is the famous Ben Thanh Market and two blocks north is the former *Hôtel de Ville* (town hall), another of the city's architectural treasures. So, by being based at the Hotel Continental, I was well placed to "do" Saigon, or central HCMC, on foot over the following few days.

There is so much to see in Saigon that I decided to omit visits to the Chu Chi tunnels, the War Remnants Museum and other reminders of the terrible years of war the city endured before the departure of the Americans in 1975. I also tended not to be attracted to the amazing modernisation of the city and the frenzy of building going on all over the place: we see enough of that at home in Australia! What I was attracted to and did admire was what is left, and indeed is now being carefully preserved, of pre-American Saigon, the Vietnamese and French colonial, both the architectural and the cultural legacies of earlier times. The Jade Emperor pagoda, the Xa Loi pagoda, the Central Mosque, the Mariamman Hindu temple and of course Notre Dame cathedral illustrated the range of the city's religious traditions and were all easily visited and were obviously popular destinations with the locals as well as with tourists. I didn't get as far as the main Cao Dai temple, which is quite a way out of town and the centre of that very Vietnamese and very eclectic religion, but I did get the impression that, at least in the south, religious beliefs are seen as in no way incompatible with nationhood, modern society or living happily. I enjoyed a show at the Water Puppet theatre that seemed in a way similar to the Miracle Plays of Europe and the Punch and Judy shows in England, and I also went to a surprisingly good presentation of Delibes's ballet *Coppélia* in the beautiful Opera House. The Opera House is apparently spreading its wings well beyond opera and ballet and now also presents concerts and musicals showcasing local artists and composers as well as a sort of Vietnamese version of the *Cirque du Soleil*! The building itself is a must for visitors to the city and to be able to see a show as well as the building is really icing on the cake!

The Vietnamese seem, in many ways, to present the best combination of Asian and French cuisines that I have seen and the only problem when mealtimes came around was selecting one from among the multitude of excellent choices available.

The Nguyen Hué boulevard, the rue Pasteur[54] and Dong Khoi are streets with many eateries of both Vietnamese and other cuisines and the *Restaurant La Fourchette*, thirty metres or so off Dong Khoi, offers great French cuisine in a beautiful setting. I also had great meals in the Hôtel Continental, where *cuisses de grenouilles à la crème* was one memorable dish; for an *apéritif* or a *digestif* while watching the world go by you can't beat the rooftop bars of the Caravelle and especially the Rex Hotel, with fabulous views of the city, particularly at night, but at similarly fabulous prices.

I had planned to include visits from Saigon to the Mekong Delta and to the beach at Mui Né in this trip, but Saigon proved to be so interesting that I abandoned the delta and spent two nights at the Coco Beach resort in Mui Né, right on the edge of the South China Sea. The train takes four hours to do the trip from Saigon to the terminus at Phan Thiet and then there is a bus or taxi ride of a few kilometres to the seaside village of Mui Né, really a stretch of the coast road with an interesting fishing port at one end and with hotels, restaurants and so on along the way. The Coco Beach resort was on the ocean side of the road and consisted of individual units disguised to look like thatched huts and set in sprawling tropical gardens running down to a long white sand beach. There was a central

---

[54] In 1975, when the North Vietnamese drove the Americans and the South Vietnamese government out of Saigon, the city was re-named HoChiMinhVille and all the streets, well almost all, were renamed too. The rue Pasteur was one street named after a French personality admired by all Vietnamese and its name was retained. The same applies to the seventeenthcentury French missionary and scholar Alexandre de Rhodes and to the nineteenthcentury French biologist Albert Calmette, the streets named in their honour still bearing their names.

swimming pool, if the ocean seemed a bit rough, as well as a beachside bar and restaurant. The French-speaking manager and staff were friendly and efficient and I found it to be a perfect place to rest and recover after the crazy pace of life in Saigon. And it was at the Coco Beach that I managed to bring my travel notes up to date before taking the train back to Saigon, one more night at the Hotel Continental and then a flight home to Australia. The flight was due to leave Tan Son Nhat at midnight and so the hotel arranged for a car to collect me at nine p.m. The driver turned out to be an elderly French-speaking chap, the streets were relatively quiet and before heading out to the airport and without any prompting from me, the driver did a "city circle" of the main sights: down Dong Khoi to the river and the Hotel Majestic, along the riverside drive to the Bitexco Tower and the Ho Chi Minh Museum, up Nguyen Hue Boulevard to the Hotel de Ville, a right turn then to drive past the cathedral and the post office, then two left turns to take us past the Reunification Palace and then on to the airport. As all of these buildings and many others were beautifully floodlit, with illuminated fountains playing at roundabouts and along Nguyen Hue boulevard, with the dark folds of night covering the less salubrious areas, the city looked absolutely beautiful and I thanked the driver for taking me on this farewell tour of the hometown of which he was so obviously very proud.

It had been a marvellous trip and I think Australians are lucky to have such a wonderful holiday destination so close: Vietnam must surely give Bali, Singapore and Thailand stiff competition in coming years for the title of "Favourite Asian Destination" among Australian travellers. I must admit, however, that I had made a foolish mistake in that I had gone there hoping to experience *Indochine* before it faded from history, and of course I was far too late. I do not like visiting countries where I am unable to speak with the locals in their own language and wrongly thought that French would still be a widely spoken second language in Vietnam, at least in urban areas. Alas, the twenty years of American presence after the French withdrawal in 1954 seem to have wiped out a century of French influence and to have made English the second language and to have largely replaced interest in *la civilization française* by an interest in Coco Cola, McDonalds and Hollywood. While I had the impression that, in and around Hanoi, France, the USA and Australia are still regarded with suspicion, as opponents, if no longer as actual aggressors and enemies, I felt that the further south one went in the country the less suspicious and resentful the people became. In Saigon, which was actually conquered and occupied by the North in 1975 and where the former seats of government, both national and municipal, are now mere branch offices of the Hanoi administration staffed by northerners, I got the impression that the locals gave a shrug of the shoulder to their defeat, a bit of lip-service to the northern government's propaganda about "reunification" and the "new Vietnam"… and quietly got on with their lives, with surviving, with building a future for their families. I felt that the magnanimity of the people, especially in the south, towards the foreign occupiers, Australian, Chinese, French, Japanese, American and even Northern, was extraordinary and was perhaps being rewarded by the way in which the economy has already boomed and by the way in which the growing prosperity does appear to be spreading among the wider population rather than concentrating in the hands of an elite. *Liberté, Egalité, Fraternité* as a national motto may well prove to be a long-lasting legacy of the French!

(ii) Réunion Island

The first Europeans to sight this island, then uninhabited, were the Portuguese who followed Vasco da Gama's 1498 discovery of a sea route from Europe to the Indies (by sailing around Africa). In 1513, Pedro de Mascarena sighted and named the archipelago which includes Réunion, Mauritius and *Rodriguez*. In 1641, France established its first colony and trading post in the Indian Ocean on the island of Madagascar, at Fort Dauphin. In 1642, France claimed possession of the whole archipelago of the Mascarenes, naming the southernmost island of the group *Ile Bourbon*, the middle island *Ile de France* and leaving the northernmost island with its Portuguese name of *Rodriguez*. A settlement was made on *Ile Bourbon* and slaves were brought in from Africa to develop the coffee and timber industries. A colony was set up by the Dutch on the *Ile de France*, which they renamed Mauritius, but it did not flourish and in 1710 was reclaimed and settled by France. In 1735, France appointed the dynamic and far-sighted Count Mahé de la Bourdonnais as governor-general of its Indian Ocean colonies, based on *Ile Bourbon*, and under his rule the three islands began a period of growth and prosperity. In 1793, the name "*Ile Bourbon*" was changed by the Revolutionary Committee in Paris to "*Ile de la Réunion*".

Réunion lies five hundred kilometres east of Madagascar and just two hundred kilometres south-west of Mauritius. It is twenty per cent larger than Mauritius and almost exactly the same size as Luxembourg but most of the island is taken up by three volcanic peaks, one of them, *Le Piton de la Fournaise*, still very active, leaving only a very narrow coastal strip plus a few small mountain valleys suitable for human settlement. I first went to La Réunion in 2004, travelling on the overnight ferry from Mauritius. It was a pleasant trip and I got a good night's sleep in a comfortable cabin and was up early next day to see the landfall and to watch the pilot coming on board. When approached from the east, the island seems to rise up out of the sea very abruptly and to be ringed by cliffs rather than by a coral reef and palm-fringed beaches as usually expected in the tropics. There is, in fact, no natural harbour anywhere around the coast of the island and for the first three hundred years of settlement, ships had to anchor offshore and hope for calm weather. Passengers and cargo had to be ferried ashore from the sailing ships by using small dinghies and barges and running them aground on the pebbles of small coves. In 1870, once he had completed the Suez Canal, the French engineer Ferdinand de Lesseps applied his mind, his men and his machines to solving the problem and was able to dredge and build an artificial harbour in the mouth of a short, wild torrent that cascaded into the ocean after heavy rains in the mountains. As the ferry approached this port, Pointe des Galets (Stony Point), we could see that there was a quite narrow entrance between two massive concrete breakwaters jutting out into the ocean, prolongations of what had been the two banks of the stream. Inside the opening, a third breakwater seemed to bar the way but the ship did a ninety-degree turn to starboard and was soon berthed in the inner harbour's deep water, protected by high, thick masonry walls from the vagaries of the open Indian Ocean.

Once the harbour had been completed in the 1880s the Messageries Maritimes Company, the French equivalent of Britain's P&O Line, (both companies having been established to guarantee the transport of mail, passengers, cargo, civil servants and troops between motherland and colonies), inaugurated a regular steamer service linking Marseille with Réunion via the Suez Canal. A little later the service was extended to Australia, New Caledonia and Tahiti with the introduction of steamships bigger and faster than those of P&O of the day[55]. While the harbour was being built, a railway line linking the new port to Saint-Denis, the main town, was built and was gradually extended to almost circle the island, omitting only the fifty kilometres or so of south-eastern coastline along the flank of the ever-rumbling volcano. All these words to explain just how mountainous and even forbidding the island seems when approached by sea (which of course most people do NOT do in these days of jet aircraft but which I certainly did and which the French settlers did for three hundred years).

I was met at Le Port by Jean, the host of the B&B I had booked and was driven in his snazzy red sports car to the beach resort of Saint-Gilles-les-Bains. I would have preferred to do the trip by train but alas, what must have been a spectacular train line had been abruptly closed down after ninety years of service and "the authorities" had begun "discussions" as to a suitable replacement form of public transport. As a temporary measure, buses were introduced and fifty years later those discussions are continuing! The big problem is that there was no road, and no room to build a road, along the coast from Le

---

[55] In the 1880s, the Messageries Maritimes ships were particular rivals of the P&O liners on the route from Europe via Suez to Australia. In 1885 the MM liner *Melbourne* and the P&O liner *Paramatta* raced one another between Suez and Aden, the *Melbourne* overtaking and then circling the *Paramatta*, dipping its flags in mock salute, and then disappearing over the horizon.

Port to Saint-Denis, a stretch of twenty kilometres of towering cliffs plunging into the ocean with no coastal plain and only occasional narrow rocky strands at the base. The single-track railway had been able to squeeze its way along these narrow ledges and where there was no more ledge the train headed in to one of the many tunnels chipped out of the mountains. After ten years of arguing, the railway bed was turned into a road but the ever-increasing number of vehicles on the island and the propensity of the cliffs to shudder and dislodge rockfalls on to passing motorists forced "the authorities" to look for a new solution. In 2009, a completely new road on a great viaduct a hundred metres out to sea from the base of the cliff was begun... and as I write, in 2020, is still a-building!

The road along the coast southwards from Le Port to Saint-Gilles was not quite so scary, even when being driven in a fast sports car open to the fresh air, as along the west coast of the island there is a bit of a coastal plain, rarely a kilometre wide but wide enough for some good beaches, a good road, the old railway line, and a narrow strip of urban development. My host had a beautiful two-storey apartment on the upper floors of a modern building just a short walk from both the beach and the seaside village, which was well equipped with shops, supermarkets, bars, restaurants, nightclubs, hotels and even a casino. I had asked for dinner, bed and breakfast for the week and so did not really need to go to Saint-Gilles very often. There was one other guest in the apartment and, along with the host's partner that made for great evenings when the four of us would begin with an *apéritif* on the terrace followed by a wonderful home-cooked meal, fine wines and endless friendly chat about the island and about the *métropole*... the other guest was a *métropolitain*, i.e., from the French mainland.

Réunion's tourism authority advertises the place, in the French-speaking world, as *"L'île intense"*. They are pushing the many opportunities there are for intense and extreme sports, like climbing an active volcano or hang-gliding over an extinct one, or swimming with seals and sharks, mountaineering, canyoning, caving, crawling along lava tubes and other things I would never think of doing. The topography of the place does lend itself to such adventures. The roughly circular island is very little more than the tops of three volcanoes, one very active and two long extinct, rising up out of the sea. The craters of the two extinct ones have collapsed and are called *cirques*, or circuses into which intrepid hikers can go bushwalking. Because this is a tropical island, the *cirques* are full of rainforests, lush undergrowth and waterfalls. In between the three peaks, there are valleys and plateaux of arable land and there are a few small patches of arable land along parts of the coast. Harvesting sandalwood and other exotic timbers was one of the early industries of the colony and cultivating coffee, sugar cane and vanilla also became important. Slaves provided the basic labour force until the French Revolution, many of them coming from Madagascar and the great African slave trading centres in Zanzibar and Mombasa. The farms and plantations would, I think, never have been very large and there are no great slave-funded mansions like George Washington's *Mount Vernon* or Thomas Jefferson's *Monticello* (or Scarlet O'Hara's *Tara*) to see as there are still in the USA. But nonetheless, there are lots of interesting things to see and do.

Saint-Denis, with a population of 200,000 and on the north coast, is the capital or *préfecture* of the island and there are *sous-préfectures* in the towns of Saint-Paul, population

170,000, Saint-Pierre, 84,000 and Saint-Benoit 38,000 in the west, south and east. A string of small towns and villages, almost all bearing the name of a Christian saint, circles the coast and a couple are found in the interior, although those do not have similarly saintly names: the curiously named Le Tampon, the island's fourth-largest town (80,000) is on the western approach to the *Piton de la Fournaise* volcano and Hell-Bourg[56] (2,300), perhaps the island's most strangely named and yet prettiest mountain village, lies in the *Cirque de Salazie* at over 1,300 metres. I made several day trips by bus to major places of interest, beginning with one to Saint-Denis, which involved the thirty kilometres long drive along the "old" *Route du Littoral*, keeping a nervous eye on the cliffs along the inland side of the road for falling rocks and sudden waterfalls after heavy rain. Though the road is very scenic I was glad to get to the end of it, both going to and coming home from the city. Saint-Denis was a little disappointing, with many rather neglected-looking, mostly two-storeyed timber buildings in the old part of town on the flat strip of land near the sea, backed by a sprawl of mostly unremarkable new, white high-rise buildings on the foothills of the great volcanic peaks that loom in the background. On the other hand, there are some beautiful

Le Tampon

---

[56] Named after Governor Louis de Hell, born in Alsace, and not after any resemblance between the mountain-top village and the underworld, volcanic or other.

colonial mansions in town, especially along the rue de Paris, and some fine old public buildings such as the town hall, the cathedral and the former headquarters of the French East India Company, now the *préfecture*. There are lots of colourful small houses in a vaguely Créole style, often with lush tropical gardens and masses of bougainvillaea tumbling over the fences. The fine arts museum, housed in the former home of the bishops of Saint-Denis, has a surprisingly rich collection of sculptures and paintings including works by Cézanne, Chagall, Gaugin, Picasso and Renoir, and the beautiful building itself is worth the detour. There are some very fine botanical gardens, the Jardins de l'Etat, and the promenade along the seashore, the *Barachois*, is a very pleasant place to stretch your legs or to have a drink or a meal.

I decided to splurge a little on lunch and made my way up to the Hôtel Créolia, which is perched high on a hill near the main football stadium and has an extraordinary view over the city and the Indian Ocean. It also has the reputation of offering one of the finest buffet lunches in town and testing that reputation was my chosen serious task for the day. I did my best and fully concurred with the view of my B&B hosts that the choice and quality of the dishes on offer was exceptional. The hotel, a modern construction, looks like a sort of vast Disney-esque plantation mansion, but do not despair: it is set in beautiful, manicured gardens on a clifftop, the buildings grouped around a huge swimming pool surrounded by palm trees and beach umbrellas, and that is where the buffet lunch was set out. The food was exceptional as was the setting and I was reluctant to leave and to do anything more with the afternoon. Indeed, when I returned to Réunion a few years later for a two-night stopover between Australia and Africa, the Créolia was my immediate choice. So much for my first day of sightseeing: I did make it back to Saint-Gilles and my B&B in time for a snooze on the terrace before perking up and joining the others for another friendly evening meal.

The next day, I took the bus to Saint-Pierre for lunch after which I visited the rum distillery and museum of one of the family companies that have been in the sugar cane industry for over a century. Recently revamped and expanded as *Le Saga au Rhum*, it is an excellent presentation. Back to base at a more respectable hour for another nap and dinner and then, the following day, a long bus trip up into the mountains to the former spa village of Hell-Bourg. It took an hour to get into Saint-Denis where I had to change bus and then two hours for that second bus to climb up into the *Cirque de Salazie* and to Hell-Bourg, negotiating I don't know how many hairpin bends and passing numerous waterfalls and lookouts or *belvédères* as the French call them. Hell-Bourg really is a mountain village and there is not much to do other than to admire the mountain views, the sub tropical gardens, the Créole architecture... and to have lunch. After a little walk around to admire what needed to be admired, I had an excellent curry, almost a national dish on Réunion, on the terrace at *Chez Alice* and answered promptly when our friendly bus driver, who had also had lunch there, summoned us with "all aboard" and we set off down the mountain, back to Saint-Denis, then along that terrifying *Route du Littoral* and back to safety at Saint-Gilles.

With some organisational help from my B&B hosts and the local tourist bureau, I was next day picked up at about six o'clock in the morning and set off with seven other tourists in a spanking new minibus for a guided day tour of the volcano, *La Fournaise* (the Furnace). It was a long drive around the coast from Saint-Gilles in the north-west, through Saint-Pierre in the south and on to Le Tampon in the south-east, and then up the western slopes of the mountain to the viewing point at the *Pas de Bellecombe*, which we reached at about nine a.m. Any later and there would have been, we were assured, a high probability of clouds forming, crowning the mountain, and blocking the view. And the view was extraordinary. The lookout was on the edge of a cliff or *rampart* as the locals say, the edge of the caldera which was about ten kilometres across. Rising up in the centre was the present cone of the volcano, another "mountain" about four hundred metres high from the base of the caldera, from which wisps of smoke drifted up. The fitter and braver visitors, and there were many other vehicles in the car park when we arrived, set off walking down into the base of the caldera and then faced a three-kilometre slog across the ash and cooled lava to the base of the central cone, passing a smaller and dormant cone on the way. They were able to climb right to the top and to look down into the active crater. I did not attempt the walk across the caldera and was content to just admire the incredible scene. It was almost lunar-like and very disorienting, but not frightening, as the *Fournaise* is a sort of polite volcano, always giving notice of impending eruptions and never emitting poisonous gases or catapulting hot rocks at sightseers. We had hot coffee and brioches at the *Gîte du Volcan*, which were very welcome after our pre-breakfast start and as it was very cold outdoors, and just before midday we all climbed into our minibus and set off down the mountainside, turning towards Saint-Benoît on the northern coast once we got to the main cross-island road. The day tour package included lunch at *Le Relais des Plaines*, a quaint little Créole restaurant in a village called La Plaine des Palmistes and that turned out to be a delightful stop with good food and a warm welcome. Then we went on down to sea level and the road along the north coast to Saint-Denis and the dreaded *Route du Littoral* back to Saint-Gilles and "home". It had been a very long day, a wonderful day, but I was certainly ready for my dinner, BED and breakfast.

I spent the following day relaxing on the terrace and around Saint-Gilles-les-Bains, which is really the best-equipped beach resort on the island. I had a light seafood lunch at a great restaurant right on the beach, *Le Bénitier*, suggested by my hosts. The only downside was the cost: as in New Caledonia and Tahiti, those other exotic bits of France *Outremer*, "beyond the seas", the cost of living is much higher than it is in metropolitan France, especially for tourists… and that is why I usually try to find package accommodation, such as a dinner+bed+breakfast deal, *demi-pension* as the French put it. By staying in small establishments, such as a B&B, one can save money and support locals rather than the big international hotel and restaurant chains!

Next day, my last full day on the island, was spent with my hosts who, their other guests having returned to Paris, loaded me into that bright red roadster and took me on a complete tour of the island, two hundred kilometres along the coast. We stopped for lunch at a little restaurant called *Les Badamiers* overlooking the sea just outside the village of Saint-Joseph and had a wonderful selection of Créole dishes, which Jean had chosen when making a reservation the evening before. It seemed a long way to go for a meal but he assured me that *Les Badamiers* offered the best Créole cooking on the island. We then continued on along the coast across the stretch of road just reopened after being covered by a lava flow of the recent eruption to the villages of Saint-Rose and then Le Bras

Panon. There we made a quick visit to the co-operative of local vanilla growers, *"Provanille"*, where the cultivation, pollinating, harvesting and processing of that fragrant flower is cleverly explained and where visitors are gently tempted to purchase all sorts of vanilla-linked products. There were also co-operatives for small-scale plantations of geraniums, *vétiver* and tea up in the highlands but time did not permit for any further detours. And so we made our way back to Saint-Gilles-les-Bains taking, just to show me, the *route de la montagne*, an inland road between Saint-Denis and the port which, while avoiding the eleven kilometres of scary coastal road, involved thirty kilometres of switchbacks up, over and then down the far side of the mountain promontory before reaching Le Port and Saint-Gilles. It had been a long but delightful day and I had enjoyed lounging across the back seat of that smart red roadster and in between wind gusts chattering away with my *Réunionnais* hosts. But all good things come to an end and the next day my by now friends escorted me back to *Le Port* for the early evening sailing of the ferry to Madagascar. The ship sailed at sunset, westwards towards the Big Island, and my last view of La Réunion was of the great, brooding black mountains sweeping up from the sea with the myriad twinkling lights of Saint-Denis spilling over the lower slopes like so many fireflies flittering around in the dusk. A wonderful visit to a most exceptional place and people!

(iii) New Caledonia

Nouméa is the capital and largest town of New Caledonia, an island group in the South Pacific a little over two hours by air east of the Australian coast and three hours by air north of New

Zealand. Called *Port de France* on its establishment in 1854, the settlement's name was soon confused with *Fort de France*, the capital of the French Caribbean island of Martinique and so, in 1866, the name was changed to Nouméa. The main island is about sixty kilometres wide and four hundred kilometres long, with a mountain chain running down the middle from one end to the other and reaching over 1,600 metres at its highest point (Mount Humboldt). It is surrounded by a coral reef second in size only to Australia's Great Barrier Reef, creating the biggest lagoon in the world. There are many smaller islands and islets within the lagoon and several large islands not far outside it (the Isle of Pines, the Bélep Islands and the Loyalty Islands). Nouméa is situated at the south-western end of the biggest island in the group, referred to nowadays as *Grande Terre*. While there is a narrow savannah-like plain along the west coast of *Grande Terre*, the mountains and valleys of the central chain run right down to the sea on the east coast, which has a much higher rainfall and is covered with tropical forest. It was Captain Cook who saw the east coast of the island in 1774 and, seeing its misty green mountains as reminiscent of those of Scotland (not far from his birthplace in North Yorkshire), he named it "New Caledonia". In 1842, British missionaries established a base on one of the offshore Loyalty Islands and, in 1843, French missionaries arrived and began a settlement near Balade in the northeast of *Grande Terre*. Both groups were stoutly resisted by the local Melanesian tribes and many missionaries were (like Cook himself later on in Hawaii) killed and eaten, as the locals were both bellicose and cannibalistic. Missionaries from both countries, along with sealers and whalers, had settled in nearby New Zealand (populated by Polynesians) and, in 1840,

Britain proclaimed New Zealand to be a British colony. In 1853, France sent warships to the Pacific, both to protect the missionaries and to proclaim a "protectorate" over Tahiti and its surrounding islands as well as the archipelago between Australia and New Zealand, which they called *Nouvelle Calédonie*. There was at the time no known Melanesian name for the islands, each tribe having its own land, usually a river valley, and its own language, of which more than thirty still survive. French is the only common language. The name Kanaky, deriving from the Polynesian *kanaka* and the French version *canaque*, meaning a man, came into frequent use only in the 1970s as the name preferred by the emerging Melanesian independence movement. Both sides of the independence argument rather endearingly refer to their island home as *Le Caillou* (the pebble), referring I suppose to the vast mineral resources resulting from its volcanic origins.

My first visit to New Caledonia was made in the 1960s onboard the Messageries Maritime liner *Mélanésien*, on her way from Sydney to Marseille via the Panama Canal. I was a recently graduated languages teacher and, with three other keen young graduates, had enrolled in a two-week summer course of French being inaugurated in Nouméa by the University of Paris (*la Sorbonne*) to help Australian and New Zealand language teachers in their work. Although I have since then made many more trips to New Caledonia, it is that first sighting of the island that remains most vivid in my mind. Soon after sunrise, I was on deck to watch landfall after two days and three nights at sea out of Sydney. The first sign that we were nearing land was the arrival of birds of one sort or another beginning to circle and then to follow the ship. Then a long, dark blue line appeared along the horizon off the starboard bow, a blue line that slowly developed into a long mountain range... the *Chaîne Centrale* of New Caledonia. Then we noticed what looked to be another ship ahead of us and, as we overtook it, we saw that it was but the wreck of a ship, stuck fast on the coral reef, a grim warning to all mariners to look carefully for an opening in the reef before attempting to enter the port. A little further ahead there was a tall white lighthouse, the Amédée light, drawing attention to the location of the safe passage through the reef and welcoming ships to harbour. It took a further hour for the *Mélanésien* to carefully thread its way through the many islets between the reef entrance and the harbour proper and it was nine a.m. before we were tied up at the *Quai des Messageries* in Nouméa.

It is only a short walk from the wharf and the *Gare Maritime* to the centre of town, the *Place des Cocotiers*, a large, rectangular tree-filled park offering a shady resting-place to people shopping or strolling in the rather narrow and treeless streets surrounding it. The flat, gridiron-planned centre of town is largely built on land reclaimed from the lagoon and quickly gives way on the eastern side to steep streets climbing up the low hills which run down the length of the peninsula on which Nouméa is built. Like Sydney, Brisbane and Hobart in Australia, Nouméa began life as a penal settlement, the convicts often being used as free or very cheap labour and it was the convicts who, with pick and shovel, reclaimed the land for the central part of town. Many of the stone barracks, storehouses and workshops, the original hospital and the commandant's residence, can still be seen in an area called Nouville, originally an island (*Ile Nou*) but now joined to Nouméa by a short causeway. The most prominent buildings of old Nouméa as seen from the harbour are the

Catholic cathedral and the Protestant temple, both built with convict labour and both interesting buildings. There are many interesting old "colonial" houses to admire in the older suburbs such as Trianon and Faubourg Blanchot. They are usually built of timber, rather than brick or stone, have corrugated iron roofs and airy verandas to help cope with the tropical climate. The verandas have, in some cases, been partially or even fully enclosed, often with wooden slats and coloured glass panels, and the roofline is very often crowned with one or two wrought iron finials, probably inspired by the *faîtages* which crown the thatched roofs of the circular chiefs' houses in the Melanesian villages.

A handsome and interesting building from the nineteenth century, but a little way out of town, is *Ma Maison*, the home for old people set up by the *Petites Soeurs des Pauvres*, an order of nuns founded in France in the 1830s. It had been opened originally to offer shelter to homeless ex-convicts when the system of penal transportation from France to New Caledonia ended in 1897 but, by the time of my visit in 1961, there was only one ex-convict among the eighty or so old people living there. He had been transported in 1897 as a young chap of twenty-two and had never seen France again. Before leaving Melbourne for Nouméa, I had been entrusted, by a friend of my parents, with a parcel to be delivered to *Ma Maison* where her daughter was stationed after having joined the *Petites Soeurs* at their convent in Melbourne. And that is how I picked up this snippet of information about Noumea's convict history!

The *Mélanésien* had arrived in Noumea a few days before Christmas and the language course was not due to start until the third of January. As my companions and I would be spending two weeks in the centre of Noumea while on the course, we had decided to spend the ten pre-course days seeing something of the rest of the country and had booked homestay accommodation on a property that was both a coffee plantation and a cattle-raising enterprise near the village of Hienghène, nearly four hundred kilometres northeast of Noumea. To get there we took the regional bus service, provided by a minibus which left the town centre at four a.m. in the cool, pre-dawn darkness. It was already almost full of passengers, luggage and mail bags when we squeezed into the last unoccupied seats. The other passengers were mostly Melanesian, Polynesian or Asian folk and it quickly became apparent that the French and other European members of the higher socio-economic classes did not normally travel by public transport! We foreigners, notoriously informal Australians, were at first met with some diffidence but our polite friendliness and valiant efforts to speak French soon won over the passengers near us and by the time we were rolling through the outskirts of Noumea all was well.

I was sitting beside a pleasant chap of Indochinese or Javanese descent in his late teens who explained that he was heading home to the East Coast for the Christmas holidays. He was in his final year of study for the French *baccalauréat* and, as the last two years of the course were not available in schools nearer to home, he attended a large secondary school in Nouméa which had both day boys and boarders and had just closed for the start of the holiday season. He laughed when I lightly complained about the early start of the trip, saying that it was unavoidable if we were to complete the seven-hour bus ride before the heat of the middle of the day (this was long before the introduction of air-conditioned buses) and if we were to arrive at the one-way stretches of the road over the *Chaîne Centrale* in time to be part of the first east-bound convoy of the day. He explained that after following the western coast of the island for about three hours north of Nouméa the bus would leave the bitumen of the *Route Nationale* and turn east on to a gravelled road to begin a torturous climb up into the mountains and over the *Col des Roussettes* (Flying Fox Pass) before descending steeply to the east coast and the village of Houaïlou. There, the gravelled road turned north and followed the coast to Hienghène and beyond, crossing more high mountain passes and several wide rivers, three of them by *bac* or ferry. The one-way stretches of road, where the direction of traffic alternated every hour and the ferries that were hauled laboriously across the rivers by means of a sort of treadmill worked by patient ferrymen, the *passeurs*, greatly slowed traffic and it was mid-morning by the time we reached the pretty coastal village of Ponérihouen where the chap next to me alighted and was greeted by a group of smiling family members. The final hundred kilometres or so along the narrow shoreline and across the wide river Tchamba was perhaps the most scenic part of the trip, with the jungle-clad mountains on our left and the reef-bound sandy beach on our right, both sides of the road being dotted with coconut palms, frangipani and hibiscus among which from time to time thatch-roofed cottages, vegetable gardens and even a few head of cattle could be seen.

It was just before midday when we reached the village of Hienghène, prettily located on the estuary of the Hienghène river, and were met by Jacques, the owner of our chosen homestay, who quickly loaded us and our luggage into his ute and drove a couple of kilometres upriver to his coffee plantation and guest house. In the 1880s, when the local tribes were still being weaned from cannibalism, the colonial authorities had built a small fort at the mouth of the river, garrisoning it with French military, and Jacques's family had been among the early French settlers in the area. The arrival of European colonists had been bitterly resisted by the Melanesian tribes on whose lands the colonists set up their farms and coffee plantations and even eighty years later, when we arrived, the tension between the Melanesians and the descendants of the early colonists was still palpable. We were, however, made very welcome by Jacques and his Polynesian wife, their adult children and by the several mixed-race workers who helped around the house and on the plantation. We were given comfortable, airy rooms overlooking the river and, beginning with an excellent midday meal which had been delayed a little to fit in with our arrival by bus, we enjoyed a week of wonderful home cooking *à la française* at that friendly family table. There were hammocks in the shady garden where one could snooze or read, there was a wonderful waterfall about halfway to the village, tumbling down about thirty metres into a pool of surprisingly cool water where we could swim (the river, we were told, was not suitable for swimming for reasons not explained), and there was a wide sweep of black (volcanic) sand beach around the bay just beyond the village which we seemed to have all to ourselves apart from the occasional Melanesian fisherman. It was an idyllic week of *farniente*, the laziest Christmas of my life!

One memory that remains very clear in my mind was of attending Midnight Mass on Christmas Eve at the nearby mission of Ouaré. The five family members, several staff members and we four guests all piled into the cabins and trays of two old utes (the second driven by the eldest son) and headed down to the river, which had to be crossed by *bac*, and then through the village and along the coast for a couple of kilometres. There was a full moon turning the coconut palms and the sandy shoreline to silver as we bowled along the unmade road, backed on one side by the dark purple mountains and on the other by the silver and grey waters of the bay. The air was warm and still, almost velvety, and there was not a sound other than the purr of the two utes and the strangely hushed voices of our companions. Quite suddenly, the road turned sharply to the left and up a small hill where we pulled up in a wide, cleared space where groups of people were emerging from the shadowy surrounding bush and walking towards the pretty white church in the middle of the clearing. Other low, white buildings flanked the church and its tower... the priest's house, the mission's elementary school and boarding house, a small clinic and the convent for the nuns who helped run the mission. We had arrived just in time to squeeze into places in the church, a large overflow of worshippers ending up in the porch and even in the grounds outside. The inside of the church was very simple, almost austere, with whitewashed walls and plain wooden benches, but the altar was a blaze of light with dozens of candles burning brightly, well-polished brass candlesticks, bookrest and lectern gleaming, and masses of flowers and palms flanking that central focal point. The Mass was said in Latin by a very old but sprightly priest, *Père Rouel*, who we learnt had been stationed at the mission for nearly fifty years and who, though a Frenchman associated with the resented colonists, had earned the respect of the local Melanesian tribes. Included in the Mass was a short homily, probably a precis of the Bethlehem story with an exhortation to spread goodwill, but as *Père Rouel* gave the homily in the local tribal language

I could only guess at its message. The congregation would have been made up of about a quarter Europeans and three-quarters Melanesians and the old man seemed to me to speak as a father or teacher admonishing naughty children, at times sounding quite angry and at times quite affectionate. He seemed to be listened to with great respect and in absolute silence, but his concluding blessing of his flock was welcomed with a very loud *Et cum spiritu tuo* and even louder and more enthusiastic "Amen". We then all streamed out of the church, milling around in front, when suddenly there was a whooshing sound and then a loud "crack"... and the first rocket of a *feu d'artifice*, a fireworks display, sailed up over the church and burst in a cascade of white stars, to the delighted "ohs" and "ahs" of the crowd. *Père Rouel* came out of the church still robed in his vestments and joined in the excitement, everybody seemingly wanting to approach or speak with him... except Jacques!

"He should never speak that native language in the church," he said, and when I asked him why he thought so he said: "Do you know what the natives call us, call you, the white people? *La chose*, that thing, that piece of shit!"

He went on to say that *Père Rouel* was old and delusional and did not understand that his labours at the mission had all been in vain, that behind his back the tribal people laughed at him and his religion and would never become "civilised". I was surprised by the bitterness of his words and although they were not backed up by anyone else in our group, they cast something of a shadow over the rest of my time in Hienghène. I was very ready to return to Nouméa at the end of the week and to start the language teaching course.

The colony in New Caledonia established in 1853 had

grown and prospered, largely through the exploitation of nickel and other mineral deposits while the coffee, timber and other agricultural industries, originally so important, gradually declined. Nouméa had spread along the peninsula on which it is built, the southern suburbs with their bays and beaches attracting the rich and the tourists, the eastern and northern suburbs inland being left for the less well-off. About forty per cent of the population of New Caledonia is of Melanesian or Kanak descent but only twenty per cent or less of the population of Nouméa is. "Up country", as in Hienghène, the majority of the population is of Melanesian descent, although the dozen or so small towns or large villages such as Bourail, Koumac, Canala and Poindimié do include people of European, Polynesian and South-East Asian descent. A number of workers came from French Indochina and the Dutch East Indies in the early twentieth century and from French Polynesia after the Second World War.

In 1986, I spent a week or two on holiday in Nouméa accompanied by my eighty-year-old maiden aunt, a lively old soul and an accomplished artist who spent much of her stay doing a series of exquisite watercolours of the bays, beaches, marinas and tropical gardens around the town. Like my stay in Hienghène years earlier, the visit was marred by an incident one day. We were walking along the Boulevard Vauban below the cathedral when a recent model Peugeot 504 draped with a large Kanaky flag and overflowing with twenty-ish Melanesian chaps slowed to keep abreast of us, one chap leaning out of the front window and waving a clenched fist in our direction and shouting *à bas les Blancs*, (down with the whites). I did not translate his shout for my aunt but feared that the intention of intimidation was clear enough. Fortunately, the car moved on and there were no other incidents to spoil the holiday.

Then in 1988, two years later, there were pro-independence riots in some parts of the country including in Hienghène, where virtually all Europeans (including Jacques's family) were forced to abandon their landholdings and to move to the safety of Nouméa and its surroundings. Calm was restored when it was agreed by the government in Paris that a binding referendum on the matter of independence would be held in 1998. The referendum was held on time and fifty-seven per cent of the voters (eighty per cent of the population voted, a quite high participation rate) voted to remain French. At the request of the Kanak leadership, it was agreed that a second referendum would be held and even a third one should independence not be supported at the second referendum. The second referendum was held in October 2020 and fifty-three per cent voted to remain French, a clear but slightly smaller majority. Most Kanaks appear to vote for independence and whether they would agree, after a likely loss at a third referendum, to live harmoniously with the majority of the population who do not seek independence seems problematic. How the archipelago could maintain its present standard of living without the current level of financial support received from France is also doubtful. Politics seems to cast a shadow over this corner of paradise in the Pacific.

I had been in Nouméa in 1988 when the worst of the *évenements* or disturbances occurred, and twenty-one people were killed. Most of the trouble was in outlying areas but a bomb was thrown at a government building in Nouméa a few doors along from where I was staying, rattling my window and throwing up lots of dust and debris but doing little damage to the government building targeted. For most tourists, there was no interruption to the rather idyllic lifestyle of a South Pacific

Island resort with French cuisine and Parisian chic added to the attractions of a bounteous nature and the mix of Melanesian and French culture. There were, however, serious cracks in society arising from the colonial past, the outnumbering of the original indigenous Melanesians by people of European, Polynesian and Asian descent (as of course had happened and to a far greater extent in Australia and New Zealand) and the obvious economic and social disadvantage most Melanesians continued to experience. I hoped, and still hope, that a peaceful solution to the problems would be found. After forty years of visiting both New Caledonia and Tahiti, I have become very fond of this corner of the Pacific and see Nouméa, which is only a thousand kilometres from my front gate in Brisbane, as the ideal place to escape from the confines of the Anglo-Saxon world and the monolingual society we have created here in Australia.

Anse Vata, Noumea

Perhaps this has all become a bit too serious for a "postcard" from Nouméa! Let me add then a little of what might be expected if visiting New Caledonia. You really need to spend a few days in Nouméa itself, where there are good hotels and restaurants in the two tourist hot spots, *Anse Vata* and the *Baie des Citrons*, which also have pleasant beaches: because of the surrounding reef, the beaches here are all suited to swimming rather than to surfing. For the family, Nouméa has a small but fine aquarium and a zoological garden that is worth a visit. For adults, there are two casinos, nightclubs and cinemas. And for those interested in French and Melanesian culture, there are the spectacular Tjibaou Centre, the Bernheim Library housed in a fine plantation-style building, several small specialist museums and a good number of interesting old government buildings along with some fine old colonial houses such as the *Château Hagen* and the *Maison Célières*. There is a very good bus service radiating from the town centre that will take you almost anywhere in Nouméa (but it operates only in daylight hours) and also on longer trips to the country. There is a ferry service several days a week to the Isle of Pines and the Loyalty Islands and there are air services from the domestic airport at Magenta to the small towns upcountry and to the outer islands. I really think all visitors should spend a day or two on the Isle of Pines which has, perhaps, the most beautiful beaches in the Pacific. Try to be there when they are not expecting a few thousand passengers to come ashore from a mega cruise liner, and take the ferry one way for the spectacular trip down through the *Canal Woodin* and take the air service from, or back to, Nouméa's domestic airport at Magenta and fly low over the lagoon and the coral reef for an enthralling display of the range of colours one can see in the sea. A slightly longer trip away from Nouméa can be made by bus or by hiring a car and heading north for a more or less complete tour of the island. That would involve covering about eight hundred kilometres, with overnight stops in pretty places such as Sarraméa, Poindimié, Hienghène, Koumac and Koné. There are some good small hotels along the way and many B&Bs, mostly run by Melanesian families and offering an introduction to Melanesian culture and cuisine. The road across the *Chaîne Centrale* from Bourail to Houaïlou and passing over the *Col des Rousettes* (Flying Fox Pass) is not to be missed, nor is the road along the east coast through Hienghène, with a crossing of the wide Ouaïème river by punt and the chance to see, a little way further north, the Tao waterfall, in a beautiful rain forest setting and, with a three-stage drop of two hundred metres, the highest in the island.

The country is so beautiful, there are so many interesting things to do, the climate is so mild... New Caledonia is the ideal place for a summer holiday, especially when it is wintry elsewhere. Moreover, with very professionally run intensive French language courses available in Nouméa through the government-backed CREIPAC,[57] New Caledonia really is the obvious choice for Australians and New Zealanders, especially language teachers, wanting to experience a foreign yet friendly culture only a couple of hours flying time from home.

(iv) Tahiti via the New Hebrides

I first went to Tahiti in the early 1960s, travelling on the Messageries Maritimes cargo-passenger liner *Tahitien* with three fellow teachers met at university. On leaving Australia, our first port of call was Nouméa, where the ship embarked a number of passengers including civil servants and military

---

[57] Centre de Rencontres et d'Echanges Internationaux du Pacifique. www.creipac.nc

personnel returning to France after several years in that distant French outpost. There were also quite a few local people, both Melanesian and European, heading for the *métropole* for tertiary studies and employment experience or, in the case of the older people, on holiday or even for a first glimpse of the land of their forebears. There were quite a few teachers, too, employees of the French Ministry of Education returning to France after completing a three-year posting to schools in New Caledonia. By chatting with some of them I learnt that a posting to New Caledonia or to the New Hebrides was a much-coveted appointment, as the pay and allowances amounted to double what young teachers could expect in mainland France. Some of them would apply for a second appointment after a six-month vacation and some teachers apparently so liked living and working in Nouméa that they sought permanent appointment there in the colonial education service. There was also a quite large contingent of Tahitians who had been attracted to work in New Caledonia by its nickel mining industry and more buoyant economy and who were returning home to Tahiti and its outlying islands either on a visit or, with a hard-earned nest-egg, to settle down.

Not long before we were due to sail from Nouméa, a detachment of soldiers accompanied by a military band marched on to the pier and lined up at the foot of the gangway. They were just in time to snap to attention and to look very professional as an older-looking officer with lots of gold on his *képi* and *épaulettes* arrived, shook hands with a group of officials, inspected the guard of honour and walked up the gangway, which was immediately raised and secured to the side of the *Tahitien*. The ship gave a loud blast of its siren, the tugs tugged gallantly and moved us slowly away from the pier, the military band played lustily, the honour guard remained stiffly to attention, the civilians on the wharf waved... and we were off. Apparently, the military man, a general no less, was returning to France after completing a three-year posting as *supremo* of all French forces in the South Pacific. Once onboard, he must have quickly changed to civvies as although I remained on board for another two weeks that was the last I saw of the rather dashing red and gold *képi* and immaculate uniform.

It took only a day and a half to steam from Nouméa to our next port of call, Port Vila, at that time the capital of the Condominium of the New Hebrides, a group of islands about five hundred kilometres northeast of New Caledonia and known since 1980 as the Republic of Vanuatu. The islands had been sighted and named [58] by the Portuguese explorer de Quiros in 1606 but had not seen European settlement until the 1800s when English and then French missionaries arrived on different islands, along with sandalwood traders, "blackbirders"[59] from Australia and, in the 1860s, settlers from Australia and France planning to make fortunes from cotton, coffee, copra etc. and from cheap labour! The two colonial powers in the region, Britain and France, prevented one

---

[58] De Quiros landed on the largest island in the group and, believing he had discovered the "great south land" thought to exist in the south Pacific, named the archipelago *Tierra Australis del Espiritu Santo*, the South Land of the Holy Spirit. When Captain Cook sighted the islands a hundred and sixty years later in 1774, he re-named them the New Hebrides.

[59] "Blackbirding" was the practice, introduced in the 1880s, of "recruiting" or kidnapping Pacific Islanders to work as "indentured labourers", or virtual slaves, on sugarcane plantations and other farms and industries in the British colonies of New South Wales and Queensland on the east coast of Australia.

another from formally claiming the archipelago until, in 1906, they agreed to establish a quite unique *Condominium* or joint-rule colonial government. The *Condominium*, or "Pandemonium" as it was often called, lasted until 1980 and the establishment of the independent Republic of Vanuatu.

Port Vila[60] was a curious place in the 1960s when the *Tahitien* arrived. There was no deep-water wharf[61] so the ship anchored in the harbour a few hundred metres from the shore and close to a small islet which had a large verandaed villa on top of a tiny hillock with a Union Jack fluttering from a tall flagpole. That was Iririki Island, and the villa was the Residence of the British Commissioner. The *Tahitien* lowered a gangway to a pontoon at its side and we passengers were ferried ashore to land at a small jetty in the centre of the main street or waterfront drive. We walked the length of this street,

---

[60] Established on Efate Island and named "Franceville" in 1880. A small group of French settlers and a few hundred Melanesians, impatient for some sort of law and order, proclaimed the independent "Commune of Franceville" in 1889, with a mayor or president elected by universal suffrage, but the self-proclaimed republic was never recognised by Britain or France and faded away by the end of the century, replaced in 1906 by the *Condominium* and the name "Port Vila".

[61] A deep-water wharf was built in 1972.

the rue Higginson[62], looking at the sights. The most prominent building was a quite magnificent modern villa on a slight rise and with a tall flagpole in the front garden, a French *tricolor* fluttering at the top. This, we learnt, was the Residence of the French Commissioner, and the very tall flagpole had been installed to ensure that the national flags of the two Commissioners were at exactly the same height!

Back at sea level, we continued our walk through the town and came across our next glimpse of quaint *Condominium* officialdom, a couple of policemen on patrol. One wore the summer uniform of a French gendarme, the other wore that of a British bobby. Presumably one spoke French, with Francophone offenders, and one spoke English with English crims. There was something almost Gilbert and Sullivan about the *Condominium* and Offenbach's "Gendarmes Duet" came to mind whenever the duo of policemen came into view.

Further along the street, we came to the shopping precinct, an open-air produce market with a corrugated iron roof, a small number of shops with signage in French and English and seemingly in the hands of Chinese or Indochinese owners, and

---

[62] I had noticed the Cinéma Higginson near the harbour in Noumea and had been mildly puzzled by the choice of name in a French-speaking country. The same name for a street in Port Vila was equally intriguing and my enquiries turned up the information that John Higginson was actually an Irishman who migrated to Australia in the 1840s and then in 1859 moved to New Caledonia and became a French citizen. He was an adventurer and speculator who tried his hand at many business ventures including sugarcane farming, mining, "blackbirding", and land development. In 1880, he was one of the three founding members of the *Société Le Nickel*, the SLN, which in due course he sold for a fortune to the Rothschild family. He died in Paris in 1904. The SLN is the largest company in New Caledonia today and is one of the biggest nickel-producers in the world.

then two big shops which were the local equivalent of department stores, where almost anything seemed to be available. These were the trading posts, one belonging to Burns Philp, an Australian company, and one belonging to *Ballande,* a family company from Nouméa and Bordeaux. My friends and I were all rather shocked to see how the goods were presented and sold to the locals. Both stores were huge, barn-like structures of corrugated iron, open to the street (there were no display windows), the items for sale being piled on trestles or counters that ran back into the depths of the store. Clothes, household goods, tools, furniture, lengths of material, rolls of chicken wire, umbrellas, footwear, children's toys, books, electrical goods etc. all seemed there but in a terrible jumble and marked at prices that as far as we could tell were often up to the double or more of what we would expect to pay for them in Australia.

There were not a lot of people about, for the main street of a capital city, but it was mid-afternoon and very hot and a nap in the shade did seem like a very good idea. We had a cold beer in the one large, pleasantly dilapidated Hotel Rossi and then took the ferry service back to the ship for that nap in the shade by the ship's pool. The *Tahitien* spent three days in Port Vila loading copra and we spent two of those days at Blacksand Beach, a long hot walk from the harbour (there was no public transport and we decided to exercise our legs rather than to open our wallets and use a taxi). Fortunately, we had discovered that strength for these long walks could be built up or recovered, as necessary, with a cold beer or two in Harry's Bar, an atmospheric little shack on rue Higginson. We never met Harry and I suspect that he lived in Venice or in the imagination of Ernest Hemingway, but the place was run by a very friendly but strange middle-aged Frenchwoman. She wore a wide-brimmed brown hat, covered in brown velvet bows and brown birds' wings all the time, indoors, and rattled as she moved about the bar, her long, dangly earrings and many strands of amber-coloured bead and glass necklaces and bracelets clinking with every movement she made. She was quick to urge us to wear big straw hats at the beach and to use lots of sunscreen and to drink plenty while in the Tropics. At times, she seemed to be mothering us but at other times she let slip that she was simply a very astute businesswoman, ensuring that we would do our drinking in her bar rather than down at the Hotel Rossi. Alas, I have forgotten her name, but she was fun!

On the third day, we did arrange with a taxi man to take us to a white sand beach, a half-hour drive over the hills from Port Vila, and to collect us later in the afternoon. We bought the ingredients of a picnic lunch in the town (where happily there was a French boulangerie selling excellent bread and right next door another French shop where we found cheese, olives, ham and wine) and we had a great day. The beach was of pure white sand, tree-lined and with plenty of shade, deserted apart from a couple of Melanesians fishing from their small outrigger canoe and the water was crystal clear. Closer to the town, where there was no sewage system and an inadequate network of septic tanks, the beaches were horribly polluted by the local practice of building "the smallest room in the house" at the end of a little jetty running fifty metres or so out from the beach. Depending on the tide, seashells were not the only things to be found on the seashore!

With the copra loaded the *Tahitien* set off again, our next stop being Luganville, the main town of the island of Santo, the biggest island in New Hebrides. This is the island in the archipelago that de Quiros had actually landed on in 1606. The island and even the town are nowadays usually referred to simply as Santo. In 1961, Santo seemed more prosperous and "go-ahead" than Port Vila: there was a newly built deep-water wharf right by the town centre and that must have facilitated the loading of cargo as we stayed only a little over a day there. There was also a quite delightful hotel right by the harbour and that is where we had lunch and spent much of our time ashore. The ship left Santo in the late afternoon, moving slowly down the *Canal du Segond* between Santo and the small island of Malo and then, once abreast of the lighthouse, turning northeast into the Coral Sea, next stop, after a week of open ocean, Tahiti!

Tahiti from across the Lagoon

Arriving in Tahiti by ship is a magical experience, from whichever direction you approach. The island, separated from its "little sister" island of Moorea by a deep channel twenty-five kilometres wide, rises up out of the South Pacific very dramatically, the highest peak, Mt Orohena, an extinct volcano, reaching over 2,200 metres, is often capped in white cloud clinging to its jungle-covered slopes. When we arrived, it was a beautiful day, the sea calm and blue like the sky and the peak of Orohena clear of cloud. The Tahitian passengers were lining the ship's rail excitedly pointing out features of the islands familiar to them, some laughing, some even crying with happiness to be coming home. And there was a strange and pleasant, even delicious, something in the air: an odour or smell are not suitable words because it was quite heavenly. Then our Tahitian companions explained that it was vanilla, wafting on the breeze from the many vanilla plantations up in the mountain valleys. The ship had, by then, entered the channel between the two islands and we could clearly make out the coral reef circling Tahiti, the ocean swell gently rolling by on our side of the reef and the water glassy calm between the reef and the shore. Then we noticed the tall tower of a red-roofed and white-painted church and when we were directly abreast of the church and aligned with a white-painted marker on a rocky escarpment behind the church the ship suddenly turned hard to starboard and we glided through a narrow gap, or *passe,* in the reef and into the prettiest little landlocked harbour you have ever seen. The centre of the island is totally taken up by steep, jungle-covered volcanic mountains although there are many short river valleys running down to the sea, many plateaux, lakes and waterfalls higher up in the interior and only a relatively narrow coastal strip of land at sea level. The actual town buildings of Papeete were, apart from a couple of handsome churches, pretty forgettable, but the lush green setting of jungle background and the proliferation of hibiscus, frangipani and palms all over the place in the foreground more than compensated for the tawdriness of the works of man. And the handsome Tahitian men and beautiful Tahitian women with their "golden bodies", as Paul Gaugin described them, flower-bedecked lustrous black hair and gracious welcoming of strangers to their corner of paradise utterly captivated us as it had Gaugin and so many others in the past.

My friends and I had not booked any accommodation and as the only French speaker of the group, I was delegated to find something quickly. This little adventure happened long before the invention of the Internet, of googling for information and the arrival of Airbnb. Until late 1960, there was no airport on Tahiti to speed up the mail service, and the Messageries Maritimes ships carried virtually all the mail on their six-week run in each direction between Marseille and Sydney via Panama. There was, however, a weekly flying-boat service[63] between Auckland and Tahiti, via Fiji and Samoa, which did carry airmail and I had written in advance to the Tahitian tourism board and had received a list of hotels. While the other chaps sat at a terrace café having a beer and minding the luggage, I set to work. There were in fact not many hotels in Papeete and very few in our price range and I soon found that all those we could afford, which were not too seedy, were fully booked. Unbeknownst to us, a very large contingent of Americans was in town making a feature film and they had booked out nearly everything. The sympathetic manager of one hotel advised me to try an estate agency that handled short-term renting and the one he suggested did, to my great relief, have something to offer, something I quickly accepted. It was

---

[63] Provided by TEAL, Tasman Empire Airways Limited, the forerunner of Air New Zealand.

a large old house in the middle of a coconut plantation a few kilometres out of town. The plantation was for sale and the house was available for rent, for a minimum period of two weeks. The price asked was bearable and included the wages of staff who would clean, maintain and, if required, even cook! We had booked a return passage to Australia via New Zealand on a German ship due in Tahiti in two weeks' time on its way from Europe to Australia[64], so the timing worked out well. A disadvantage was the distance from town but we solved that by hiring a rather tired old car and using it sparingly to keep the daily kilometres and petrol costs low.

By late afternoon, we had everything organised and the agent drove me out to the plantation followed by my friends and the luggage in the old Peugeot. The house was about five hundred metres in from the main road around the island and was approached along a crushed coral drive that wound its way among the coconut trees. There was a huge, sparsely furnished living room, a kitchen, a bathroom and four bedrooms, each with a double bed, a chair, a table, a wardrobe and basic linen. There was a wide veranda front and back and the whole

---

[64] That ship, a strange vessel built in the USA in 1940 as a cargo ship, had spent the war years converted to become an "assistant" aircraft-carrier and after the war had been converted to become a migrant-carrier owned by the Swiss but staffed by German officers and crew. Named *Seven Seas*, it made several round-the-world voyages via Panama and Suez and, in 1961, took us from Tahiti to Pago Pago in Samoa and then to Auckland and Sydney. In Pago Pago, we had a few drinks at the hotel stayed in by Somerset Maugham when he wrote his short story *Rain*. The hotel is now called the "Sadie Thompson", that lady being the temptress who so troubled the missionary in Maugham's tale. We had enjoyed the film version, *Miss Sadie Thompson*, starring Rita Heyworth, before the trip to Tahiti and I suppose it had coloured our expectations of both Tahiti and Samoa!

building, though of timber and galvanised iron, was raised on concrete piers three metres high. We could not actually see the sea but we did get a cooling sea breeze on the veranda whenever one blew. The agent handed us the keys and was about to leave when two Tahitian girls in their early twenties wandered in and were casually introduced as Sarah and Léah, our "staff" and Elisabeth, the agent, then drove off!

Sarah was very pretty, Léah less so but the more friendly. Neither spoke any English and so I suddenly found myself in full-time employment as a translator and interpreter again. Sarah explained how the place was run and said that they were happy to do breakfast and the evening meal if given notice a day in advance. So no evening meal that day and did we want breakfast or the evening meal on the next day? We decided not to make any such decisions just then and said we'd let them know either verbally or by a written note around nine in the morning. They apparently lived somewhere else on the plantation and saw no difficulty with that arrangement. Sarah asked us what we would do about the evening meal that day and we (I) replied that we'd drive into town and find something.

Léah then said: "Would you like to go dancing?"

At least I think that is how I translated her question for the others but I had been so flustered by it, by the choice of words and the speed and suddenness of the development that I'm no longer sure of exactly what happened. We four, anyway, perhaps because of my inaccurate interpreting, thought that we were being asked whether we wanted to go dancing and then to "go on somewhere". Léah was all giggles at our confusion but Sarah said briskly that when she said "dancing", she meant "dancing", and NOTHING more. I translated quickly. She went on to say that they both went to the Seventh Day Adventist Church we had passed on our way and that the church tolerated dancing but NOT further fraternising. I can't at this stage remember her exact words, in French, but I think she tried to stress that she and Léah would like us, all of us or some of us, as dancing partners but were NOT looking for friends. It was a strange conversation, made all the stranger by the fact that the girls never stopped smiling while we four, shaken if not shocked, tried to recover our composure. In the end, it was agreed that we would have a light meal and a quiet night on that first day in Tahiti and that we would "go dancing" the following night... and that is what we did the next day and for most of the fortnight we spent in Tahiti.

The centre of nightlife in Tahiti then was *Tommy Quinn's Tahitian Hut* and that is where Sarah and Léah took us. It was high grunge, years before grunge became fashionable. I have read many amusing stories about *Tommy Quinn's*, one of them titled: *The Toughest Bar in the World* by Randolph Wolfe and it was indeed a pretty basic place, a big, corrugated iron shed really, with bits of lacquered bamboo here and there by way of decoration. Wolfe and others talk about it as a bar, a drinking and fisticuffs sort of place, but in the two weeks that we frequented it every second night we saw no fights and no drunks. This may have been because of the presence in town of those big spenders from Hollywood who would have been looking for "local colour" of the hip-swaying Tahitian dancing kind rather than of the waterfront brawling kind. The constant presence in the streets of Papeete, and particularly around *Quinn's* and the waterfront, of large numbers of smartly uniformed and no-nonsense-looking French *gendarmes* probably also helped keep things on the relaxed side of respectable while the American money was in town.

There certainly was a big bar just inside the door and there was lots of drinking, mostly the light blond local beer, Hinano. There was a huge dance floor and there was a fantastic band of Polynesians playing both Tahitian and Western music. There were lots of handsome men and pretty women looking to make some quick and easy money and there were even more people there, like Sarah, intent on dancing. The place was often packed by eight p.m. and it closed on the dot of midnight[65] so Sarah trained us to eat in the middle of the day on "dancing days" and to be ready to drive into town by seven p.m., she and Léah and we four fellows all squeezing into the old Peugeot. She always arrived with a bunch of *tiare* (frangipani) and taught us how to tuck the flower behind our right ear. Anyone, male or female, with a flower on the right was available for dancing: those with the flower on the left side were already taken and had to be approached with circumspection, if at all. The music was just wonderful, the beer cold and cheap and we had the most marvellous times. *Quinn's* burnt down ten or so years later and, like much of Papeete from the sixties, has been replaced by concrete and glass and modern architecture. I made four more visits to

---

[65] When *Quinn's* and the other bars in Papeete closed at midnight another similar establishment, the *Lafayette Bar-Dancing*, opened. The *Lafayette* was out on the edge of town where the sound of its music and patrons was less likely to disturb the slumbers of honest, hard-working citizens, and it remained open until sunrise. Sarah always insisted we return to our plantation when *Quinn's* closed, while Léah always looked a little disappointed at our acquiescence. We gradually formed the view that things were even wilder out there than in town at *Tommy's* but our holiday came to an end before we gathered the courage to demur!

Tahiti over the years and French Polynesia remains a beautiful place, especially once you get away from modern civilisation. But oh, for those good old days!

We did of course see a bit more of Tahiti than the dancefloor at *Tommy Quinn's*. We did a one-day tour right around the island on *le truck*, a real truck with a vertical ladder at the back for access to the open tray and seats around the sides of the tray leaving room for a tiny dance space in the middle whenever the truck stopped and somebody started playing a guitar or ukulele. We took a ferry across to Moorea[66] one day, hired four cycles and pedalled over to Cook Bay where we had a memorable seafood lunch in a small restaurant right on the beach. Cycling back to the ferry proved to be a bit of a challenge! Another day we went to the black sand beach at Matavai Bay and walked out to the lighthouse at Point Vénus. That was where Captain Cook anchored in 1770 to take his astronomical observations of the planet Venus and that is where, believe it or not, we came across the sailing ship *Bounty* along with its crew of "mutineers". The Americans who had booked out much of Papeete were in fact filming *Mutiny on the Bounty*, with Marlon Brando as Fletcher Christian and Trevor Howard as Captain Bligh. We often saw Marlon Brando and his beautiful Tahitian girlfriend (whom I think he married and carried off to California) dancing cheek to cheek at *Tommy Quinn's*. They didn't notice us and we did not intrude on the filming at Matavai Bay and ask for autographs. I remember laughing a little, however, on seeing the sailing ship

---

[66] The inspiration for the Bali Hai Island of the James A. Michener's book *Tales of the South Pacific*, and the Rogers and Hammerstein musical, *South Pacific*.

Bounty, an exact replica of the original, zipping out of the bay with all its sails furled: what was propelling it? It had a diesel engine hidden below decks, of course, and would have been hurrying to some other location around the island where the sails would have been unfurled just for show, if needed!

Another place where we might have seen or met Brando and the film people was at a fire walking ceremony or *Umu-ti*. Alone among my group I decided on the Sunday to go to Mass in the cathedral in Papeete, not that I was feeling religious but because I wanted to hear the music and the singing. The Polynesians are a musical people and while the Mass had been celebrated in Latin, the singing was in French and Tahitian, with the people's voices harmonising naturally in a most beautiful way. In between bursts of harmony and the old familiar Latin prayers, there was a short sermon and the priest spent most of the time exhorting his flock NOT to take part in the "pagan" fire walking ceremony scheduled for that afternoon in one of the town parks. I sped "home" to our plantation in the old Peugeot and told the other chaps about this forbidden ceremony and, of course, we immediately decided to attend. Sarah and Léah affected to be shocked by our interest and had no information to give us but they did advise us to talk to Pierre, another plantation worker, if we really wanted to go. Pierre cheerfully told us all about it and volunteered to accompany us and "hold our hands"! So at about six in the evening, we all turned up at the park and found a large crowd had gathered, some having been there since morning getting things ready. A shallow pit about three metres wide and thirty metres long had been dug and lined with fairly large river pebbles. A log fire had then been built covering the pebbles and it had been fed and stoked all day. When we arrived, the fire had been allowed to burn out and men were raking the hot coals to spread them evenly on the stones. The pit, or path of hot rocks, was now ready.

Pierre explained that we were witnessing a religious ceremony, one that had been carried out there for centuries before the arrival of the Christian missionaries. It was some sort of act of respect to the moon goddess, an acknowledgement of the importance of light over darkness... He seemed to see no conflict between this religious ceremony and those of the missionaries and cheerfully said that "*oui oui, pourquoi pas?*" he took part in both.

The ceremony began, with the elders or priests chanting rhythmically and dancing in line, waving branches of a holy shrub called *ti* (which looked like cordilyne, common along the Australian northeast coast). They then smacked the soles of their feet with the *ti* branches and walked slowly, one after the other, across the hot rocks, turned around, and walked back. The women, who had been somehow kept well in the background, started singing wildly at this stage and this apparently encouraged the men, the "lay congregation", Pierre among them, to follow the priests' example and to cross the hot rocks.

A large crowd of young and old Tahitian men did so, but first of all held up the soles of their feet to be smacked and blessed with a branch of sacred *ti*. Then came the turn of the Europeans and tourists (and probably some of the chaps from Hollywood, but we did not actually identify anybody) and we four joined the queue! I will admit that I politely stepped back several times to let impatient fellows get in front of me (to let their feet absorb some of the heat lingering in the rocks before I had to step up) but in the end, it was my turn to remove my sandals, present my feet to the Tahitian priest for a swishing, and then to walk ahead. "Walk, don't run," Pierre had said and, to my surprise, the rocks though hot were not unbearably so, and I got across without yelling or flinching or hopping... as did nearly everybody else. I suppose the rocks really had cooled down by the time we put our soft, white feet on them, but I remain mystified as to how the first few pairs of feet, those of the three priests in particular, had not been burnt or blistered.

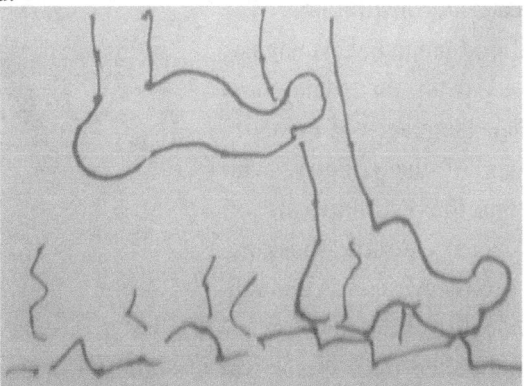

At the Umu-ti on Tahiti

It is now hard to believe that my first visit to Tahiti, when I was a twenty-seven-year-old looking for adventure and romance, was so far in the past, but that is a fact as I was there when *Mutiny on the Bounty* was being made and that was sixty years ago. How time flies, how quickly life goes by, how wonderful it all is!

(v) Madagascar

Madagascar is no longer a French territory but French is still one of its two official languages and is the language of instruction used in all educational institutions. The other official language, Malagasy, is derived from the Malay and Polynesian languages of the early inhabitants of the country, with input from the later arrivals of Bantu and Arabic-speaking people from Africa. Although geographically close to Africa, Madagascar seems to have been uninhabited until the arrival of settlers from Southeast Asia between 300 AD and 600 AD. These people, now known as the Merina, chose to live on the highland plateaux rather than on the hotter, humid coast and from their highland fastness they came to dominate later-arriving peoples, mostly from Africa, who settled in the coastal areas. The first Europeans to visit Madagascar were Portuguese navigators on their way in 1500 from Lisbon around the Cape to India. They were Diego Dias and Fernando Suarez and they landed near the northeast tip of the island, where the port of Diego Suarez was in time developed by the French to become the biggest naval base in the Indian Ocean. In 1641, the French East India Company was authorised by Cardinal Richelieu, Chief Minister of King Louis XIII, to establish a fort and trading post in the south of the island at what is still known as Fort

Lemurs everywhere

Dauphin [67], and in 1750 the local rulers of northeast Madagascar ceded a large island off the coast of Diego Suarez, the Ile Sainte Marie, to the French Crown. In 1840, the island of Nosy Bé off the northwest coast was ceded to France, in 1880 Tamatave followed suit and then in 1895 the rest of the island was occupied and became a French colony.

When I was a student in France in the 1950s, I met my first *Malgache*, as the people of Madagascar are termed in French. He was a dark-skinned *côtier*, a person from a coastal tribe, and like me, he was a student in Bordeaux. His French was better than mine, but mine was good enough to chat away with him and to share, among other things, our impressions of life in France: we were both lonely chaps from far away islands and from lifestyles very different from those of metropolitan France. It was nearly fifty years before I managed to visit Madagascar and, in the interim, the country had become politically independent of France and had then gone through years of civil war and economic decline. I had lost contact with my student friend but was still determined to visit the "Big Island" and to see something of the life and landscapes he had described and had sorely missed... especially in the depths of a European winter!

It is, I believe, best to approach an island nation by ship rather than by plane. The sea voyage allows the traveller time to gently free himself from the culture left behind and to approach the destination with an open mind and in the lively expectation of new experiences and cultures. As a result, I travelled by ship from Mauritius to Réunion Island and after a

---

[67] So named in honour of the then young Dauphin of France who later became king Louis XIV.

week or so there boarded a second ship of the same company for the two-night trip on to Madagascar. There were about fifty passengers on the *Mauritius Trochetia*, many of them Malgache returning home after working in Réunion and Mauritius where stronger economies offered better chances of employment than in Madagascar. I shared a very comfortable en-suite cabin with a handsome young Malgache and had many an interesting chat with him, in his impeccable French, about Madagascar, Australia and the wide world around us. The sea was calm and the ship made good time, arriving off Tamatave/Toamasina just after dark on the second evening and anchored in the bay, the harbour lights twinkling tantalisingly a kilometre or so away.

In the morning, the ship moved to its berth and we all disembarked. In broad daylight, what had seemed the night before to be a mysterious and enchanting harbour city turned out to be the most ramshackle and chaotic port I had ever seen. In the deep background, there was a blue-green mountain range, in the middle background were the roofs and walls of a sprawling two- or three-storeyed town, and in the immediate foreground was the wharf, with disused railway lines and ancient, rusting cranes lined up in front of a row of dilapidated sheds and warehouses. A battered old bus waited for the passengers as we struggled down the gangway with our luggage and once all were loaded it rumbled along the wharf to a large tin shed where we all filed off and entered under the sign *Immigration Contrôle*. It took nearly an hour for our passports to be checked (manually, as there were no computers or other modern technologies in sight) and stamped and then we were invited back on to the bus for the short run of about a kilometre into the town centre.

I hesitated about getting back on to the bus and explained that I had made a reservation at the Hôtel Joffre and that the hotel had promised to send someone to meet me at the ship. The immigration officer or policewoman in charge of proceedings laughed at that and said, "*Pas possible!*" And then in English, to make sure I understood: "Hotel not allowed at wharf. You want walk or come in bus?"

It was by then nearly midday, very hot and sticky and there was not the slightest breeze. I boarded the bus meekly, which then slowly made its way towards town along a road pitted with potholes and between corrugated iron and crumbling concrete warehouses that all looked as if no maintenance at all had been carried out since the French had withdrawn thirty or more years earlier. Eventually, the bus reached what once may have been a handsome, tree-lined boulevard, turned the corner and stopped. "*Monsieur*," the driver called to me, "*Monsieur! Voilà l'Hôtel Joffre.*"

I alighted, watched with some amusement by the other passengers who remained on the bus as it pulled away, and dragged my case through the dust and rubble to the hotel.

The Hôtel Joffre was a substantial, three-storeyed building dating from colonial times. Despite the shuttered verandas on two sides, it had a vaguely Art Deco look about it. It was painted, or perhaps had been rendered, white but was now a little faded or perhaps it was coated with dust from the crumbling buildings around it. I was politely welcomed by the *réception* staff and taken up to a first floor en-suite room which was spacious, clean, comfortable, cool and airy. *Le Déjeuner* had just begun to be served in the hotel's dining-room and, as I had had nothing since a coffee at about seven a.m. before leaving the ship, I had a quick shower and change of clothes and went down for lunch. I had a delightful meal in the large, high-ceilinged room which opened out on to a shady terrace. The cuisine was good, basic French but with local ingredients and specialities available too. In the following days, I took most of my meals there and got to chat a little with some of the staff. The manager was French, the first Frenchman I met in Madagascar, rather reserved, quiet, and eagle-eyed as far as the running of the hotel was concerned. The *réception* was staffed by charming Malgache girls who spoke very good French and did their best to handle my enquiries about sightseeing, transport, shopping and so on. The chef, whom I only glimpsed now and then, looked to be Indochinese, and the waiters and general helpers were all Malgache.

I was very happy and comfortable at the Joffre and quickly came to think of it as "home". After a leisurely lunch and a bit of a siesta, I took my first stroll down the street, intent on finding a shop or Internet centre where I might get assistance with a problem that had cropped up with my laptop. I had not walked a hundred yards down the boulevard before a wizened old man slowly pedalling a *pousse-pousse*, or rickshaw, appeared at the kerbside and timed his pedalling to keep right beside me as I walked. This was just what I had dreaded might happen: having emerged from the Hôtel Joffre I was seen by the locals as a rich tourist and fair game for the impoverished citizenry whether beggars, pedlars or *pousse-pousse* drivers. They did not know that I was more likely to hand over a few ariary to a beggar than to get up into a rickshaw and be pulled along by a poor human being doing the work of a horse! I looked steadily ahead and tried to ignore the old man. "*Monsieur, Monsieur! Montez, Montez, s'il vous plaît! Donnez-moi du travail! Monsieur, Monsieur!*" That "give me some work" was so heart-breaking. I stopped and turned and gave him a handful of ariary, the local paper currency, and said that I was not going far and actually wanted to walk. The poor old chap probably didn't believe anybody would actually want to walk in that heat and he followed me for another few minutes until, fortunately, I came to a forecourt where I managed to duck into an arcade of shops where he was unable to follow. I'd not done my homework properly and did not know that rickshaws still existed in Madagascar: the *cyclos* and motorised *tuk-tuks* of Southeast Asia I could cope with, and even use at a pinch, but the idea of being pulled along by that worn-out old man was really upsetting. To my surprise, there was an Internet store in the arcade where I had sought shelter and in next to no time a bright young chap had produced a USB and other gadgets I did not understand and had my laptop problem fixed. He quoted me a price in ariary and when I paid in euros, and included a few extra, his eyes shone with gratitude and, presumably in response to some coded signal from him, the rest of the staff in the shop gave a little bow, a smile and a "*Merci, monsieur!*" in unison as I left.

Baobab trees

Back at the hotel, I sought advice for a bit of sightseeing the next day and was soon fixed up with a car and driver. When I went down to breakfast in the morning, the driver was already there and waiting for me. He was a nice young chap with a long Malgache name and the conveniently shorter French name of Michel. The car turned out to be a large, old Simca Versailles and we soon set off in the cool of the morning on a day trip to the curiously named Foulpointe, some seventy kilometres north along the coast. Michel spoke good French and a little English, and chatted easily as we bowled along, pointing out the sights and asking me about Australia and kangaroos and I countered with questions about Madagascar and its lemurs.

The lemurs, of various sizes and colours, seemed to be everywhere, sitting on telegraph poles and fence posts, scampering around gardens and rubbish bins. They looked so cute and cuddly, just like possums in Australia but, unlike the possums, they were not nocturnal and seemed quite unafraid of humans. They had become quite an iconic tourist attraction and were almost the first thing that visitors like me wanted to see.

More lemurs

The drive along the tropical coast was very pleasant, with lots of palm-fringed beaches on the ocean side and pockets of farmland and fruit gardens on the inland side. All along the way, there were brightly dressed but often bare-footed people, men and women, walking along the road or working in the fields. I suspect that the simple country life looked pleasanter to the passer-by than it actually was. It was hot and humid, as it is all the year there, and most of the people we passed would not have been as assured as I was of having food on the table and a roof over the head at the end of the day.

We visited the ruins of a fort built by King Radama I before the arrival of the French in Madagascar (it had been built to keep the French and other foreigners away), admired the beach at Foulpointe and then drove on a further twenty kilometres to a small seaside town called Mahambo where we had an excellent lunch of locally caught lobster at the very picturesque Hôtel La Pirogue.

We were a little late setting off on the return leg of the trip and perhaps I had enjoyed a little too much Muscadet with the lobster (Michel did not touch alcohol) and it was dusk when we arrived at the river Ivoloina. The Ivoloina was wide but shallow, so they said, and on the way north we had crossed it by means of a ford, the high-level, all-weather concrete bridge just upstream from the ford being still under construction. On our return, we joined the queue of vehicles waiting to use the ford, mostly trucks and pick-ups loaded with farm produce and minibuses loaded with cheerful country folk heading into town for a night out, so Michel told me. By the time we actually got to the river's edge, night had fallen and it was very dark. I thought that the river was quieter than when we had crossed it earlier in the day and Michel said that yes, it was quieter because it was deeper and no longer gurgling over the stones in the riverbed: we were near the river mouth and the tide had come in! A little more than halfway across the car stalled, made a glug-glug sort of noise and stopped dead. The water level was just above the hubcaps and just below door level. I knew we were not going to drown and could wade to the riverbank but wondered whether the car would be a write-off and whether the rich tourist would be expected to pay up.

I had forgotten that we were not alone: the vehicles in front of us were all crossing safely and those behind us began tooting and honking, their drivers shouting and laughing and waving us onwards. Suddenly, a chap appeared striding towards us from the far bank waving a flash-lamp and holding up a large coil of rope. In a matter of minutes, he had the rope secured to the front of the car and back he waded to the river bank where he fastened the other end to the tow-bar of a large truck loaded with vegetables. To the cheers of the onlookers and other drivers, the truck moved slowly off and, like Aphrodite, the Versailles emerged slowly from its watery bed. Once we were on dry land, the truck driver, instead of stopping, undoing the towrope and leaving us to dry out and make our own way home, simply sped up and headed for town. It turned out that Michel had quickly concluded that the Simca's engine would be too waterlogged to re-start that night and so he had told the truck driver that *monsieur l'Australien* would certainly pay for us to be hauled out of the river and towed the twenty or so kilometres back to Tamatave. And that is what happened. The truck cast us off in the suburb where Michel lived and we pushed the *Simca* into a large shed that served as its garage. I handed over a bundle of ariary and the truck driver took off. Michel invited me into his humble home for *souper* but I carefully declined, not wanting to embarrass him and the extended family gathered goggle-eyed at the door. I asked him to summon a taxi for me, to tell the driver to take me directly to the Hôtel Joffre and to pay the driver the proper fare, plus an appropriate tip, so that I would not have to do any haggling on arrival at the hotel. I gave Michel another bundle of ariary to cover the taxi costs and arranged that he would come to the hotel in a day or so, once the Simca was running again and we would make another trip somewhere. He said nothing about paying for repairs to the waterlogged engine and thanked ME for the *bonne journée*. My suspicions had been unfounded, he and the truck driver had not conspired to rip the elderly tourist off. The Malgache were indeed lovely people! Or perhaps I had undervalued the bundles of ariary I had been handing out?

The next day I spent on foot seeing the sights of the town, such as they were, although the destruction caused by years of civil war was everywhere in evidence and was depressing. I had intended travelling by train up to the capital, Tananarive, high on the central plateau, but found that passenger services on the railway built in colonial times had been suspended because of poor maintenance, so with the help of the Joffre staff, I flew up with Air Madagascar, leaving most of my things in my room in the hotel. I arrived in Tananarive in the late afternoon after a smooth and scenic flight over the jungle-clad mountains and the carefully tended farms up on the plateaux.

The Joffre had booked me in to the Hôtel Colbert in the capital and the Colbert[68] had indeed sent a car and driver to the airport to collect me. Everything went very smoothly but I could see both at the airport and along the ten kilometres drive into town that many people even here in the major city struggled to survive. The car was an old but well-maintained

---

[68] Jean-Baptiste Colbert was one of Louis XIV's chief ministers and something of a financial genius.

Mercedes, and the driver was a grizzled, grey, retired military chap who spoke excellent French and said that he had served in both the French and, later, the Malgache army. It was thanks to his indexed French military pension that he and his family were able to manage financially, he said, as the political and economic situation in Madagascar had been so unstable since independence.

The Colbert was another very atmospheric old colonial hotel and I was made very welcome and felt very comfortable there. It was very close to the railway station and so I was able to walk over and admire the *Belle Epoque* architecture even though I had not been able to buy and use a train ticket. But that was the only bit of walking I did do there in 'Tana. It was almost dusk, the ill-lit streets were full of hurrying people and of beggars and touts and I felt quite intimidated as an elderly, lone foreigner. Perhaps it was my grey hair that protected me but I was extremely glad to arrive back safely at the front door of the hotel. Even there, it was a bit unpleasant as there was a flight of broad, shallow steps up to the glass double doors and the bright lights and safety inside. A uniformed concierge stood guard and, while he did not admit any of the men and women squatting on the steps soliciting sales or help of some sort, running the gauntlet of those poor and desperate people was, for me, quite a challenge. Fortunately, the concierge recognised me as I got to the steps and sallied forth, taking my arm and helping me up and into the warmth and comfort of my temporary home. (Tananarive is at 1,400 metres above sea level and by comparison with Tamatave down on the coast, the nights are quite cool, with temperatures dropping to near zero Centigrade in June, the coldest month. I was there in April and the temperature dropped to seven degrees at night.)

The next day was spent having a quick look at the city from the safety of the old Mercedes and with the guidance of my friendly driver. Tananarive, as the French called the city, or Antananarivo to give it its less often heard Malgache name, or simply 'Tana', for short to everyone, is built on a series of steep, small hills around a man-made lake, Lake Anosy. On top of the highest hill is the Rova, the royal compound and principal site of interest in the city. Originally a sort of fortress consisting of a wooden palisade and earthworks surrounding a number of timber buildings, it had become by the eighteenth century the favoured seat of the Imerina dynasty which ruled about two-thirds of the island. In 1841, Queen Ranavalona I, who had assumed power on the death of her husband King Radama I, had a large, new royal residence built. Though built of timber like the smaller residence of Radama I, twenty years later it was encased in stone, with arcaded balconies and towers added in a rather Italianate style. A grand stone gateway to the Rova was also built, surmounted by a huge bronze eagle and flanked by a very large stone phallus!

The royal succession in Madagascar in the nineteenth century was rather curious. There were two kings regnant and four queens regnant. There were five chief ministers between 1810 and 1897, three of them in office for less than a year, one in office for thirteen years and one (the latter's younger brother) for thirty-one years. Queen Ranavalona I had seized the throne on her husband's death and, to secure her position, had married her husband's chief minister. Her only child was born eleven months after the king's death but was nonetheless accepted as his heir and on her death that child, then a grown man, succeeded to the throne as Radama II. In the intervening thirty years, the queen successively had and married two more chief ministers. On his mother's death, Radama II was thought to be too liberal in his ideas and after eighteen months on the throne, he was assassinated by order of the chief minister (his stepfather!). Radama II was succeeded by his number one wife, Queen Rasoherina. The chief minister was then assassinated by his younger brother, who was commander-in-chief of the army and the younger brother then took over as chief minister… and married the new queen, Rasoherina, who reigned for six years until her death from dysentery. She was followed by her cousin (and number two wife of Radama II) as Queen Ranavalona II. The new queen married the chief minister she had inherited along with the crown and this same procedure occurred again in 1883 when she died and she was followed by her twenty-two-year-old niece, Queen Ranavalona III. By then, the chief minister whom the young queen was to marry was sixty years old and the widower of the two previous queens, so presumably he had learnt quite a bit about how to handle a reigning monarch who was also his wife. After the fall of Tananarive to the French army in 1895 and the surrender of her government (and chief minister-cum-husband), Queen Ranavalona III is said to have tearfully asked the French commander whether she was expected to marry the conquering general. The conquering commander was forty-five-year-old General Joseph Gallieni and the Queen was said to have been greatly relieved on being told by the general that such was not the custom of the French Republic. Ranavalona III died in comfortable exile in Algiers in 1917, her exiled chief minister and husband having died there twenty years earlier.

The whole royal compound including the grand Queen's House was swept by fire in 1995 and almost every building was damaged or destroyed. Restoration is proceeding very slowly and the public is still excluded from most of the compound as it is nearly all a construction site. By far the biggest building in the Rova, the Queen's House still dominates the city from its position high on the hill. Knowing this, we nonetheless drove up the hill if only to admire the stunning view of the lake and city below and of the carefully cultivated farms and rice paddies stretching around on all sides.

After my quick look at Tananarive, I returned by Air Madagascar to Tamatave and was met at the airport by Michel and his Simca Versailles, once again in running order. No garage bill was presented or even mentioned. My room at the Hôtel Joffre was as I had left it, my clothes pressed and hanging in the wardrobe or neatly folded and placed in the drawers and after another pleasant dinner and night at the hotel, I decided to follow the manager's suggestion and do the trip on the Pangalanes Canal on the following day. The Canal had been begun by King Radama I in the early 1800s and had been greatly enlarged and extended during colonial times to provide a safe, cheap and easy form of transport along the east coast, where road and rail construction was proving immensely difficult and expensive. The Canal is really a series of short man-made navigable links that connect numerous lagoons, creeks, and other bodies of water, turning them into a very useful six-hundred-and-fifty-kilometre network now busily plied by barges and boats and all sorts of craft carrying passengers, goods and cattle. Along with four other guests, I met our guide for the day in the hotel lobby after breakfast and we all boarded the hotel's minibus and were ferried down to the harbour where we boarded a quite smart motor launch, crewed by what I guessed were father and son, both smiling and friendly. The launch chugged away from the jetty and across the harbour to an entrance to the Canal and in a very short space of time we had left behind the noise and chaos and pollution of the harbour and were gliding along the calm waters of the Canal. Both banks were covered in dense jungle, broken up by frequent clearings and signs of human activity such as steep-roofed thatched houses, some on stilts, small vegetable plots with people working in them, women hanging out washing, men working on building or repairing their fishing boats and nets. The Canal was really quite busy with traffic in both directions and almost as many motorised craft as manually propelled canoes.

After some time, we reached a widening of the Canal where it entered Lake Ampitabe. The eastern shore of the lake was a fairly narrow strip of land covered in jungle and separating the lake from the Indian Ocean. In a cleared area, there was a large resort which our guide said faced on to a very good ocean beach. On the western side of the lake, just before it narrowed and fed into the continuing Canal, there was our destination, the Hôtel Palmarium and its Nature Reserve. The hotel buildings had all mod cons but had been built to look like traditional, steep-roofed, Malgache thatched houses, set in a beautiful tropical garden. We had lunch on the shady terrace, distracted from the excellent food by the lemurs of the locality who scampered about quite unafraid and in some cases game enough to balance on the veranda railings right next to the tables and to twitch their noses and roll their big soft eyes at us as we ate. After lunch we had a guided tour of the park and, although the tropical flora were splendid, it was the antics of the many different types of lemur there that had us all enthralled. The launch got us back to the city and the Hôtel

Joffre just in time to avoid a heavy downpour: our guide laughingly told us that that was a "normal afternoon" and added that they kept a supply of waterproof ponchos on the launch for such eventualities. Something they didn't keep on hand was a supply of anti-mosquito spray or lotion and as the little critters were in abundance along the Canal I would recommend all visitors to be prepared!

The next day it was time to leave Madagascar. Michel and his Simca arrived after breakfast to take me to the harbour where I was to board the ship for Europe. I said my goodbyes to my friends at the Hôtel Joffre and off we went, bumping over the dreadful road to the port gates. There I had my passport, visa and ticket checked and stamped and then had to say goodbye to Michel and to transfer to a regular taxi as private vehicles were not permitted within the port precinct. The whole area seemed thick with armed guards or police as the taxi drove a few hundred metres to another set of gates and another guard box where we were again stopped. I did not get out of the taxi but passed my documents to the driver who handed them out through his window for inspection. The officer in charge barely glanced at the papers but stared and scowled at me and said something very quickly in Malagasy to my driver. The taxi driver turned to me and said in French that I could go no further until I paid a fifty-euro fee. The people at the Joffre had warned me that this might happen whenever documents were being checked. They assured me that there were no official departure fees or taxes and that such demands were simply petty extortion rackets. I therefore screwed up my courage and said loudly in French that there were no more charges to be paid and that I insisted on being taken to the ship immediately. I added that I was the only passenger boarding that particular cargo ship and the captain was expecting me at that very hour. To my great surprise, the bluff worked; with a bit of a grunt the officer thrust the documents back at the driver without any pretence of stamping them, grumpily waved us through and went back to his little desk. The taxi headed off along the wharf and pulled up at the foot of the ship's gangway. I was about to leave Madagascar!

(vi) Madagascar to Marseille

I had, with great difficulty, arranged to travel by ship from Tamatave to Marseille. The regular passenger services on that route run for over a century by Messageries Maritimes had stopped in the 1970s and I was lucky to secure a berth on the *La Bourdonnais*, a cargo ship belonging to that line's successor, the CMA-CGM company. The ship was of about 9000 tonnes, had six double cabins available for passengers and would take me to my preferred European port, Marseille. The three weeks on board looked like being spent in the company of French officers and passengers, enjoying good French food. So it was with high hopes of an interesting voyage that I made my way up the steep steps of the ship's gangway, followed by my taxi driver struggling with my luggage.

At the top of the gangway stood two white-uniformed officers, an older grey-haired man with a fair bit of gold braid on his jacket and a younger, dark-haired chap who seemed to be the sidekick (and who would, I surmised, have the French title of *Capitaine* for the position which on English ships was termed the First Officer). So, confidant in my knowledge from earlier voyages on French ships that the man really in charge would be, not the *capitaine* but the *Commandant*, I smiled at the older man and said, "*Bonjour Commandant*," as I reached the top of the gangway, "*Je suis votre passager Australien, de Tamatave jusqu'à Marseille.*"

"I hope you speak English," he replied, with what I was amazed to hear was a thick German accent.

"Well, yes, I do", I replied, "but I prefer to speak French on a French ship."

"Ha ha ha," he guffawed, "this ship is French-owned but German-speaking. Do you speak German?"

"Not a word," I answered.

"Ha! Well, the other passengers und mein officer speak German, but English you can speak with me! Now we are ready to sail. Mein steward will show you to your cabin. Go und wait there until I send for you to come to the bridge to watch us leave Tamatave."

What a disappointment! An ardent Francophile since my schooldays in the care of a gifted French teacher, I had been looking forward to spending the three weeks of the voyage in a French atmosphere. Instead, I was facing three weeks with a shipload of Germans! *Les Boches*! Germany had started two world wars and before them the Franco-Prussian War. I did not like Wagner or Mahler, was no fan of Krupps engineering and was not keen on beer or sauerkraut! I had, at that stage, no option other than to grin and bear it so I did as I was told und followed mein steward. Happily, the cabin turned out to be very pleasant, large and bright with two big windows on two sides (it was in a corner of the superstructure, just under the bridge) and had its own tiled bathroom. With a *danke* to the steward for carrying my case (I did know a couple of German words), I made myself a cup of coffee and did a bit of unpacking while waiting for the call from *Herr Kapitän* to go up to the bridge. It came fairly quickly but the ship had cast off and was backing away from the wharf as I got out on deck. There were two women leaning on the rail watching proceedings and one of them turned to me and said something in German followed quickly by: "Hello, my name is Inge. You must be the Australian passenger joining us. Come over to the railing and join Irma and me!"

Again, I did as I was told. Inge was very nice: mid-forties, 175 centimetres, trim, sensibly wearing a light cotton dress and a big sunhat. Irma was much older, in her seventies, with steel-rimmed glasses and grey hair cut like a storm-trooper's helmet; no hat but dark sunglasses. She turned slightly towards me and said "hello" and then turned back to watch the ship dropping the pilot and manoeuvring out of the harbour. I leant on the railing and did the same, the two women resuming their chat in German.

After a while, the kapitän came along and walked over to us, saying something in German and then to me, in English: "So you have met your travel companions! I hope you enjoy your voyage with us."

He then reverted to German and continued to chat with Inge and Irma. I said something about unpacking and "excuse me" and went back to my cabin where I did indeed finish unpacking. The cabin had a sitting area in one corner with a sofa, two armchairs and a coffee table and so I made myself comfortable and decided to relax by reading the Safety Procedures and Ship's Instructions and Information for Passengers while I waited for lunchtime to come around. Fortunately, this printed material was in both German and French and I soon learnt that while the ship did indeed belong to a French company, it was deployed to the Hamburg–Rotterdam–Le Havre–Marseille–La Spezia–Port Said–Mauritius–Réunion–Madagascar–Mayotte–Mombasa–Suez and return run. While mostly involved in carrying cargo containers between those ports, it was widely advertised in Germany as offering an idyllic cruise to exotic ports for small numbers of savvy passengers. The officers were all based in Hamburg and the "crew" (the cooks, stewards and sailors who did all the hard work around the place) were Filipino or Eastern European engaged through an agency in Hamburg. Inge came from Munich and Irma from Berlin. I was told that all six cabins were usually booked except in the "off" or cyclone season, which was just ending.

The information sheet set out the hours of mealtimes: breakfast between eight and nine; lunch at noon; dinner at seven. There were tea and coffee making facilities in the cabin and in the lounge, where there was also a television set (which only worked when in port and didn't work in any of the ports we visited). On the dot of twelve, I made my way to the dining-room, on the deck below the cabins and alongside the lounge. The passengers shared both the lounge and the dining-room with the officers, the *kapitän* and his officers sitting at one large round table and we three passengers at another. There was no menu but the food was reasonable, plain stuff with always the option of asking for an omelette or a sandwich if one did not fancy the meal the cook had chosen for the day. Breakfast was the only slight problem for me as there were no freshly baked croissants or baguettes but lots of cheese, sliced cold meats and "cake" of some unidentifiable kind, along with a plentiful supply of sliced white bread, all breakfast elements looking as if they had been purchased in an Aldi store in

Hamburg and stored in a cold room for the duration of the voyage. What did rather spoil meals for me was the way all the others chattered away all the time in German, the *kapitän* often firing off remarks from the far side of his table to the two women sitting with me. They being ladies did not shout back, although Irma usually did reply, quietly enough to indicate that she found the shouting rather tedious. Inge was actually embarrassed and more than once apologised to me for the *kapitän*'s rudeness in speaking so loudly and so often in German, which he knew I could not understand. However, I learnt to be amused rather than irritated by the Germanic atmosphere on board and soon acknowledged that the *kapitän* seemed competent at his job of running the ship and meant well.

On leaving Tamatave, the ship headed north along the coast of Madagascar, always within sight of land and the jungle-covered mountain range that runs for 1500 kilometres along the central spine of the island. On the afternoon of the second day, we steamed slowly past the entrance to the harbour of Diego Suarez at the northern end of Madagascar and then turned west into the Mozambique Channel and towards the Comoro Islands. Our first port of call was to be Mayotte, one of the volcanic *Iles des Comores* between Madagascar and Mozambique. Like parts of Madagascar, the islands had been a French possession since 1840 and, in 1974, France had offered them independence. While the three northern islands had accepted with alacrity and become a small independent nation, the island of Mayotte had voted to remain French and, in 2011, had been named as an overseas *département* of metropolitan France, as are Réunion, Guadeloupe and Martinique. In 2014, some ninety-five per cent of the Mayotte electorate voted to become part of the EU. French is the only official language, and the euro is the local currency. Mayotte now has a border control problem in that people from the other Comoro Islands constantly try to get to Mayotte, by boat or plane or even by swimming, as Mayotte's standards of living and of social, health and educational services are so much higher than those of the other islands. Moreover, as Mayotte is technically and legally part of France and therefore of the EU, it is seen as a sort of doorway to Europe for the inhabitants of this impoverished part of Africa.

The port and main town on Mayotte, Mamoudzou, turned out to be a moderately attractive little place, mostly low-rise white- or sand-coloured buildings brightened by lots of palm trees and French *tricolors* waving in the breeze. The day before we arrived there my left eye had become very bloodshot and the *kapitän*, Irma and Inge all advised me to get a doctor to look at it while we were in port. I agreed and so Irma, Inge and I took a taxi to the town centre. I quickly spied a green neon cross on one of the buildings, the standard sign in the French world for a pharmacy, and so we stopped the taxi and walked across the road. The pharmacy was, in fact, the first shop in a big, air-conditioned shopping arcade and there was a taxi rank a short distance further down the street: it seemed a good place for us to meet up again once I had had my eye checked and *Meine Damen* had done a bit of shopping. The pharmacy was big and bright and busy and pleasantly air-conditioned and looked just like any modern pharmacy in metropolitan France. There were several white-coated African shop assistants moving about and two similarly dressed older European men behind a glass panel at the back of the premises in what I took to be the dispensary. As I went in, one of these men looked up, no doubt recognised that I was not a local and walked towards me saying in French "Can I help you, *monsieur*?" It was so pleasant to hear French again instead of German and German-accented English!

I explained my problem and the pharmacist nodded and said that I should see a doctor rather than self-prescribe an eye ointment. There was, he said, a medical centre on the floor above the shopping arcade and so I made my way up there, asked for an early appointment and was invited to sit in the pleasantly appointed waiting room. Instead of going shopping as originally planned, Irma and Inge opted to stay with me, probably because of their inability to speak French but also, I think, out of friendship for a fellow passenger having a little health incident, *un mauvais moment*, as the French would say. I was grateful for their solidarity and offered to go shopping and translating with them once we had finished with the medics! After a very short wait, I was shown in to see the doctor who, like the pharmacist, turned out to be a Frenchman from the *métropole*, and both charming and professional. After examining my eye, listening to my summarised account of the troubles I had earlier had with it and, noting that I was about to resume a three-week voyage on a ship with no doctor on board, he recommended that I see an ophthalmologist "just to be sure there is nothing serious". I agreed, he rang his ophthalmologist colleague and made arrangements, and Irma, Inge and I went down to the taxi rank and were soon at the specialist medical centre not far away. The thought did occur to me that the French health professionals were as successful as the Malgache transport people in subtracting cash from this elderly Australian tourist but I put such an uncharitable thought behind me and continued to enjoy my brief contact with these Frenchmen far from metropolitan France. The ophthalmologist was another pleasant Frenchman and he examined my eye and ran a few tests and decided that there was in fact nothing new to worry about. He said the haemorrhaging would slowly clear and that there was no need for any treatment or ointment... and wished me *un bon voyage* for the rest of the trip.

So, it had been a case of "Much Ado About Nothing" and had cost me quite a few euros in doctor's fees and taxi charges. I had, however, rather enjoyed the little foray into everyday life in this remnant of the French colonial world and had also enjoyed showing off to my German companions the way in which the civilising influence of *Douce France* is still felt and appreciated around the world. I suppose that elderly Australian tourists were something of a rarity on Mayotte but, for whatever reason, I was treated with courtesy and even kindness everywhere I went. On leaving the ophthalmologist, Irma, Inge and I headed for a charming little bistro nearby and, choosing the air-conditioned inside rather than the terrace, had a bit of lunch and several long, cold drinks. And that was really all we saw of Mayotte, *Meine Damen* gracefully giving up their idea of a spot of shopping and, as the ship was to sail at four p.m., once lunch was over and we were rested we asked the bistro staff to call us a taxi. I asked the driver to take us to the ship via a quick tour of the town centre and we were back at the wharf by three p.m. I don't know what the ladies told the *kapitän* about their visit to Mayotte... "all terribly French" would be my guess... but I really enjoyed the visit and was happy and confident about re-boarding that ship without a doctor.

We left Mayotte just before sunset and then headed northeast past the other Comoro Islands, Dar-es-Salaam and

Zanzibar to Mombasa, where the ship was to spend a day or two loading and unloading cargo. The *kapitän* said that Mombasa was always unpleasantly hot and noisy onboard during that process and he always recommended that passengers go ashore and find an air-conditioned hotel in which to wait. On this trip, the ship's agent in Mombasa had organised a "mini safari" for Irma and Inge, a twelve-hour drive through a nearby game reserve in a private vehicle with an English-speaking guide. I was invited to join them and to divide the costs between three rather than two. I needed no persuasion and so it was that we were awakened at four a.m. one day as the ship was approaching the harbour in Mombasa and by five a.m. we were ashore and aboard our own safari SUV and heading off out of town towards the Tsavo National Park.

First, there was a drive of two hours or so along the "highway" towards Nairobi. Parts of the highway were sealed and in reasonable condition and parts just a dirt road full of potholes and teeming with traffic... old, overladen trucks, vans, cars and bicycles, and scores of people walking, walking, walking. We stopped for breakfast in Voi, a dusty town on the old Mombasa-Nairobi railway line that had featured in the film *Out of Africa*. It was during the construction of this railway in the 1890s that a hundred or more construction workers had been killed and eaten by the lions of Tsavo and work on the line stopped for several months while the lions were tracked and eventually shot. At Voi, we turned off the highway, crossed the railway line and headed in to spend the day driving around the park with our very knowledgeable guide. Visitors are forbidden to alight from the safari vehicles while game spotting and, as only a few miles inside the gates we came across a pride of lions sprawled across the dirt track and blocking our way as they snoozed and groomed in the morning sun, we needed no further reminder to be very careful. Our driver slowly detoured around the lions and continued deeper into the park and past numerous zebra, giraffe, antelope, hyena and a small herd of elephant.

We stopped for lunch and a rest in a luxurious safari lodge built on a rise overlooking a waterhole where another herd of elephant arrived and spent nearly half an hour drinking and splashing around. We hit the road again after lunch for the drive back to the park gates, passing more zebra, two adults and a juvenile giraffe, lots of gazelle, several of those strange secretary birds almost as big as an ostrich and definitely looking neater, trimmer and almost prim and then, suddenly, a huge lone male elephant approached our SUV as if intending to ram us or roll us over, trunk raised, ears flapping and bellowing. Our driver stopped the vehicle and advised us to be very quiet and very still, whispering that the elephant could toss the car in the air or crush it and its passengers if he wanted to. The elephant stopped about twenty metres away, gave a sort of snort… and let us see his rather impressive erection. "He's letting us see that he is male and he is boss," said our guide. That done, the elephant eyed us for a few minutes more and then ambled off into the bush. A few minutes later, we were out of the park and back in the safety of Voi, where we stopped for a breather and a cool drink before setting off back to Mombasa. We reached the port and the ship just after dark and in time for a shower, late dinner and bed. It had been a long but eventful day and I was grateful that I had decided to join Irma and Inge on the trip.

The loading of cargo was completed by lunchtime next

day and we quickly up-anchored and set off, leaving the harbour under the (very antique) guns of Fort Jesus, built in the sixteenth century by the Portuguese, and then turning north along the African coast to Cape Guardafui, the Red Sea and the Suez Canal, which we reached after a further week or so. We arrived off Suez in the late afternoon and dropped anchor in the bay to wait our turn to enter the Canal. The procedure was that ships were formed up into batches or convoys, a day one and a night one, the transit of the Canal taking about twelve hours. A dozen or more ships had arrived ahead of us and so we joined the end of the queue but, instead of moving off into the Canal at sunset, the convoy was ordered by radio from the Egyptian Canal Authority to remain anchored and wait: an American warship had radioed that it was approaching and required immediate and priority transit! As the night wore on with no sign of the Americans, the *kapitän* advised us to go to bed, promising to phone our cabins as soon as we were given the "all-clear" to enter the Canal. The phone call came at sunrise next morning and I emerged on deck just in time to see a huge aircraft carrier and its two escorting frigates steam past. Then it was the turn of our convoy and anchors began to be raised and the first ships to have arrived began to move slowly forward, ours following towards the rear.

Transiting the Canal is a weird experience as you know you are on board a ship and yet, when you look to either side, you see nothing but miles and miles of sandy desert. There is, it is true, a railway line running beside the Canal for much of its length and crossing it about halfway along by means of a big swing bridge. After four transits of the Canal, I have never seen a train and, of course, have never seen the bridge in use: it has always been open to the ships gliding along the Canal, each half of the bridge having pivoted on its pylon and sitting motionless parallel to the Canal bank. Until 1869, and the building of the Canal by de Lesseps and those French engineers, there had been a busy train service between Alexandria, Cairo and Suez, transferring passengers, their luggage and ships' cargoes between the eastern Mediterranean and the Red Sea, where they were all loaded onboard ships waiting to head off towards East Africa, India, Asia and Australasia. The opening of the Canal had eliminated the need for this huge transhipment exercise and so the development of Port Said at the northern end of the Canal had seen the decline in importance of the port at Suez and of its once-busy railway station. The one thing I did notice that had changed since my first time through the Canal was that an enormous but elegant road bridge had been built across it and completed in 1999. As the desert on each side is perfectly flat and as the central span is seventy metres above the Canal (to allow large ships to pass under), the approach ramps are nearly two kilometres long on each side; to support such a high and long central span the main towers are one hundred and fifty metres tall, designed to look like great obelisks from pharaonic times. The whole bridge quite deceivingly looks as if it were built in stone, just like the pyramids and temples of ancient Egypt and the overall impression was that this is the Great Gateway to Egypt.

It was evening by the time we reached Port Said and, stopping only to drop the Canal pilot, we left the Canal and entered the Mediterranean. By morning, the temperature had dropped (it was in April), the sea had become a bit choppy, the officers had abandoned their summer white uniforms for dark blue and warmer ones and we passengers wrapped up in pullovers or jackets before venturing out on deck. The next day, we slowly passed along the southern coast of Crete, a much bigger island than I had expected, its long mountain chain capped with snow. Another day saw us off Malta and then we rounded the toe of Italy and headed between the Italian mainland and Sicily and the Straits of Messina, the abode of Scylla and Charybdis in Greek mythology. Once through, with no sign of monster or whirlpool, we veered slightly north-west towards the Aeolian Islands. It was just on sunset on a cold, clear night when we passed Stromboli, the northernmost island of the group, an almost perfectly pyramid-shaped volcano rising nearly a thousand metres up from the sea, hurling rocks, lava and orange-coloured smoke skywards and topped by a great spiral of black smoke and cloud drifting slowly away to the west... a wonderful sort of welcome show for an Antipodean visiting Europe. We were off Cap Corse next morning with Nice and the French coast in the distance. The ship slowed so as not to arrive in Marseille during the night and, sure enough, soon after daybreak, we were approaching our berth in the outer harbour. Irma and Inge were staying on board for another week while the ship made its way home to Hamburg but I availed myself of the taxi that the ship's agent had used to come and meet us and with "goodbyes" all round I was soon whizzing along the Boulevard de la République and into the Vieux Port. I had arrived in France.

(vii) Quebec to Europe on the *Marco Polo*

In the northern autumn of 2016, I set off from Australia to Canada with the delightful Air Tahiti Nui and after stops in Tahiti and Los Angeles, as I abhor flying long distances non-stop, I spent a night recovering in a comfortable hotel bed in Vancouver. I flew on at noon next day to Quebec City arriving, after a change of plane in Montreal, at nine-thirty p.m. There I was met by my B&B host and driven the few kilometres to my base for the next few days. My host, a retired academic, had a really nice duplex apartment on the edge of the Quebec CBD and overlooking a linear park along the banks of the St Charles River, a tributary of the St Lawrence. It had been twenty-eight degrees during the day, an unheard-of phenomenon in Quebec City in September apparently, and I was offered, of all things, *un gin and tonic* in this that I had thought would be the least anglophile city in Canada! But I too was hot and thirsty so I accepted gratefully and after a bit of chat, hit the sack and was asleep in a wink, mightily relieved to have, at the age of eighty-two, flown halfway around the world without mishap.

The next day, after breakfasting carefully from a lavish spread of croissants, tartines, home-made jams and fresh fruit, I set off sightseeing. My host had rather optimistically urged me to walk in to town along the linear park but I opted for the bus from the corner of the street and alighted at Parliament Square at the top of the hill on which the city is built. From there, I could walk down the winding streets to the *Place Royale* and the river's edge… and the linear park in the unlikely eventuality that I should feel like walking home. Before wandering down to the river, I walked over to the citadel, which is absolutely amazing. While the city centre, *Vieux Québec*, is still surrounded on three sides by the gated walls built by the French in the seventeenth century (the fourth side fronts on to the mighty St Lawrence which acts as a natural moat), the main defence of the city was provided by a huge fortress outside but adjoining the walls in the north-west corner. This "citadel" was built during the reign of Louis XIV, it and the city ramparts being designed by Vauban, Louis's great military engineer and the designer of the French frontier fortresses at Besançon, Lille, Metz and so on. Apart from the massively thick walls and fortified gates, however, the citadel looks more like one of the fairy-tale châteaux of the Loire Valley than a military fortress. It includes a quite palatial residence originally built for the French governor of New France and now used as the summer residence of the Canadian governor-general and, during the rest of the year, it is used for state receptions and other posh functions. Agreed, it is built of grim, grey granite rather than of gleaming white limestone as along the Loire but the architecture, the steeply sloping and many-angled roofs, the towers and turrets with their candle snuffer tops and the delicate stone tracery of the residence windows opening on to the inner courtyards really do emphasise Quebec's links with France in the heyday of the Sun King. And I am sure that the citadel was the inspiration behind the iconic Château Frontenac Hotel, the roofline of which closely resembles that of the citadel.

I had not realised, until I got to Quebec and started to read some of the local history books in the B&B, that the French had arrived in Quebec at the time of Francis I (and of Henry VIII in England), i.e., the French in North America crossed the Atlantic well before the Dutch and English arrived in Nieuw Amsterdam and Virginia. Cardinal Richelieu approved many of the colonial projects and it was all going so well until the time of Louis XV, who gave more attention to his love-life than to politics, to Madame de Pompadour than to his military advisers! When told in 1757 that the fortress of Quebec had been captured by the English, Louis is said to have brushed aside the defeat as the loss of "a few hectares of snow". The word *'Québec'* in the local Algonquin language means the narrows and identifies the first place where the river becomes narrow enough for passage to be defended against seafarers venturing up the St Lawrence from the Atlantic... Quebec is truly the gateway to Canada, the ideal place for a fortress with cannons that could sink any enemy ship attempting to pass upriver. It is the spot where a bridge would eventually be built (in 1909, the then longest cantilever bridge in the world, the *Pont de Québec*). In losing Quebec and its command of all movement up the St Lawrence, Louis XV lost the fortress that was the key to Canada... much more than *quelques hectares de neige*!

The citadel was being restored after damage in a great fire a few years earlier and when I was there they were installing a shiny new copper roof, which looked like beaten gold in the midday sun. From the citadel I walked back to one of the city gates, through the ramparts and down to the river. The *Place Royale* on the river's edge is the site of the original settlement and the buildings along two sides of the *Place* all date from the seventeenth century and are now well maintained and ready for inspection by the many tourists. *Vieux Québec*, I discovered, is regarded in Canada as a national treasure, and rightly so.

Man does not live by bread alone but cannot live without it and I had fun selecting a suitable place for lunch from among the many cafés, bistros and restaurants which seemed to be doing a pretty brisk trade. I eventually settled on a place off the rue St Jean called *Le 8½*. It had a large sun-drenched terrace sheltered from the coolish breeze and there I enjoyed some quiche and salad, a maple syrup crêpe, and a glass of wine. My determination to eat as the locals were doing did not stretch to asking for a serve of *poutine*, aggressively marketed to the passing tourists. My B&B host warned me that it consists of cubes of cheddar cheese and chips all smothered in brown gravy! Sounded horrible but he said it is a very popular snack, on a par with hamburgers, hot dogs and fries in the USA! The influence of the culinary tastes of the big neighbour to the south seems very evident! After lunch, I visited the cathedral of *Notre Dame de Québec*, an interesting building dating from the early eighteenth century with a very elaborate gilded *baldaquin* over the high altar and apparently very much frequented by the locals. There were many churches scattered around the city, including a small and pretty Anglican cathedral that seemed to be little used. I was told that at the most recent census ninety-seven per cent of the population of Quebec City reported that they were practising Catholics, while in Montreal only half made that claim. The tallest building in the city, outside the walls of Vieux Quebec and of about twenty storeys, houses the provincial Department of Education and is named after an Ursuline nun, Marie Guyart, recently canonised who, with another Ursuline, Marguerite Bourgeois, opened the first school for girls in Canada in the late seventeenth century. The Ursuline convent and college they established are still flourishing although the original building, in the centre of the city, is now a museum. Another similar convent and college had been established by the Augustinian nuns and its impressive buildings are close by the cathedral. I saw a number of priests in their soutanes walking about the streets but no nuns in traditional habits. Perhaps the women have been faster off the mark than the men in adopting the modernising spirit of Vatican II!

  The next day was one of warm drizzle and so after a late start, I took the bus in to town, poked about the shops looking for a warm jacket in preparation for my coming transatlantic voyage, had a lunch of soup and shepherd's pie (*hachis*

Parmentier in Quebec) and then did a hop-on, hop-off bus tour of the city, which brought it all together nicely for me. Then "home" for another evening meal (and G&T or two) with my hosts. The next day my hosts drove me out in the morning to the Montmorency Falls, four or five kilometres out of the city, thirty per cent higher than the Niagara Falls but only thirty per cent as wide... impressive nonetheless, particularly when viewed from the zip-line that foolhardy sightseers can take to skim across the falls a hundred metres or so above the rushing waters. After an early lunch, we set off by car for Montreal, where we arrived at about five p.m., rush hour, with traffic backed up chaotically as everybody tried to cross the St Lawrence by the Jacques Cartier Bridge and gain access to the city centre. Eventually, I was deposited at the B&B run by friends of my Quebec hosts and settled into my room for dinner, bed and breakfast. The house, a converted warehouse, was about a hundred metres down a side street off the rue St Catherine, surprisingly quiet and yet close to everything. The next day, I was able to board the *Marco Polo* which had arrived at seven a.m. and was not due to sail until the following day, Sunday, at four p.m. As a result, I was able to settle into my cabin, unpack, have lunch on board, and then go ashore and "do" Montreal. Although much bigger than Quebec, Montreal seemed less interesting to me, more Anglo and less French but an interesting mixture of the two cultures nonetheless.

The *Marco Polo* left Montreal on time and sailed off down the mighty St Lawrence for Ireland, with the next six days given to daylight stops in Saguenay, Sept Iles, Corner Brook, Cap aux Meules and Sydney. The weather was mild and the ports of call interesting but I would NOT like to be there in winter (which lasts for five months!). The ship was fine, the food very good and too plentiful and after only four days of open ocean, we had crossed the Atlantic and were promised we should see the coast of Ireland at sunrise next day.

Indeed, the *Marco Polo* arrived ahead of schedule in Ireland and soon after daybreak we were off Mizzen Head, the westernmost point of Ireland and of Europe. An hour or so later, we were moving slowly into Cork harbour and up the river Lee to our berth at the passenger terminal in Cobh. This is where the *Titanic* had made her last call in Europe in 1911 before setting out on her voyage across the Atlantic. Both Cobh in Ireland and Halifax in Canada, where many of those drowned from the *Titanic* were buried, make much of the *Titanic* connection, with museums, galleries, memorabilia shops, bars and guest houses abounding. I was one of only four passengers disembarking in Cobh (the rest going on to Liverpool) and by nine thirty a.m. I was at the foot of the gangway and on Irish soil, looking for the customs and immigration control people. It was apparently too early in the day for them and a friendly wharfie, whom I asked, told me to just walk on over across the road to the station and catch my train in to Cork. There were no railway people at the station, just a couple of ticket machines, so I joined the short queue, bought a ticket and was waiting on the platform when the train glided in a few minutes later. It was a pleasant thirty-minute trip along the banks of the Lee to Cork City itself and then a short taxi ride to the B&B, "Emerson House", less than a kilometre from the railway station but up a hill too steep for elderly passengers with large suitcases.

The place turned out to be a lovely eighteenth-century house, beautifully furnished and run by a very friendly couple, and who seemed perfectly willing to put down the duster or the vacuum cleaner at any time and to engage in lively conversation ("*creaic*" in Irish) about what to see in Cork or about family history, politics, sex or religion: no subject was taboo in that relaxing household! Once settled into my room and sort of unpacked I walked down the hill to the CBD in search of lunch and the exact location of the bus terminal from which I would be getting the shuttle bus next day for the overnight ferry sailing to France. I found the bus terminal without trouble and then walked on down Saint Patrick Street, as advised by my hosts, to have a soup and sandwich lunch in the central market, the "English Market".

This turned out to be an architecturally interesting two-hundred-year-old produce market, full of well-stocked stalls, stall-keepers and customers... a smaller version of the Victoria Market in Melbourne and just as lively. I had my lunch, including a big bowl of delicious seafood chowder, and then caught a bus back up the hill to my B&B for a well-earned nap. I did ask my hosts about the somewhat incongruous name of the market and was told that yes, there had been an "Irish Market" as well as an "English Market" two hundred years ago: sure, it was where the Irish had been obliged to shop and were sold very inferior produce to what was available in the "English Market", the preserve of the Ascendancy and the English army of occupation. When the English left (three-quarters of) Ireland in 1922, the "Irish Market" was closed, and the Irish moved in to the until then forbidden premises of the former occupying power! When I suggested that they ought to change the name, my hosts laughed and said, "Why bother? That's all over now. The future's more important than the past." So, I stopped my politics and religion natter and went upstairs for my nap. Although the sun was still shining through a cloudy sky it had started to drizzle... "a lovely soft afternoon," said the locals. When I woke it was almost dark and still a bit damp, so I followed suggestions and walked a little further up the hill to the slightly grand Montenotte Hotel where I had an excellent meal of Lough Corrib salmon, Chablis, Irish brown bread and butter, and Irish coffee... and thence an easy (st)roll downhill to bed.

After a fine Irish breakfast next morning with lashings of bacon and eggs and tomatoes and mushrooms and fried bread and fresh toast with Kerry Gold butter and home-made marmalade and a big pot of tea, slowed down by wonderful *creaic*, I was very kindly driven down to the station where I was to meet my cousin, Helen, arriving on the twelve o'clock train from Limerick and Athenry, where she had been doing a little bit of research into our shared Irish family history. Unfortunately, Helen was not among the passengers who alighted from the train and so I sought help from the station staff. White hair, a foreign accent and a good Irish name worked wonders and I was shown to a seat, offered a cup of tea and helped with my luggage! A staff member phoned the station at Limerick, where Helen was to have made a train connection and then came over to me and said that because of "works on the line" the train had been changed to a bus, which would be arriving at the bus station, not the train station, at a quarter past one and that "an Australian lady" was indeed a passenger on board. They then offered to provide a complimentary taxi to take me to the bus station but as it was only a ten-minute walk and I had plenty of time I politely declined, thanked them all for their extraordinary help, and set off.

Helen's bus arrived on time and fitted in nicely with the

two p.m. departure of our shuttle bus to the ferry port for our four p.m. sailing to France. So, by about three-thirty p.m. we were comfortably installed onboard the *Pont Aven*, 42,000 tonnes, making a reservation for dinner in the elegant restaurant at seven-thirty, and heading for the bar and a drink. There was a cold wind blowing as the ship moved down Cork harbour but, happily, the sea remained pretty calm even when we turned north-east into the Irish Sea and headed for Roscoff in Brittany. Although the ship averaged twenty-five knots and arrived ahead of schedule there was no noise or vibration and very little movement to make passengers uneasy. Helen and I had an excellent meal, a good night's sleep and, when the ship docked at seven a.m., we were ready and keen to disembark and begin another trip through France.

MORLAIX

The shuttle bus from the ship to the railway station failed, however, to materialise and the three other passengers counting on it like us joined us in phoning for and organising two taxis (five people plus five large suitcases) for the fifteen-kilometre journey to the *Gare sncf* in Morlaix. There we all boarded the nine-twenty train for Paris, relishing the warmth and comfort of the double-decked TGV and the coffee and croissants in the upper-deck bar and then relaxing in our window seats and watching the Breton and Norman scenery glide by on the four-hour trip to Paris.

Chapter 12
The Last Time I Saw Paris

The first time I saw Paris was in the autumn of 1956 when, as a twenty-two-year-old from the Antipodes, I arrived by train in the *Gare de Lyon*. I clutched a passport which, to my annoyance, on its cover had the words "British Passport" embossed and which on the inside described me not as an Australian citizen but as a "subject of Her Britannic Majesty".[69] I had been whisked away by a fairy godmother with a taxi in to the city centre, along the rue de Rivoli, past the Louvre on my left and the Comédie Française on my right, then into a long avenue with, at the far end, the Opéra, the gilded statues on the roof and Apollo with his golden lyre gleaming in the sunlight. To actually be there, in Paris, seemed like a dream coming true. Over the following sixty-four years, I visited Paris many times, sometimes for a few days,

---

[69] The only time I liked that passport was on arriving later on at Dover on the ferry from Calais. There, in the immigration and customs control area, all passengers were formed in to two queues, one quite fast moving and one very slow moving. Beyond that area was direct access to the platform of the Dover Maritime Station and the waiting London train, which appeared to be filling rapidly as people hurried across from the passport-checking area. The fast-moving queue was restricted to British passport holders and the other was for "Aliens". I swallowed my pride and agreed temporarily to be a British subject, managed to get one of the last seats on the train and left the "Aliens" to stand or to sit on their cases all the way to London.

sometimes for a few weeks. It was always wonderful, exciting, stimulating, fulfilling, endlessly showing me something new, unexpected, different, as well as always delivering the hoped-for experiences and discoveries that attracted me from the other side of the world. For someone interested in history, architecture, theatre and music, as I was, it was a bottomless treasure-trove. And in all those years and visits, I only once experienced anything other than friendliness from the people of Paris, no rude words for an outsider, never an attempt to con me or to take advantage of my foreigner's lack of understanding of how things work in France.

The <u>last</u> time I saw Paris was four years ago, when I was eighty-six and, perhaps surprisingly, still healthy and active, and when Paris was still, for me, the dream-come-true, the City of Light, "the heart that pumps the lifeblood of civilisation". This time, however, I <u>did</u> have an unpleasant experience and in the interest of leaving a truly honest record of my travels in France I feel obliged to tell the story here. I had just left the metro station at the *Gare du Nord* one day in April 2018 and was walking down the rue de Compiègne when I bumped in to, or perhaps I was bumped in to by, two North African-looking chaps. Mutual apologies were expressed, politely on both sides, and I walked on. A short distance further, I entered a small restaurant, the name of which alas escapes me, and had a very pleasant light lunch. When I reached for my wallet to pay at the desk on my way out I discovered, to my horror, that I had no wallet, and no money at all. I immediately went to the manager and told him my story, surmising that I had been pickpocketed near the *Gare du Nord*. I told him that I did have another credit card but it was in my hotel room and I asked him if he would accept my wristwatch as a surety while I went to the hotel to get my backup card. The manager sighed and said that pickpocketing was a constant problem around the station. He told me not to worry about the bill and to have the meal with his compliments. I insisted that I would come back and pay and as they were about to close (at three p.m. and would not reopen until six for the evening meal) he said that if I really insisted, I could bring the money to their coffee shop, a few doors down the street, which would stay open all afternoon. He absolutely refused to take my watch as surety and said he was sorry I had had such an unpleasant experience in his city. When I returned to the area a couple of hours later and presented the bill with a cash payment the manager of the coffee shop could not hide his surprise that I had come back and paid and he, too, asked me not to judge Paris by the chaps who had robbed me.

And there you are: my last visit to Paris included being pickpocketed and facing a possible police charge of defrauding the restauranteur but it also included yet another experience of a pleasant social exchange with those often-maligned Parisians. I suspect that my white hair and obvious age had earned me some sympathy with the restaurant staff, although I am sure that the same characteristics had already identified me as a good target for the pickpockets. I am equally sure that the fact that I did my best to speak politely in my fading French helped forestall the police being called in. So, along with Dean Martin, Odette, Edith Piaf and many others, I can say (but not sing) that:

"The last time I saw Paris
Her heart was warm and gay...
And no matter how they change her
I'll remember her that way".

P.S.

I did, in fact, attempt another visit to Paris but got no closer than the airport at Lyon. In March 2020, I flew from Brisbane to Singapore and then on to Dubai where I boarded the MSC *Splendida* for a two-week voyage to Genoa. Once in Genoa, I planned to take a train along that fabulous *Côte d'Azur* to Nice, Marseille and then deeper into France. The day after the ship's departure from the port of Dubai passengers were advised that, because of the Covid-19 pandemic, Dubai and other ports on the Arabian peninsula had suddenly been closed to all passenger ship arrivals and departures. As the *Splendida* proceeded towards Europe, the same thing occurred at each of the expected ports of call in the Arabian Sea, the Red Sea and the Mediterranean. We were alarmed to learn that Genoa and all the European ports on the Mediterranean had closed too and wondered whether we would all have to stay on board until the ship reached Southampton, the first port on its itinerary not closed at that stage. Then, a few days later, we were relieved to be told that France had agreed to make an exception for us and to allow the ship to berth and to terminate its voyage in Marseille. There was a catch, however. Marseille, like the rest of France and much of Europe, was by then in lockdown and only residents of France and of other Schengen countries would be allowed to freely disembark and make their way home. Others, like me, would only be allowed to disembark in order to proceed, *under security guard escort*, to an airport and to leave the country immediately.

By the time we arrived in Marseille three days later, I had, with great difficulty, secured an online reservation for a flight from Lyon to London and then to Singapore and Sydney and so after spending two days in quarantine onboard the ship at an isolated berth in the outer harbour of Marseille I was able to go ashore and, under strict supervision, board a bus on the wharf and make the three-hour drive to Lyon-Saint-Exupéry airport, about twenty-five kilometres out of the city which sadly I never glimpsed. The twenty-four-hour flight back to Australia was unpleasant, to say the least, with a packed aircraft, minimum staff, masked and gloved, and two meals consisting of a bottle of water plus a ham roll. On arriving in Sydney, we were transferred under police supervision to a city hotel where I spent two weeks in strict quarantine, alone in a room with sealed windows and with meals of a very basic kind being placed outside my door in a brown paper bag three times a day. I was allowed to open the door to retrieve the food but not to step out into the corridor. After two weeks of quarantine and with daily health checks at the door or by telephone revealing no sign of any illness, I was allowed to go, again under escort, to the airport and to fly on to Brisbane. There, on disembarking, my health was again checked before I was allowed to leave the arrival gate after signing an undertaking to go straight home and to self-isolate at home for fourteen days. I did as I was told and finally emerged from the "trip to nowhere" five weeks after I had set out.

Of course, I was disappointed that all I saw of France on this my last trip was the harbour in Marseille, about three hundred kilometres of the motorway between Marseille and Lyon, and the virtually deserted Lyon-Saint-Exupéry airport. I was disappointed, too, at missing interesting ports of call in Oman, Egypt, Jordan, Greece and Italy. My two weeks on board the *Splendida* were, however, very pleasant. Like all of these megaships of over 100,000 tonnes and designed to carry several thousand passengers, it is far too big ever to be described as "beautiful", but as it was only half full, we were confined in great comfort, indulged with fine Italian cuisine at every meal, cosseted by attentive and not overworked crew members and were all the time in the company of interesting passengers from many different countries and cultures.

The two weeks at sea were, moreover, a time for reflection on the planned and unfolding, and finally aborted, trip as well as on the many other trips I had already taken and, indeed, at the age of eighty-six, on the great trip of life itself which for me was nearing completion. What a wonderful trip life has in fact been! How fortunate I have been in the circumstances of my birth: in a country with a reasonably open and egalitarian society and with a strong economy, into an educated and caring family, receiving a good education, enjoying full employment throughout one's working life and able to enrich life by visiting other countries and cultures around the world. Travel can, if one's eyes and ears and mind are truly open, broaden one's understanding of what life is, help get things in perspective and deepen one's appreciation of home. Home is, after all, where the heart, not the hearth, is and the best moments in travel are those where one makes contact with other hearts, even fleetingly. Life is really one long search for such contacts and many a traveller after years on the road finds that that contact was available, indeed waiting, at home. But would he have realised that if he had not gone away?